The Defenses in Psychoanalysis

The Defenses in Psychoanalysis explores the nature and assessment of defense mechanisms through an integration of psychoanalytic theory and empirical research in contemporary psychoanalysis.

Presented in two parts, the first section offers a comprehensive overview of major psychoanalytic contributions to the understanding of defense, from Freud's foundational ideas to contemporary developments. This section serves as a conceptual foundation for the empirical work that follows and provides a coherent synthesis of key perspectives, aimed especially at readers less familiar with psychoanalytic thinking. The second section presents the development and validation of the Comprehensive Rorschach Defense System (CRDS), a tool developed in collaboration with Carl B. Gacono for coding defense mechanisms in Rorschach protocols. The structure and coding criteria of the CRDS are explained and illustrated with numerous examples, followed by the presentation of data from a validation study supporting its reliability and clinical significance. The book concludes with a clinical chapter demonstrating how the CRDS can be used to deepen psychoanalytic understanding of defensive functioning.

The Defenses in Psychoanalysis will be of interest to psychoanalysts in practice and in training and to psychologists with psychodynamic training.

Anna Maria Rosso, Psy.D., is a clinical psychologist, psychoanalyst, and Associate Professor of Psychodynamic Psychology at eCampus University, Italy. A full member of the Italian Psychoanalytical Society and the IPA, she is in private practice and serves as co-delegate for Italy to the Comprehensive System International Rorschach Association (CSIRA).

The International Psychoanalytical Association Current Challenges in Psychoanalysis Series
Series Editor: Silvia Flechner

IPA Publications Committee
Natacha Delgado, Nergis Güleç, Thomas Marcacci, Carlos Moguillansky, Rafael Mondrzak, Angela M. Vuotto, Gabriela Legorreta (consultant)

Recent titles in the Series include

Psychoanalysis and Severe Disorders in Young Children
Clinical and Community Work with Autism Spectrum Disorder and Child Mental Health
Nahir Bonifacino

Couple Work, Work with Couples
Éric Smadja

Narcissism
Psychoanalytic Clinicians and Researchers in Dialogue
Edited by Marianne Leuzinger-Bohleber, Stephan Hau, Rogério Lerner, Erik Stänicke & Siri Erika Gullestad

Art and Psychoanalysis
Between the Dialectics of the Other and Poetic Estrangement
Gabriela Goldstein

The Defenses in Psychoanalysis
Theoretical Concepts to Empirical Research
Anna Maria Rosso

Paths of Symbolization
Alain Gibeault

The Defenses in Psychoanalysis
Theoretical Concepts to Empirical Research

Anna Maria Rosso

R Routledge
Taylor & Francis Group

LONDON AND NEW YORK

Designed cover image: Getty | Wirestock

First published 2026
by Routledge
4 Park Square, Milton Park, Abingdon, Oxon OX14 4RN

and by Routledge
605 Third Avenue, New York, NY 10158

Routledge is an imprint of the Taylor & Francis Group, an informa business

For Product Safety Concerns and Information please contact our EU
representative GPSR@taylorandfrancis.com. Taylor & Francis Verlag
GmbH, Kaufingerstraße 24, 80331 München, Germany.

British Library Cataloguing-in-Publication Data
A catalogue record for this book is available from the British Library

ISBN: 9781032882741 (hbk)
ISBN: 9781032882734 (pbk)
ISBN: 9781003536994 (ebk)

DOI: 10.4324/9781003536994

Typeset in Palatino
by KnowledgeWorks Global Ltd.

To you, who, without knowing or meaning to, brought a brief light to my eyes, and more enduringly, new life into my days.

Contents

List of contributors   *ix*
Acknowledgments   *x*
Series editor's foreword   *xi*
SILVIA FLECHNER

Introduction   1
ANNA MARIA ROSSO

PART I
**A journey through the changing landscape of defenses
in psychoanalysis**   3

1   **A journey through Freud's conceptualization of defense
    mechanisms**   5
    ANNA MARIA ROSSO

2   **Forty years on: Anna Freud's re-examination of defense
    mechanisms in dialogue with Joseph Sandler**   21
    ANNA MARIA ROSSO

3   **The Klein–Bion paradigm shift**   35
    ANNA MARIA ROSSO

4   **The British Independents' twist**   53
    ANNA MARIA ROSSO

5   **Insight into defenses in North American psychoanalysis**   69
    ANNA MARIA ROSSO

6   **Does the concept of defense still hold water in psychoanalysis?:
    Notes from the current psychoanalytic literature**   79
    ANNA MARIA ROSSO

PART II
**The heuristic utility of defense mechanisms in
empirical research in psychoanalysis**   97

 7 Exploring the defenses in outcome research in
    psychoanalysis   99
    ANNA MARIA ROSSO

 8 Historical developments of assessing defenses on
    the Rorschach   118
    JASON M. SMITH AND CARL B. GACONO

 9 The Comprehensive Rorschach Defense System:
    A new coding system   129
    CARL B. GACONO AND ANNA MARIA ROSSO

10 The validation of the Comprehensive Rorschach
    Defense System   156
    ANNA MARIA ROSSO AND ANDREA CAMOIRANO

11 Exploring psychic functioning through the
    Comprehensive Rorschach Defense System:
    A case study   175
    ANNA MARIA ROSSO

    References   *192*
    Index   *208*

List of contributors

Andrea Camoirano, Psy.D., is a licensed Clinical Psychologist and Psychotherapist, Candidate of the Italian Psychoanalytical Society, IPSO member. As a psychotherapist, he is in private practice with adolescents and adults. Since 2010, he has collaborated with the University of Genoa as an assistant lecturer in clinical psychology.

Since 2014, he has worked as a consultant in a therapeutic clinic specializing in the treatment of personality disorders, affective disorders, psychotic disorders, and eating disorders.

Carl B. Gacono, PhD, ABAP, formerly an Assessment Center Director (Atascadero State Hospital, CA), and a Chief Psychologist (FCI Bastrop, TX), worked for over 20 years in correctional & forensic psychiatric facilities. He is the recipient of the 1994 Beck Award & 2000 W. Klopfer Award. He is a member of the American Board of Assessment Psychology and a Fellow of the Society for Personality Assessment.

Anna Maria Rosso, Psy.D., is a licensed clinical psychologist and psychoanalyst. She is a full member of the Italian Psychoanalytical Society and the International Psychoanalytical Association (IPA), and Associate Professor of Psychodynamic Psychology at eCampus University (Italy). As a psychoanalyst, she is in private practice with children, adolescents, and adults. She practiced in the National Health Service as a psychologist-psychotherapist from 1987 to 2003. Since 2002, she has been teaching in the degree course in psychology at the University of Genoa, Italy. She is a member of the Council of Administration of the Comprehensive System International Rorschach Association (CSIRA) and a member of the Society for Personality Assessment.

Jason M. Smith, Psy.D., ABPP, is a licensed Clinical Psychologist who is currently a Chief Psychologist at a female prison in the United States. He is a founding member of the International Rorschach Institute (IRI) and a member of the Comprehensive System International Rorschach Association (CSIRA). He was awarded the APA Division 18 Criminal Justice Section Outstanding Dissertation Award (2014) and the SPA John E. Exner Scholar Award in 2019.

Acknowledgments

The development of this research project—and, later, the idea for this book—was made possible thanks to Carl B. Gacono, one of the most experienced psychodynamically trained Rorschach experts, whose reputation is widely recognized internationally.

Three and a half years ago, he was the one who realized that we were both, independently, studying the validity of the Lerner Defense Scale and the Rorschach Defense Scales, and he was the one who invited me to collaborate. The idea of creating a new system that would integrate the strengths of both scales while addressing their respective limitations was entirely his; I doubt I would ever have had the boldness to conceive such a project on my own.

For this—and for so much more—I am deeply grateful to him. His contribution to this volume includes co-authoring Chapter 8 with Jason M. Smith, to whom I am equally grateful for his valuable input, as well as co-authoring with me Chapter 9, which presents the coding system of the Comprehensive Rorschach Defense System (CRDS).

I also wish to express my heartfelt thanks to Andrea Camoirano, whose collaboration and friendship I have cherished for nearly 20 years. Together, we conducted the validation study of the CRDS, and he is also the co-author of Chapter 10.

Series editor's foreword

Silvia Flechner

The International Psychoanalytic Association Publications Committee is honored to present a new book from the Current Challenges in Psychoanalysis series. This series explores the evolving landscape of psychoanalytic practice, addressing contemporary issues such as trauma, cultural diversity, the influence of technology, and shifts in psychoanalytic dynamics. Each volume offers concise, interdisciplinary insights from leading experts, bridging classical psychoanalytic theory with modern challenges. Designed for clinicians and researchers, this series is a vital resource for those seeking to navigate and innovate within today's complex therapeutic environment.

The IPA Publications Committee is pleased to publish Ana Maria Rosso's Book *"The Defences in Psychoanalysis, Theoretical Concepts and Empirical Research."* Developing the Comprehensive Rorschach Defense System (CRDS), a new coding system designed to assess defensive functioning within a psychoanalytic framework.

This book is the result of a conceptual and empirical exploration into the assessment of defense mechanisms. The first part offers a synthesis of theoretical developments, tracing a trajectory from Freud's foundational ideas to contemporary psychoanalytic models. It aims to provide a coherent and integrated overview of significant psychoanalytic contributions to the study of defense. It seeks to assemble a range of perspectives in a cohesive and accessible way, particularly for psychologists with a psychodynamic background or an interest in psychoanalytic thinking, in addition to trained psychoanalysts. The theoretical section is intended as a contextual foundation to help readers unfamiliar with psychoanalytic models better understand the conceptual premises that informed the development of the coding system presented in the second part of the book.

The second part, called *"The Heuristic Utility of Defense Mechanisms in Empirical Research in Psychoanalysis,"* presents empirical research that led to the development and validation of the CRDS. The structure and coding criteria of the CRDS are illustrated with numerous examples, followed by the results of the validation study. The final chapter offers a clinical application, demonstrating how psychoanalysts can use this instrument to deepen both clinical and research-based understanding of defensive functioning.

The author introduces us to the journey through Freud's conceptualization of defense mechanisms, outlining the evolution of Freud's theory of defense mechanisms through three key phases: affective-traumatic, topographical, and structural.

In her next chapter, she examines Anna Freud's contributions to the theory of defense mechanisms, with particular attention to her dialogue with Joseph Sandler and her critical reassessment of key psychoanalytic concepts. Central themes include the underlying motivations for defensive functioning, the distinction between defense mechanisms and defensive measures, and the role of defense analysis in psychoanalytic treatment. Building on the contributions of Melanie Klein and Wilfred Bion, the British Independents, including psychoanalysts like Michael Balint, Ronald Fairbairn, and Donald Winnicott, developed their frameworks to conceptualize defense mechanisms. Examining also the concept of defense in North American Psychoanalysis through the contributions of Heinz Hartmann, Otto Kernberg, and Heinz Kohut. Including also some notes from the current psychoanalytic literature.

The author continues exploring the defenses in outcome research in psychoanalysis. She delves into the CRDS, stating that a new coding system was developed to address the limitations of the Lerner Defense Scales (LDS) and the Rorschach Defense Scales (RDS), while integrating their conceptual strengths.

Anna Maria Rosso is a licensed clinical psychologist and psychoanalyst. She is a full Member of the Italian Psychoanalytical Society and the International Psychoanalytical Association (IPA), and Associate Professor of Psychodynamic Psychology at the University campus (Italy). As a psychoanalyst, she works in private practice with children, adolescents, and adults.

This book will be an essential resource for psychoanalysts and psychologists interested in empirical research and also the value of psychoanalysis, showcasing the interest in the CRDS, a new coding system designed to assess defensive functioning within a psychoanalytic framework.

Silvia Flechner
Series Editor
Chair, IPA Publications Committee

Introduction

Anna Maria Rosso

Three years ago, I submitted a research grant proposal to the International Psychoanalytical Association (IPA), serving as principal investigator for a study entitled *"Beyond LDS and RDS: Toward the Development of a Valid and Reliable Measure of Defenses,"* in collaboration with Carl B. Gacono, Andrea Camoirano, and Jason M. Smith. The primary aim was to develop a clinically useful instrument for assessing defense mechanisms in psychoanalytic research, with particular attention to treatment processes and outcomes.

Acknowledging the inherent challenge of measuring unconscious psychic processes, we explored the use of performance-based tools and identified the Rorschach test as a promising option. This decision aligned with Lerner's (2005) perspective on the Rorschach's utility in operationalizing unobservable aspects of psychic functioning.

The ultimate goal was to create a new system that could integrate the strengths and address the limitations of two existing instruments: the Lerner Defense Scale (Lerner & Lerner, 1980) and the Rorschach Defense Scales (Cooper & Arnow, 1986). At the time, the most widely used instruments in empirical research—the Defense Mechanism Rating Scales (DMRS; Perry, 1990) and its Q-sort adaptation (Di Giuseppe et al., 2014)—presented significant limitations: they were not explicitly psychoanalytic in their theoretical foundations, required extensive training, were time-consuming, and, importantly, risked interfering with the analyst–analysand relationship.

Given the widely acknowledged reluctance among analysts to employ intrusive instruments within the analytic setting, the development of non-intrusive tools for studying psychoanalytic treatment processes and outcomes became essential.

The Rorschach test, when administered outside the analytic setting—such as during initial consultations at psychoanalytic institutes—emerged as a viable and ethically appropriate solution. These consultations, conducted prior to assigning an analysand to a treating analyst, offer an ideal opportunity to introduce the Rorschach. Research participation can be initiated by the consulting analyst, without involving the future treating analyst. The analysand may choose to discuss the assessment with their analyst, thereby integrating it into the analytic process itself.

DOI: 10.4324/9781003536994-1

Thanks to the support of the IPA, this project was made possible.

This book is the result of a conceptual and empirical exploration into the nature and assessment of defense mechanisms. The first part offers a synthesis of theoretical developments, tracing a trajectory from Freud's foundational ideas to contemporary psychoanalytic models. While it does not claim originality, it aims to provide a coherent and integrated overview of major psychoanalytic contributions to the study of defense. It seeks to assemble a range of perspectives in a coherent and accessible way, particularly for psychologists with a psychodynamic background or an interest in psychoanalytic thinking, in addition to trained psychoanalysts. The theoretical section is intended as a contextual foundation to help readers unfamiliar with psychoanalytic models better understand the conceptual premises that informed the development of the coding system presented in the second part of the book.

The second part presents the empirical research that led to the development and validation of the Comprehensive Rorschach Defense System (CRDS). The structure and coding criteria of the CRDS are illustrated with numerous examples, followed by the results of the validation study. The final chapter offers a clinical application, demonstrating how psychoanalysts can use this instrument to deepen both clinical and research-based understanding of defensive functioning.

Part I

A journey through the changing landscape of defenses in psychoanalysis

1 A journey through Freud's conceptualization of defense mechanisms

Anna Maria Rosso

In this chapter, I explore the evolution of Freud's thinking on defense mechanisms, following the chronological order of his key writings. The choice to proceed chronologically is based on the idea that it offers a straightforward way to navigate a complex path, reducing the risk of overly personal interpretations or, more importantly, misleading misunderstandings.

As outlined by Sandler, Holder, Dare, and Dreher (1997), Freud's theoretical journey unfolds in three distinct phases: the affective-traumatic, the topographical, and the structural—each providing a distinct theoretical framework. In examining the development of defense conceptualization in this chapter, the progression will move through these phases, discerning the re-adjustments or changes each implies.

The conceptualization of defense mechanisms in the affect-trauma frame of reference

During the initial phase, Freud increasingly asserted that hysteria in his patients primarily resulted from the deliberate repression of genuinely experienced sexually traumatic events. This repression led to the emergence of painful and overwhelming affects that individuals could not effectively process.

In collaboration with his Viennese colleague Breuer and Freud observed that hysterical symptoms ameliorated when patients, initially through hypnosis and suggestion, could recollect events tied to the onset of their symptoms and engage with the associated emotions (Breuer and Freud, 1893). Consequently, Freud concluded that repression impeded the discharge of psychic excitement, resulting in its conversion into somatic phenomena, and giving rise to hysterical conversion symptoms.

Treatment during this phase aimed to bring repressed memories into consciousness, enabling patients to release emotions through abreaction (Freud, 1893e).

In this phase, Freud, aligning with the principles of the physics of his time, considered the economic perspective as crucial to psychic

DOI: 10.4324/9781003536994-3

functioning. According to Fechner's principle of constancy, the generated energy must be discharged; when there is an accumulation, as seen after traumatic experiences, neurotic symptoms emerge due to increased arousal that necessitates discharge, but it is impeded by repression (Freud, 1895).

Typically, when the energy level is manageable, discharge occurs through actions and expression of emotions. However, when the energy surpasses the capacity for discharge, and when the idea conflicts with social norms, personal ideals, or desires, the ego employs defense mechanisms to push the idea and associated emotions out of consciousness.

Freud identifies repression as a key defense mechanism, describing it as the act of relegating the incompatible idea and associated emotions to the unconscious mind. The repressed idea may attract other ideas that, while not incompatible with the ego, are pushed into the unconscious due to associative connections with the incompatible idea.

In his clinical cases on hysteria, Freud (1893a, 1893b, 1893c, 1893d) illustrates how he brought the incompatible idea to consciousness only after making the associated ideas conscious.

In addition to repression, Freud identifies other defenses, such as substitution, in which the affect associated with the incompatible idea is shifted to another idea acceptable to the ego, and affect transformation, which involves the substitution of one emotion for another.

At this early stage, the dominant perspective is the economic one, in which defense is aimed at managing emotions that cannot be discharged. Psychopathology, in this perspective, is viewed as a consequence of defense: in individuals with a constitutional predisposition, unexpressed arousal manifests as symptoms.

It is noteworthy that at this early stage, Freud placed significant emphasis on actually experienced traumatic events. He argued that in relation to external stimuli, an individual might experience an uncontrollable increase in arousal. He assumed the presence of a protective shield against external stimuli, serving to safeguard the psychic apparatus, while he did not consider such a shield necessary in relation to internal stimuli, as he did not believe that the amount of internally generated energy could be incapable of discharge (Freud, 1895).

Referring to external events capable of triggering emotional reactions that exceeded the discharge capacity of the mental apparatus, Freud distinguishes between actual and retroactive traumas. He focused on the latter and built much of his theoretical framework around them. These are events, particularly sexual seductions suffered passively in early childhood, which were not perceived as traumatic at the time but acquire intense traumatic significance when awakened by an event later in life. At this stage, Freud hypothesizes that childhood memories are repressed and remain unconscious and inactive until triggered by later events, eliciting intense anxious emotional reactions.

These concepts are extensively examined in some key papers from this early period: *Studies on Hysteria* (1893), *The Neuro-Psychoses of Defense* (1894b), and *Further Remarks on the Neuro-Psychoses of Defense* (1896).

In *The Neuro-Psychoses of Defense* (1894b), Freud acknowledged that intentionally pushing away disturbing ideas might not inherently indicate psychopathology. He was unsure whether such intentional distancing from consciousness is effective and lasting in mentally healthy individuals. However, in the patients he analyzes, intentional repression is not achieved. Instead, the attempt to repress disturbing ideas results in psychopathological manifestations, encompassing not only hysteria but also obsessive states and hallucinatory psychosis.

Drawing from his clinical experience, Freud developed the notion that both the memory traces and the affect associated with the incompatible idea cannot be entirely erased. While defense may weaken affect, the portion of affect detached from the idea must seek alternative ways for discharge.

This was the first writing in which Freud described the different ways through which the sum of excitement, separated from the idea, is utilized in phobias, obsessions, and psychoses.

Whereas in hysteria the conversion occurs from the psychic to the somatic, in individuals without a predisposition for conversion, the idea remains conscious but becomes dissociated from its affect. This liberated affect, now free, adheres to other ideas that, in themselves, are not incompatible but become obsessive due to a "false connection." Freud reported that, in the cases of phobias and obsessions he analyzed, as well as in cases of hysteria, the incompatible idea was of a sexual nature. However, he did not exclude the possibility that incompatible ideas of a different nature may occur. In phobias, the liberated anxiety could project onto "common primary phobias" (e.g., animals, storms, darkness) or onto activities associated with sexuality (e.g., urinating, defecating, soiling, infecting).

In these psychopathological conditions, the transposition of affect onto another idea does not diminish its intensity because the excitement remains in the psychic sphere, with only the incompatible idea excluded from memory.

In cases of hallucinatory psychosis, both the incompatible idea and its affect are rejected. In these instances, the ego detaches not only from the painful idea but also from reality: withdrawal into psychosis serves as a defense against the incompatible idea. Notably, Freud refers to asylum patients who struggle with the loss of a loved one, such as mothers mourning the death of their children by cradling a piece of wood, and women who, elegantly dressed, waited for years for the return of their betrothed.

Even more intriguing is Freud's consideration of the possibility that the same individual may manifest both obsessive and hysterical symptoms, and individuals with mixed neuroses may experience psychotic episodes.

As previously emphasized, however, the economic perspective holds a central position in this work, particularly in the concluding section, where

Freud points out that affective quantity, though currently immeasurable, possesses all the properties of quantity: it is capable of

> increase, diminution, displacement, and discharge, and is spread over the memory-traces of ideas somewhat like an electric charge is spread over the surface of a body.
>
> (Freud, 1894b, p. 60)

Two years later, in *Further Remarks on the Neuro-Psychoses of Defense*, Freud (1896) reiterates that the symptoms of hysteria, obsessive neurosis, and paranoia stem from the psychic mechanism of defense, now explicitly considered unconscious. Defense is defined as the attempt to remove an idea incompatible with the patient's ego, which has entered into painful conflict.

The new perspective, clearly articulated in this paper and only foreshadowed in the *Project for a Scientific Psychology* (1950 [1895]), introduces the concept of "deferred action," which refers to the retrospective impact of childhood sexual trauma—still regarded at this stage as a real event.

Freud explicitly states that for the traumatic event of a sexual nature to be pathogenic, it must not only have constituted an actual irritation of the genitals but must also have taken place in childhood. It is not the childhood event itself that is traumatic, but the recollection relived after puberty, at the onset of sexual maturity. Subsequent sexual experiences, even if entirely normal and thus not inherently traumatic, become pathogenic as they reawaken the memory trace of childhood traumas, leading to the release of affect and repression.

In this writing, a second element of novelty concerns the assertion that in cases of hysteria, the sexual seduction must have been passive, while in cases of obsessive neurosis, it would involve active aggressions following a previous experience of endured seduction. This statement introduces a deepening of the obsessive defensive mechanism. As long as the defense against the repressed content succeeds, the individual exhibits traits of meticulousness, shame, and self-distrust. However, when the defense fails, the resurgence of repressed material leads to self-accusations related to the aggression, manifesting themselves in a disguised form through obsessive ideas. Freud peremptorily stated,

> Wherever a neurotic obsession emerges in the psychological sphere, it comes from repression.
>
> (Freud, 1896, p. 171)

When self-accusation is also repressed, affect can undergo further and different transformations (e.g., transforming into hypochondriac anxiety, social anxiety, religious anxiety, delusions of attention, etc.). It is noteworthy that in this paper, Freud explicitly mentions the connection between affect and obsessive ideas and "periodic melancholia," a theme that will be developed in the chapter on the Kleinian perspective of defenses. The investment of thinking activity in content distant from the incompatible idea, frequently observed in obsessive thinking and lingering doubt, proves to be another protective measure. Obsessive actions (e.g., rituals, arithmomania) and phobias, along with superstition, pedantry, and extreme fastidiousness, also serve as protective measures.

In this essay, Freud reiterates that paranoia is also a defensive psychosis, originating in the repression of painful memories, and that its symptoms emerge from the very material that has been repressed. Through a detailed clinical illustration concerning a woman with hallucinatory psychosis, Freud presents his perspective that the hallucinations were also fragments of repressed childhood sexual experiences, that is, symptoms of the return of the repressed. Whereas in obsessive neurosis, self-accusation is repressed and self-confidence is replaced by marked meticulousness, in paranoia, self-accusation is repressed through a process of projection. Instead of self-confidence, the individual defensively develops distrust of others, although self-accusation returns in delusional ideas and auditory hallucinations.

It is clear that in these early writings, Freud, while often using the terms repression and defense interchangeably, was already highlighting the emergence of different defensive mechanisms. Repression, up to this point, seems to indicate the general inability to recall traumatic childhood sexual events that become pathogenic as a result of sexual maturation after puberty. However, additional and specific defenses underlie different psychopathological manifestations, as seen above, and may also coexist: conversion in hysteria, displacement in obsessive neurosis, and projection in psychosis. What was expressed in the *Further Remarks on the Neuro-Psychoses of Defense* had been anticipated in *Draft K* of Christmas (Freud, 1895) addressed to Fliess, while in *Draft H* of January 24, 1894, Freud (1894a) had addressed the psychopathological condition of paranoia for the first time, identifying the defensive recourse to projection, a theme that would later be explored in greater depth in the essay on President Schreber (1911b).

The conceptualization of defense mechanisms in the topographical frame of reference

Freud is known to have declared in 1897, in a letter to his friend Fliess, that he no longer subscribed to the theory that neurosis was solely caused by infantile sexual seduction. Although he never dismissed the possibility of this being a cause of psychopathology, he began to attribute greater importance to the phantasies of sexual seduction elaborated by his patients during childhood.

These fantasies were repressed from consciousness and continued to operate as if they were memories of actual experiences. This significant shift in perspective marked the beginning of a new phase in his theoretical development, leading to a prolific scientific output.

The exploration of dreams (Freud, 1900) and the analysis of common phenomena like slips of the tongue (Freud, 1901) led Freud to identify other manifestations of repressed fantasies, even outside of psychopathological conditions.

It was in *The Interpretation of Dreams* (1900) that he formulated the topographical model of the mind, comprising three systems, namely Conscious, Preconscious, and Unconscious. According to this conceptualization, the Unconscious system contained instinctual drives and was characterized by a primitive functioning based on the primary process and the pleasure principle. In other words, its functioning was solely aimed at the discharge of arousal and the gratification of desires, without logical and formal relations between its elements. In contrast, the Preconscious and Conscious systems, operating according to secondary processes based on logic and the reality principle, were thought to adhere to conscious ideals and norms of behavior.

During this period, Freud (1905) also developed a theory of sexual development that identified several developmental stages (oral, anal, phallic-oedipal), during which, depending on the source of sensual pleasure, the child invests different bodily erotic zones with libidinal energy.

In the phallic phase, a crucial element is the positive form of the Oedipus complex, in which the child grapples with both loving and hostile desires toward the parents. Freud identifies a positive form in which love for the opposite-sex parent is accompanied by rivalry toward the same-sex parent, and a negative form in which love for the same-sex parent is associated with rivalry toward the opposite-sex parent. The conceptualization of infantile sexuality and oedipal conflict is crucial to understanding the development of defense mechanisms at this stage, as castration anxiety, feared as a consequence of one's oedipal desires, would be what gives rise to the defense mechanisms. Indeed, until 1920, Freud believed that the individual fought against sexual urges.

In Freud's conceptualization during this second phase of his work, the individual is considered to grapple with instinctual libidinal impulses emerging from within. Freud defines the drive

> as a concept on the frontier between the mental and the somatic, ...
> the psychical representative of the stimuli originating from within the
> organism and reaching the mind.
>
> (Freud 1915a, p. 112)

It is characterized by its source, aims, and objects. In other words, the drive is a force that originates in a part of the body, exerts an excitation that must be satisfied through an object that can change over time, and can be either external to the individual or the individual itself. Within this theoretical framework, Freud (1915a) perceived conflict as the opposition between sexual instincts, aimed at the attainment of sexual pleasure, and ego-instincts, directed toward self-preservation.

Attempting to resolve the conflict can lead to a compromise formation: dreams, daydreams, symptoms, character traits, and artistic productions can all be seen as compromises between the desire for gratification and the opposing forces. Simultaneously, the compromise formation allows for the satisfaction of the desire while revealing the defense mobilized against it.

In this theoretical perspective, the danger an individual faces is that of being punished for his or her desires or being overwhelmed by the arousal of instinctual drives. Defense mechanisms come into play to counter these dangers.

At this stage of his theoretical development, more than in earlier or later stages, Freud, when addressing the topic of defense, refers predominantly to repression. At this stage, more than ever before, repression is synonymous with defense. In this topographical model of the mind, Freud is primarily concerned with understanding the psychic mechanisms that facilitate or hinder the passage of content from one system of the mental apparatus to another.

In the seventh chapter of *The Interpretation of Dreams*, Freud (1900) hypothesized that censorship acts between the Unconscious and the Preconscious, as well as between the Preconscious and the Conscious, functioning as a psychic mechanism at the origin of repression that blocks the passage of contents from one system to another. Censorship allows only pleasant contents to pass through and excludes unpleasant contents, which consequently constitute the repressed elements that can only manifest in dreams in a disguised form, as a compromise formation, following the mechanisms of condensation and displacement. Repression is thus understood as a psychic mechanism that protects individuals from the awareness of painful contents, not always the cause of neurotic or psychotic conditions.

In *The Psychical Mechanism of Forgetfulness*, Freud (1898) had already considered those episodes that sometimes occur for every individual when unexpectedly, while realizing that we cannot remember a proper name, another name comes to mind as a substitute, or we mistakenly convince ourselves that the forgotten name starts with a certain letter. Only after giving up the persistent attempt to remember the name does it eventually resurface in our memory.

Through the recounting of a personal experience, Freud explained that repression is found in qualitatively similar forms even in normal individuals. The analysis of a normal episode of forgetting a proper name reveals the same psychic processes involved in the formation of neurotic symptoms: a repressed ideational sequence attracts a recent idea entirely innocuous and produces compromise representations associated with an unpleasant affect that fades when the repressed (in this case, the forgotten name) returns to consciousness. However, Freud asserts that hysterical individuals do not know what they do not want to know, so a certain resistance must be addressed in treatment to bring the repressed content into conscious awareness.

Shortly thereafter, Freud (1901) expanded on the content of this writing in *Psychopathology of Everyday Life*, in which he examined various forms of slips (various forgetfulness, lapses, absentmindedness) to support the idea that they are expressions of a repressed desire in the unconscious, much like dreams and psychopathological symptoms, determined by the same mechanisms (condensation, displacement, substitution, or exchange of opposites).

In 1915, Freud's theorization on the relationships between the unconscious, instincts, and repression reached a certain level of systematization. In these writings, he introduces the topographical model of the mind, describing it in both normal and pathological states, and delving into the theory of instincts, where defenses play a central role. As mentioned earlier, at that time, he believed that the origin of neurosis lay in a conflict between the two types of instincts governing psychic life: self-preservation instincts and sexual instincts. The conflict referred to the idea that sexual instincts, capable of being satisfied phantastically, can follow the pleasure principle, whereas self-preservation instincts, needing a real object for satisfaction, must adhere to the reality principle (Freud, 1911a).

In *Repression*, Freud (1915b) initially defines it as something midway between flight and condemnation: actual flight is not possible because the individual cannot escape from an internal drive. The instinctual drive, which inherently tends toward satisfaction and is thus a source of pleasure, would be repressed because its fulfillment would bring more displeasure than pleasure. According to Freud, the essence of repression is to expel and keep away from consciousness. However, this would only be possible in a period of psychic development where a clear separation has already formed between conscious and unconscious psychic activity. Previously, according to Freud, individuals would defend against instinctual drives through other defense mechanisms (namely, the reversal into the opposite and in turning round upon the subject's own self) described in *Instincts and Their Vicissitudes* (1915a), where Freud examines the psychic processes involved in sadism–masochism and voyeurism–exhibitionism antithetical pairs illustrating that in these pairs, the active goal is replaced by the passive goal, and the object is changed.

Returning to the concept of repression, Freud distinguishes primary repression, in which ideas are denied access to consciousness, and post-repression, or repression proper, involving the removal of contents related through associative pathways to the ideas that have been previously barred from consciousness, even if they originate differently.

Primal repression constitutes the fixation of libidinal development within the Unconscious system, exerting a magnetic pull on ideas repelled by the Conscious system with which it can connect. Thus, the instinctual impulse to which access to consciousness was denied lingers in the Unconscious, organizing, proliferating, and forming connections.

> It proliferates in the dark, as it were, and takes on extreme forms of expression, which when they are translated and presented to the neurotic are not only bound seem alien to him, but frighten him by giving him the picture of an extraordinary and dangerous strength of instinct. This deceptive strength of instinct is the result of an uninhibited development in phantasy and of the damming-up consequent on frustrated satisfaction.
>
> (Freud, 1915b, p. 149)

Repressed contents, however, can breach consciousness in disguised ways, as seen in dreams and symptom formation. Furthermore, repression demands continuous energy expenditure and does not yield permanent effects. Since the repressed constantly exerts pressure toward consciousness, counter-pressure must be maintained. Freud's analogy is illuminating: just as unwanted guests can be prevented from entering a house or expelled once inside, a vigilant guard must remain at the door to prevent their desire to enter or re-enter.

Freud contends that the psychic representation of instinct comprises two elements: the idea and the quota of affect—the quantitative factor of the instinct—with distinct destinies. While the idea can be kept distant from consciousness, the affect can transform into anxiety. As repression aims to avert displeasure, the fate of affect assumes greater importance than that of the idea.

Freud explores zoophobia in this context, where, due to displacement along a chain of associations, an animal replaces the libidinal attitude toward the repressed father, as seen in the case of little Hans (Freud, 1909a). Though the idea is repressed, the affect transforms into anxiety, making the substitution effective requires avoiding the animal.

In obsessive neurosis, a hostile impulse directed toward a loved one is repressed. Initially, the effect dissipates, leading to an ego alteration marked by heightened conscientiousness. Repression employs a reaction formation, reinforcing an opposing sentiment, and the repressed hostile affect resurfaces as social anxiety, moral anxiety, and self-reproach. The repressed idea undergoes displacement toward trivial things (as seen in the *Rat Man*, Freud, 1909b), prompting the individual to impose avoidance thoughts and prohibitions akin to phobias. The failure of repression can result in any of the three neuroses.

In conversion hysteria, the affective intensity can be entirely eliminated (observed as "beautiful indifference") but at a considerable cost.

In *The Unconscious*, Freud reiterates that repression doesn't involve suppressing an idea representing the instinct but rather prevents it from reaching consciousness. Consequently, it continues to exert effects that permeate consciousness while remaining unconscious. Freud revisits the fate of affect, initially asserting that only ideas can become unconscious through repression, whereas sensations, feelings, and affects can only vary quantitatively. While affects can be repressed, blocked, or denied, they cannot be repressed in the same way as ideas can. However, an affect can become unconscious by attaching to another idea (which, as an idea, can be repressed) or by transforming into anxiety. Ideas primarily function as memory traces, while affects and feelings correspond to discharge processes, with their ultimate manifestations perceived as (internal) sensations.

Returning to the economic theory of repression, Freud (1915c) hypothesized that an idea can remain unconscious because the Preconscious defends against its pressure through the defense of anti-cathexis, as observed in the case of *Little Hans* (Freud, 1909a), who counter-invested the idea of the horse. In proper repression, anti-cathexis keeps the idea repressed, while in primal repression, anti-cathexis allows for both the establishment and duration of repression. However, anti-cathexis requires a continuous energy expenditure. Freud suggests that the energy subtracted from the idea during repression is likely utilized for anti-cathexis.

In anxiety hysteria, a series of substitutes is produced, typically through displacement. Over time, these substitute ideas are counter-invested, enabling the individual to project instinctual danger externally. While anxiety can be contained within certain limits, it comes at the cost of restricting personal freedom.

In conversion hysteria, the role played by anti-cathexis is evident in symptom formation.

In obsessive neurosis, anti-cathexis, organized as a reaction formation, facilitates repression and subsequently becomes the point through which the repressed idea manages to resurface.

Before delving into the subsequent phases of Freud's conceptualization, his foundational studies on projection, early observations on introjection, and the evolution of the concept of sublimation must be addressed.

The term projection carries various meanings, potentially leading to conceptual confusion that warrants clarification. Laplanche and Pontalis (1973) identify interpretations differing from the psychoanalytic perspective, such as a tendency to perceive the environment based on one's inclinations and emotional states, assimilating one person to another (e.g., projecting one's sister onto a friend), and assimilating oneself to another person (e.g., projecting oneself into the protagonist of a movie, a process referred to as identification in psychoanalysis).

However, for Freud, projection is the psychic process by which an individual attributes to others desires that they do not recognize within themselves. Freud employs this term to describe psychic processes in normalcy, phobia, and particularly in paranoia.

In Freud's framework, projection emerges as a central process in understanding various mental phenomena. It involves displacing one's own unacceptable desires or emotions onto another person or external object, enabling the individual to sidestep confronting these elements within themselves. This mechanism operates both in everyday life and in more pronounced psychopathological conditions, such as paranoia.

Regarding phobia, Freud (1915c) describes the projection of instinctual danger onto reality, acknowledging that the constitution of the phobic object allows for self-defense through avoidance of the perceived external danger. However, when addressing the formation of phobic symptoms, he predominantly refers to this process as displacement (Freud, 1909a).

In the context of paranoia, Freud had introduced the concept of projection much earlier (Freud, 1894b, 1895, 1896). When examining the case of President Schreber (Freud, 1911b), he expands the concept, reaffirming its role as the defensive mechanism underlying the development of paranoia. While noting that projection is not exclusive to psychosis, Freud emphasizes its significant role in paranoia. In the case of President Schreber, the initial defensive movement is identified in the transformation of affection into its opposite ("I don't love you, I hate you"). Subsequently, the hatred is externalized, attributed to another. Analogous to how neurosis develops after the return of the repressed, paranoia allegedly develops after the "return of the projected." The contents eliminated internally return from the outside through the experience of persecution. In this sense, paranoia can be considered the result of the failure of projection, just as neurosis can be seen as the outcome of the failure of repression.

However, projection alone is insufficient to explain the onset of paranoia. A few years later, Freud (1913) elucidates animism and some beliefs of primitive peoples using the mechanism of projection. In animism, projections of impulses take shape in spirits and demons. Similarly, hostile impulses projected onto the deceased by the living give rise to beliefs that the departed will haunt them throughout the mourning period.

In relation to mourning, it is in the essay *Mourning and Melancholia* (Freud, 1917), written a few years after *Totem and Taboo*, that Freud considers the mechanism of introjection in the context of melancholic pathology resulting from mourning. In the case of the melancholic individual, we observe the mechanism whereby the survivor identifies with the deceased, so to speak, "ingests" them to defend oneself from the pain of loss and the hostile impulses, which now are turned inward.

This is not the appropriate context to delve more deeply into the revolutionary implications of this writing; I will return to it in the third chapter when discussing the extraordinary development that Freud's thoughts on projection and introjection have had in the evolution of Melanie Klein's thinking.

I would like to conclude the examination of Freud's writings on defenses within the topographical frame of reference by recalling the concept of sublimation. Although not strictly understood as a defense, in Freud's thought, it represents one of the possible fates of the sexual drive when repression is excessive. The concept of sublimation, briefly mentioned in the *Three Essays on the Theory of Sexuality* (Freud, 1905), where he argues that during the latency period, sexual drives deviate from the sexual aim and redirect toward new goals in the form of cultural interests, is more extensively addressed in the paper on Leonardo da Vinci (1910).

In this writing, Freud suggests that the drive for knowledge, so pronounced in Leonardo, arises from infantile sexual curiosity, namely the desire to know where babies come from and the roles of the father and mother. When infantile sexual curiosity undergoes excessive repression, as Freud hypothesizes happened to Leonardo, sexual energy transforms into intellectual curiosity without sexual content, through the process that Freud calls sublimation. It would be, as in the case of latency, a substitution of the drive's aim. Freud (1910, p. 75) states:

> A man who was won his way to a state of knowledge cannot properly be said to love and hate: he remains beyond love and hatred. He has investigated instead of loving.

Freud argues that in cases of excessive repression, three solutions to the fate of sexual drive can be envisaged: one is sublimation, the other is a generalized neurotic inhibition of thought, and finally, the third is observed in obsessive neurosis where "eroticized" thought has become an equivalent of the sexual activity it has replaced.

The conceptualization of defense mechanisms in the structural frame of reference

Based on clinical experience and dissatisfaction with certain confounding aspects in the topographical model, Freud developed a new conceptualization of the mental apparatus, finalized in *The Ego and the Id* (1923). His theoretical refinement concluded with the essay *Inhibitions, Symptoms, and Anxiety* (1926). In Freud's latest model, the mental apparatus comprises three structures: id, ego, and superego.

The id, roughly corresponding to the Unconscious system in the topographical model, encompasses primitive instinctual drives. Operating under the pleasure principle and the primary process, its contents are primarily unconscious. The ego, evolving gradually through development, results from the child's interaction with reality. Despite functioning partially unconsciously, it adheres to the reality principle and secondary process, aiming to satisfy the needs of the id while considering both reality and superego demands. The ego serves self-preservation, utilizing defensive mechanisms to navigate instinctual needs in accordance with reality and moral norms.

The superego houses moral norms, cultural values, and personal ideals developed in childhood through interactions with parents and the environment. Both the ego and superego operate largely unconsciously.

Freud's introduction of the structural model coincided with a significant revision of anxiety theory. Previously viewed as a consequence of the repression of sexual instincts, anxiety is now seen as a signal of danger perceived by the ego. This perception prompts the ego to enact defenses against the threat. In the topographical model, anxiety and repression were linked solely to sexual instincts. However, in the structural model, danger can arise from both sexual and destructive drives. This is consistent with Freud's revised theory of instincts in *Beyond the Pleasure Principle* (1920), where he introduces the duality between Eros—encompassing both sexual and self-preservative drives—and the death drive.

The centrality of the ego in mental functioning, emphasized in the structural model, implies a significant increase in attention to defensive mechanisms. These mechanisms are now conceptualized as primary tools used by the ego to satisfy instinctual needs in accordance with the demands of reality and the superego.

The emphasis on defensive mechanisms also leads to changes in treatment technique. In the earlier theoretical phase, treatment was primarily aimed at making the unconscious conscious through free associations, dream analysis, and transference. Now the psychoanalyst's attention is also focused on the analysis and interpretation of defenses.

The radical changes regarding the theorization of defenses introduced in the 1926 can be summarized as follows: (a) The ego can confront conflict through specific inhibitions (when an organ or activity is excessively eroticized, and its unconscious symbolic meaning is heightened) or through different defensive mechanisms, (b) anxiety is the engine of defense, not its effect, (c) repression is to be understood as one of the various defensive mechanisms the ego employs to defend itself against anxiety, and (d) castration anxiety is to be understood as a sort of prototype of the anxiety of loss.

From this point forward, anxiety, according to Freud, is a psychological condition in which the ego, anticipating a situation of danger where it may feel powerless—a situation that can also be compared to a previously experienced traumatic event—triggers defensive mechanisms.

Therefore, the state of anxiety that leads the ego to employ defenses is conceptualized as signal anxiety. Freud likens this to a kind of vaccine that reproduces in attenuated form the reaction of anxiety originally experienced in a traumatic situation, thus enabling defense mechanisms to come into play. This concept is distinct from automatic anxiety, described as a psychological condition where the individual cannot control an excess of stimuli, whether from external or internal sources. This state has a traumatic effect precisely because the ego, in a state of profound psychic helplessness, is overwhelmed by it.

Freud pointed out that in obsessive neurosis, the ego employs defensive mechanisms other than repression: regression, reaction formation, undoing, and isolation. The ego regresses the genital organization to the sadistic-anal stage. In addition to using repression, it develops marked traits of conscientiousness and cleanliness, through which the struggle against instinctual impulses takes place "under the banner of ethical principles" (Freud, 1926, p. 116). Moreover, the obsessive neurotic may resort defensively to undoing and isolation. Laplanche and Pontalis (1973) define undoing as a psychological mechanism whereby the subject strives to make sure that past thoughts, words, gestures, and actions have not occurred. To this end, the subject uses a thought or behavior that has an opposite meaning.

Freud (1909b) had previously described this mechanism as a conflict between love and hate, exemplified by the *Rat man*, who initially removes and then replaces the stone on the road where the carriage of his beloved woman would have passed. Isolation, a mechanism Freud had already addressed in one of his earliest writings on defenses (Freud, 1894b), serves as a defensive function of the ego. It involves stripping an idea of its effects and/or preventing associative relations between representations, a condition often observed in the analysis of individuals who exhibit significant difficulty in free associations.

Concerning the source of anxiety, in the 1926 writing, Freud identifies it in the perception of a danger linked to separation and loss of the object. He refers to the universal experience of loss that every individual undergoes, including the loss of the maternal breast during weaning. Loss, as described in this writing, extends beyond the loss of the penis. Freud recalls infantile experiences of anxiety in the face of solitude, strangers, darkness—in other words, the absence of the mother. Only in the phallic phase does the fear of losing the mother transform into castration anxiety. Subsequently, due to the fear of losing the love of the superego, castration anxiety evolves into moral and social anxiety.

In this writing, Freud also addresses the distinction between males and females, asserting that in females, never having possessed a penis, one cannot speak of the fear of castration. There wouldn't be a sensation of lack and actual loss of the object but rather the loss of love from the object.

> Since there is no doubt that hysteria has a strong affinity with femininity, just as obsessional neurosis has with masculinity, it appears probable that, as a determinant of anxiety, loss of love plays much the same part in hysteria as the threat of castration does in phobias and fear of the super-ego in obsessional neurosis.
>
> (Freud, 1926, p. 173)

In this paper, Freud emphasizes that repression is not a one-time event; instead, it demands an ongoing expenditure of energy. In the context of psychoanalytic treatment, this continuous effort is experienced as resistance, implying a necessary anti-cathexis.

In cases of hysteria and phobia, the anti-cathexis is external, evident in the avoidance of perceived dangers. Conversely, in obsessive neurosis, the anti-cathexis is internal, giving rise to alterations in the ego through reaction formations.

In this recent period, Freud presents his more systematic reflections on the defensive processes at play in psychoses. In these psychopathological conditions, the ego, overwhelmed by the id, no longer manages to come to terms with the demands imposed by reality (Freud, 1924a), which would be intolerably frustrating to the point of denial. While in neurosis, the incompatible idea is repressed, in psychosis, it is reality itself that is denied.

In *The Loss of Reality in Neurosis and Psychosis* (Freud, 1924b), he revisits the case of Elisabeth von R. (Freud, 1893d), recalling that she was consumed by the incompatible idea of marrying her brother-in-law when her sister was dying. As a defense, she forgot about this and, as a compromise formation, developed hysterical symptoms. In the case of psychosis, Freud suggests that the girl, instead of removing her unacceptable idea, would have denied the very fact of her sister's death. In neurosis, therefore, an aspect of internal reality is avoided, while in psychosis, the individual first detaches from reality and then constructs a new one.

> Neurosis does not disavows the reality, it only ignores it; psychosis disavows it and tries to replace it.
>
> (Freud, 1924b, p. 185)

Just as in neurosis, anxiety warns of the danger of the return of the repressed; in psychosis, anxiety arises because the denied reality constantly resurfaces. The neurotic creates a new reality, but only in his imagination, while the psychotic loses the ability to distinguish their delusional constructions from external reality.

In a later writing, *Negation* (Freud, 1925), Freud addresses another type of negation (in German, *Verneinung*), distinguishing it from the denial of reality (in German, *Verleugnung*). He defines it as the rejection of an already expressed desire. Through negation, a repressed content can come to consciousness on the condition that it is immediately denied. An example given by Freud is that of a patient who asserts that the person he dreamt of could not be his mother. This linguistic denial is interpreted by Freud as "therefore, she is the mother." Saying no, denying an idea, is, for Freud, the hallmark of the repressed.

The exploration of the theme of denial later led Freud to compose the writings *Fetishism* (1927) and *Splitting of the Ego in the Process of Defence* (1938a), where he observes that the denial of the perception of reality is never complete. For example, the fetishist simultaneously recognizes and denies the lack of a penis in a woman, and in pathological mourning, an individual can simultaneously deny and accept the death of a loved one. When the defense process involves the denial of reality, a split in the ego is thus constituted, destined not only to never heal but to deepen further.

These themes are revisited in Freud's last paper, *An Outline of Psycho-Analysis* (Freud, 1938b), in which he not only reaffirms the conceptualization of the splitting of the ego in the defense process, asserting that even individuals affected by the most severe forms of psychosis retain a part of the ego that takes reality into account, but also adds that the coexistence of two contradictory psychic attitudes (i.e., accepting and denying reality) is also observed in cases of neurosis. Normality and the degree of severity of psychopathology would thus depend on a quantitative factor, relying on the intensity of each of the two attitudes.

It must be clear that the concept of ego splitting to which Freud refers is not related to the defense mechanism of splitting, explored by Melanie Klein (1946), which will be discussed in the third chapter.

As is well known, Freud never systematically addressed the issue of defense mechanisms. Instead, this task was taken on by his daughter Anna, whose work will be examined in the next chapter.

2   Forty years on

Anna Freud's re-examination of defense mechanisms in dialogue with Joseph Sandler

Anna Maria Rosso

In 1936, Anna Freud authored the renowned book *The Ego and the Mechanisms of Defence*, offering a singular and comprehensive exploration of Sigmund Freud's theories on defense mechanisms. Thirty years later, she reissued the book without alterations. Nineteen years thereafter, Joseph Sandler (1985) published a valuable volume recounting discussions held with Anna Freud in 1972–1973. These conversations took place as part of the effort by Sandler and a group of colleagues to compile the Hampstead Psychoanalytic Index, aiming to clarify controversial conceptual issues related to the definition of defenses.

In this chapter, I provide a concise review of these discussions, with a specific focus on the motives behind defense mechanisms, the differentiation between defense mechanisms and defensive measures, and Anna Freud's distinctive contributions to identifying additional defense mechanisms in children and adolescents. Additionally, I explore her role in advancing the theory of psychoanalytic technique in the analysis of defenses.

The motives for defense

Aligned with structural theory and the last theory of instincts, Anna Freud (1936) consistently underscores that defense mechanisms, orchestrated by the ego to regulate the id, aim to ward off anxiety or displeasure provoked by desire. Three motives underlie the defense against instincts: the anxiety of the superego in adults, the anxiety of parental punishment in children, and the anxiety stemming from the power of the instinct.

In neurotic adults, defense against instincts is driven by the anxiety imposed by the superego, advocating an ideal condemning both sexuality and aggression. In contrast, young children defend against their instincts to comply with parental expectations. Although the outcome is identical, the distinction lies in the fact that a child's anxiety is tangible, originating from the external world, whereas an adult's anxiety emanates from a psychic structure.

DOI: 10.4324/9781003536994-4

Defense is set into motion by the anxiety stemming from the power of instinct, particularly when instinctual demands become excessive or when the ego feels abandoned by the superego or the external world. This underscores Anna Freud's keen observation of the child and their relationship with the external world, encompassing the influence of parental and educational relationships on the child. The issue of anxiety regarding instinctual power takes center stage during puberty, a life phase where characteristic defenses (such as asceticism and intellectualization) can be observed, and will be discussed in further detail later on.

Anna Freud goes beyond the conventional understanding that defense mechanisms exclusively counter instinctual impulses. She consistently emphasizes a more comprehensive scope, asserting that defense encompasses not only instinct but also the effects associated. When an emotion becomes intricately entwined with a prohibited instinctual desire, the ego initiates defensive measures. The overarching objective remains constant: to fortify against anxiety, even in the presence of affect-laden experiences such as grief, longing, or sadness.

In the discussion with Sandler (1985) on this subject, Anna Freud emphasizes that when she wrote the book on defense mechanisms, there was no discourse addressing defense against affects. During that period, affects were exclusively regarded as accompaniments or derivatives of instinct. Sandler underscores the importance of not limiting the conceptualization of affect to instinctual derivatives, acknowledging that emotions can also emerge under the influence of the external world. He notes that instincts are theoretical constructs, and Anna Freud's discourse centers around desires. Articulating the concept of desire, as opposed to instinct, proves beneficial as it enables the examination of the emotional facet as an integral component of desire.

The theme of defense against affects holds particular significance regarding technique theory, especially in the context of treating children. Anna Freud specifies that sexual instincts may elicit affective states such as love, intense desire, jealousy, humiliation, distress, and mourning for the loss of a loved one. In contrast, aggressive desires are often accompanied by emotions such as hatred, anger, and fury. As the ego grapples with these instincts, it must quell the accompanying affects through transformation. By scrutinizing the defenses against these effects, the analyst gains insights into the defenses employed against the instincts.

In this regard, Anna Freud discusses the defense mechanism of transforming into its opposite, frequently observed in children. For instance, she cites the case of a male child patient who assumed the role of a soldier and displayed overt aggression as a defense against the anxiety of castration. Similarly, she references a female child patient who engaged in imaginative play, portraying herself as a magician capable of altering the entire world, thus defending herself against the envy she harbored toward her younger sibling.

Defense mechanisms and defensive measures

One of the most intriguing aspects of the dialogue between Anna Freud and Sandler (Sandler, 1985) revolves around the distinction between defense mechanisms and defensive measures. The discussion underscores the idea that nearly anything can be employed as a defense, prompting the question of whether, for instance, engaging in clown-like behavior is a defensive measure or an inherent aspect of an individual's personality. This consideration opens up the fascinating possibility of an infinite array of potential defenses.

Anna Freud counters by noting that even seemingly mundane actions, like falling asleep, can function as defenses against aggression. However, she refrains from categorizing these actions as either mechanisms or defensive measures. In a sense, anything intended to keep an id content or affect (or whatever the ego is unwilling to accept) at bay is considered defensive. However, it is crucial to distinguish between behaviors that may be used for defensive purposes, defensive measures, and authentic defense mechanisms.

Anna Freud analogizes defenses to weapons that exist solely as such, akin to rifles or lances. She illustrates this concept with the example of a young individual accused of matricide with a frying pan. Although a frying pan is not inherently a weapon, it was momentarily utilized as one. Similarly, engaging in clown-like behavior may serve a defensive function, much like numerous other activities chosen only temporarily.

Defense mechanisms, including repression and projection, are inherently defensive. Furthermore, she posits a meaningful distinction between defense mechanisms and defensive measures, affirming that only the former is closely intertwined with neuroses, which can be discerned by the specific types of defenses employed, for example, repression in hysteria, regression, isolation, undoing, and reaction formation in obsessive neurosis, and displacement in phobias.

Sandler raises the objection that repression is commonly used to avoid being continually overwhelmed by the return of what has been repressed. Anna Freud counters, maintaining that this does not alter the fact that repression is always and solely a protective tool, specifically employed to keep something out of consciousness. Conversely, she deems it more appropriate to designate as defensive measures those closer to normalcy and character structure.

This point, as will be elucidated subsequently, proves crucial in contemporary psychoanalytic taxonomic formulations, particularly concerning patterns and personality disorders.

Referring to Reich's writing (1933) on *character "armor-plating,"* Anna Freud defines character as a more or less enduring balance between the id and the ego. This equilibrium represents a stable interplay of quantities, giving rise to a more or less permanent style of interaction between the two.

In this context, the *character "armor-plating,"* described by Reich, emerges as a stabilizing defense system.

In her discussions with Sandler, she regards body attitudes and character traits as remnants of past defenses that have, over time, become autonomous from the original conflictual situation. In these cases, present defenses are no longer contingent on the particular impulse against which one defended; instead, they have become integral to what could be termed the individual's "style."

These reflections raise the question of how defenses can alter the ego, leading to limitations and a significant impoverishment of psychic functioning that extend beyond mere personality style, even though they don't manifest as true neuroses.

Anna Freud herself (1936) illustrates the case of a woman who, during childhood, experienced intense hostile feelings toward her mother. Initially, she attempted to defend herself by redirecting her hatred toward other women, then turning it inward, and finally projecting the hatred outward. This process led her to perceive herself as a victim of others' malice, ultimately developing what we would now characterize as a paranoid personality. Furthermore, Anna Freud underscores the danger associated with repression itself for the integrity of the personality, as it can result in the splitting of entire areas of instinctual and affective life.

Anna Freud makes an original contribution by addressing two additional defensive measures that have a lasting impact on the entire personality: inhibitions and a form of altruism. Regarding the former, Anna Freud shares observations on children who progressively relinquish certain activities and confine themselves to roles as passive spectators. Among these children, some accept certain limitations and successfully invest in other activities. However, there are also those who can no longer engage in their activities because, despite being innocuous in themselves, they have become associated with past sexual experiences. Once these activities become sexualized, they fall under the purview of the ego's defenses. These sexualized activities become a source of conflict, causing more distress than pleasure, and consequently, they are avoided. In some cases, inhibitions are so extensive that they result in a considerable impoverishment of the ego and a stable alteration of its structure. I will return to the topic of altruism shortly.

Anna Freud cautions that completely successful defenses, i.e., those that have led to the complete disappearance of awareness of what has been repressed, are always perilous. This is because they lead to a reduction in the area of consciousness, overly limit the functionalities of the ego, or distort reality, thereby diminishing the efficiency of ego functions.

She adds that all defensive mechanisms arise in normal development, and it is the quantitative factor that determines the normality of the defensive functioning outcome. Sublimation, however, holds a different position as it is always normal or leads to a normal result.

It is now time to ponder how many and which defensive mechanisms exist. Anna Freud, summarizing her father's conceptualization of defenses, lists nine: regression, repression, reaction formation, isolation, undoing, projection, introjection, turning against the self, and turning into the opposite. To these, she adds sublimation, the displacement of the instinct's aim, considered more characteristic of normalcy than of the neurotic realm.

Reflecting on her writing nearly 40 years earlier, she recalls her initial reluctance to define nine defensive mechanisms. She had the feeling that by stating there were nine, there could easily have been ten. "One should never count these things," she asserts (Sandler & Freud, 1981a, p. 155).

In her 1936 book, Anna Freud devotes a brief chapter of just 11 pages to a concise description of the defense mechanisms identified by her father. However, Sandler (1985), known for his meticulous attention to clear conceptual definitions, expands on this chapter in his book for a substantial 90 pages. At a certain point, responding to his persistent requests for conceptual clarification, Anna Freud says to him:

If you look at them [the defense mechanisms] microscopically, they all merge into each other. You will find repression anywhere you look. You will find bits of reaction formation or identification. You will find five or six defenses compressed into one attitude. The point is that one should not look at them microscopically, but macroscopically, as big and separate mechanisms, structures, events, whatever you want to call them. Then they will stand out from each other, and the problems of separating them theoretically become negligible. You have to take off your glasses to look at them, not put them on.

(Sandler & Freud, 1981a, pp. 196–197)

I have included this entire quote from Anna Freud because I believe it can be helpful and reassuring for all of us navigating this intricate theoretical landscape, often feeling like we've entered a maze with the fear of not finding our way out. An American friend of mine, upon learning about my intention to write a book on the topic of defenses in psychoanalysis, cautioned me about the perils, saying, "Forget it, you'll end up down the rabbit hole!"

To avoid "ending up down the rabbit hole," I will focus only on a few aspects related to repression and the discussion of undoing and projection. These highlight crucial issues that will be explored in the next chapter dedicated to the Kleinian model.

In relation to the notion of repression, Anna Freud elucidates a clear distinction that is commonly challenging to grasp, delineating between primary repression and repression proper. She suggests that this distinction is related to psychic development: during the division between the id and the ego, certain elements of the id do not progress further, remaining anchored at their initial stage. In this context, it is not so much a defense mechanism per se, but rather the lack of further elaboration of these contents in the developmental process. They remain confined to a more primitive level of functioning. On the other hand, repression proper involves the fact that other contents develop later at higher levels and are subsequently rejected.

In the case of primary repression, the contents are neither incorporated nor expelled; rather, they are set aside without undergoing complete assimilation. It is noteworthy that impulses subjected to primary repression create their own underground world, remaining foreign to the secondary process due to a lack of words that represent them. Being unqualified to emerge to the surface, they attract other surface contents, exerting a kind of "pull from below."

Another notable clarification is Anna Freud's explicit statement that repression also combats aggressive impulses, contrary to her 1936 assertion, when she focused mainly on sexual desires. This shift in perspective may also arise from her clinical work with children and theoretical developments in psychoanalysis over the preceding 40 years.

Finally, a crucial point is the assertion that mental health in adulthood is based on the ability to use repression in early childhood. This assertion is supported by clinical observation that identifies a normal lack of the repression mechanism in children defined as "borderline" (a term not further specified).

The discussion on undoing is particularly intriguing because, despite Sandler's insistence on regarding it as a defense mechanism typically employed in obsessive neurosis, the discourse that unfolds highlights the proximity of this concept to the Kleinian notion of reparation. Sandler emphasizes how in "doing and undoing," desire is gratified through a specific action, and the defense lies in undoing it, signaling the typical defense mechanism of obsessive neurosis. However, Anna Freud herself recounts the example of a child who, after pulling a girl's hair and being scolded by the educator, unsuccessfully attempted to put the hair back on the girl's head. Another colleague's association involves a patient who searched for banana peels on the street to gather them and prevent someone from slipping and getting hurt. I will delve further into this issue in the following chapter.

Regarding projection, the discussion takes an intriguing turn to clarify its conceptual definition. Sandler proposes labeling projection as the attribution of an impulse to another person only when the projecting subject perceives the projected impulse as directed against oneself. He suggests using the term "externalization" in all other cases where this "reflective" quality is not present. Anna Freud concurs, stating that the term "externalization" can be applied in other contexts, such as when a child externalizes a conflict by narrating a story.

Sandler further probes whether projection necessarily involves a prior stage of identification, allowing the utilization of real perception for the purpose of projection. This is observed in individuals who can identify specific aspects of others, employing real elements to justify their projections. Anna Freud agrees with this, emphasizing that the intensification of empathy is an essential prerequisite for the mechanism of projection. In this sense, the individual first identifies an aspect of reality truly belonging to the other and subsequently employs it for projective purposes, an aspect of projection that was already well delineated by Freud (1922).

In addition to the previously mentioned defense mechanisms, Anna Freud explores instances of denial, both within the realm of fantasy and through verbal and behavioral expressions, commonly observed in children. Before delving into her clinical experiences, she refers to the daydreams recounted by Little Hans (Freud, 1909a) at the end of his analysis.

Within these daydreams, the child describes a fantasy where he attends to other children in a bathroom and is subsequently visited by a plumber. In this narrative, the plumber removes the child's buttocks and penis, replacing them with larger and more aesthetically pleasing ones. As widely recognized, these daydreams were interpreted as the fulfillment of the desire to possess a penis similar to that of the father and to personally care for children, mirroring his mother's role toward his sister.

In the course of normal development, the capacity to fulfill desires through fantasy enables children to temporarily deny painful reality, awaiting the psychic maturity necessary to confront it. Anna Freud recounts the experience of a young patient who engaged in fantasies of caring for a domesticated lion, a captivating creature that instilled fear in others but harbored unique affection solely for him. While Hans had developed a phobia, this child had circumvented neurosis through the power of fantasy: the feared father had been transfigured into a protective and obedient lion, and the anxiety the child sought to evade was betrayed only in imagining others frightened by the lion's presence.

Anna Freud explains how, in adulthood under normal conditions, the efficacy of daydreams is limited and transient. Adults lose the ability to confront real anxiety through fantasy, as the function of the ego prevails in recognizing and facing reality. When adults defend themselves through the denial of reality, they inevitably open the door to delusional and/or hallucinatory disorders that seriously compromise their functioning.

In contrast to adults, children do not find the disparity between their fantasies and reality disturbing. Under normal conditions, they can clearly distinguish between the two worlds. The child, in fact, engages in the play of pretending to believe, a mode far removed from genuinely believing.

Denying the effect might be considered a subsequent step, a mechanism adopted when the denial of reality is impeded by an individual's sense of reality. Anna Freud suggests that various forms of denial may follow a developmental progression wherein there is a transition from the rejection of external reality to its acceptance while still maintaining the ability to shield oneself from associated emotions.

For instance, a three-year-old child playfully assuming the role of a traffic officer at preschool might require a helmet for this purpose. By the age of eight, if the child continues to harbor the fantasy of being a traffic officer, the need for the helmet might diminish, and the child could comfortably sit, forsaking the pursuit of other children while fantasizing within himself that he is a traffic officer.

Sandler postulates that during childhood, drawing a clear line between denial in fantasy as a defense mechanism and the normal function of fantasy for comfort and gratification is challenging. Anna Freud replies that the presence of a significant defense mechanism may be considered when the child, instead of confronting the real world, excessively retreats into denial, both in fantasy and action.

An open question concerns the chronological sequence in the classification of defense mechanisms. Initially, Anna Freud suggests that the attainment of differentiation between the ego and the id, between the self and the external world, and the formation of the superego are prerequisites for the use of repression, projection, and sublimation, respectively. At a certain point, she emphasizes that the use of repression requires an already structured personality, stating,

> If you haven't yet built the house, you can't throw somebody out of it.
>
> (Sandler & Freud, 1981b, p. 267)

Conversely, she asserts that regression, transformation into the opposite, and turning inward on the Self seem to be independent of developmental stages, hypothesizing that they may constitute the very first defense mechanisms of the ego.

However, immediately afterward, she retracts these statements and abandons the attempt to classify defense mechanisms chronologically. She notes that early neurotic symptoms in children are often hysterical, thus connected to repression, while genuine masochistic phenomena are rarely encountered in early childhood.

In this regard, one might question whether it is naive to interpret physical symptoms in children as hysterical manifestations and consequently infer the use of repression. Today, most, if not all, contemporary psychoanalysts would raise this objection.

The issue of the chronological development of defense mechanisms will be thoroughly addressed and explored in the next chapter, examining Melanie Klein's perspective.

Anna Freud's distinctive contributions to the identification of additional defense mechanisms

Anna Freud made significant contributions to the study of defense mechanisms, particularly by identifying additional ones, including identification with the aggressor, altruism, asceticism, and intellectualization.

It is essential to note that the concept of identification with the aggressor had been previously explored by Ferenczi (1932, 1933), and Anna Freud's interpretation differs significantly from Ferenczi's under the same name.

While Anna Freud views it as a defensive process frequently observed in children's development, resulting in transient modifications of the ego, Ferenczi contextualizes it within situations of abuse. In abusive circumstances, the child, overwhelmed by fear, submits to the aggressor's will, internalizing their desires and experiencing their guilt. These harrowing experiences have profound and lasting consequences on the child's psychic development.

Identification with the aggressor

Anna Freud observed the defense of identification with the aggressor in children facing normal conditions. For example, a girl overcoming the fear of encountering a ghost by running through a dark corridor pretending to be the ghost herself, or a boy, fearing scolding for ringing the doorbell insistently, aggressing the maid for her slowness in opening the door. Another instance involved a girl advising her frightened little brother to "pretend to be a little dog" to avoid being bitten by dogs.

In these situations, Anna Freud noted that the child identified with an object inducing fear. She hypothesized that this defense mechanism could represent an intermediate phase in the normal development of the superego as well as a step toward the development of paranoia. According to her perspective, by identifying with the punitive attitude of parents, the child internalizes criticism, progressing toward superego formation. At this stage, external criticism is internalized, while transgression is externalized, indicating the projection of guilt.

During discussions with Sandler, the relationship between identification with the aggressor and the mechanism of turning the passive into the active is explored for greater conceptual clarity. Anna Freud specifies that, despite similarities, these concepts do not coincide. The child transforms into the aggressor to protect oneself, not to aggress. For instance, the girl pretending to be a ghost masters the fear of being aggressed without intending to aggress in return. Anna Freud emphasizes that, in the defense of identification with the aggressor, the source of anxiety is external, not involving instinctual aggression. The child mobilizes aggression to master anxiety, but is not inherently aggressive.

In subsequent discussions, Anna Freud grapples with the intricate nature of these issues, acknowledging their unresolved complexity. To illuminate this intricacy, she provides an example of an exceptionally aggressive child exposed to the father's aggression, witnessing violent actions against the mother. The pivotal question arises: does the child defend itself by adopting aggression to master anxiety, or does the father's aggressiveness trigger the child's innate aggressive tendencies? The prognosis would be more favorable in the former case, assuming it involves an imitation of the father's aggressive behavior.

Despite these considerations, the matter appears only vaguely outlined, leaving numerous questions unanswered.

It is somewhat surprising that neither Anna Freud, Joseph Sandler, nor the participants in her research group made even a brief allusion to Ferenczi's (1932, 1933) distinct conceptualization of identification with the aggressor.

Altruism

In her examination of altruism, Anna Freud delves into the lives of individuals who willingly relinquish their own desires to wholeheartedly devote themselves to others. Drawing inspiration from Edmond Rostand's literary character Cyrano de Bergerac, who, in expressing love for his beloved under the cover of darkness, orchestrates his rival Christian's triumph in winning her affection, Freud identifies a parallel disposition of renunciation in one of her patients.

This woman, like Cyrano, sacrifices her romantic life and personal ambitions to selflessly assist friends, arranging marriages and tending to their children. Anna Freud posits that this early renunciation of instincts involves the formation of an exceptionally rigid superego, hindering the patient from gratifying her own desires. Rather than being repressed, these desires find fulfillment through substitutes in the external world, treated as conduits for instinctual satisfaction.

Instinctual desires get projected onto others, with whom the patient identifies. This allows for the satisfaction of instincts through vicarious living and the use of mechanisms like projection and identification. This intricate process serves a dual purpose: by altruistically fulfilling the instincts of others, the individual discovers satisfaction for their own instincts, defying the prohibitions imposed by the superego. Simultaneously, this unleashes previously inhibited aggression and activity.

As an extreme illustration, Anna Freud cites the murderer who, in the name of the oppressed, slays the oppressor. In such instances, the target of aggression consistently remains the representative of authority, the figure who enforced instinctual renunciation in childhood. The gratification of instinct in these scenarios emanates from the exhilaration derived from giving and aiding, facilitating the transformation of passivity into activity and compensating for narcissistic humiliation through the perceived empowerment inherent in the role of a benefactor.

Asceticism and intellectualization

During adolescence, asceticism and intellectualization occasionally manifest as defense mechanisms in response to heightened instincts and the subsequent recognition of their potency. The surge in instinctual energy prompts the imposition of stringent prohibitions against these desires, leading to their outright rejection. As the conflict between the id and the ego intensifies in adolescence, so too does the escalation of these defense mechanisms.

In this developmental phase, a latent interest in tangible objects gives way to a pronounced fascination with abstract thinking. Themes central to conflicts among psychic entities, such as freedom and control, rebellion, submission to authority, and the concept of free will, captivate the adolescent mind. This signifies a translation of instinctual processes into the language of intellect—an intentional effort by the ego to harness and regulate instincts through the power of thought.

Anna Freud (1936) posits that instinctual danger cultivates human intelligence, sparking a quest for solutions akin to responses to actual danger. Asceticism seeks to thwart the id through categorical prohibitions, while intellectualization adeptly manages instinctual impulses by rendering them accessible to consciousness through their integration with ideational content. As long as asceticism and intellectualization refrain from causing enduring alterations to the ego, they serve as normal defense mechanisms during adolescence, protecting against significant risks stemming from unrestrained breaches of psychological defenses.

The analysis of defense mechanisms in psychoanalytic treatment

Anna Freud emphasizes that, in the early stages of psychoanalysis, the focus rested on the id or the Unconscious system, with the initial objective of "disabling" the ego. This pursuit began with hypnosis, evolved through suggestion, and culminated in applying the basic rule of free associations. However, instances of failure or only temporary success led to the realization that the essence lay not in "disabling" the ego but in comprehending its resistance and analyzing the defenses it employed. By observing the defensive transformations of instincts, the analyst gains a deeper understanding of the patient's instinctual life and the process of ego development. In a sense, the analyst proceeds akin to decoding a dream, comprehending the mechanisms of condensation and displacement.

The approach aims to heighten awareness of defensive functioning, facilitating the surfacing of unconscious content. Considering that, according to the structural model of the mind, substantial portions of the ego remain unconscious, including its defensive functioning, it becomes crucial to bring them into consciousness alongside the derivatives of the id.

As the analyst's primary task is to render conscious that which is unconscious, irrespective of the psychic instance to which it belongs, the analysis of defenses occupies a central position. Like any endeavor by the analyst to delve into the unconscious, the analysis of defenses inevitably prompts resistance from the ego, albeit partially collaborative.

The resistances emerge through a reinforcement of defensive measures and may manifest as hostility toward the analyst. Understanding the timing and manner in which these resistances appear aids the analyst in comprehending the defenses. Interpreting them in the context of what the patient is defending against allows the patient to feel more liberated in bringing forth the repressed material.

Sandler (1985) asserts that when interpreting defense mechanisms, we are essentially deciphering the mechanics of the unconscious ego. This allows us to present the patient, perhaps for the first time, with a representation of the mechanisms they have employed. Once these mechanisms are brought into consciousness, they cease to operate with the same efficiency.

In this context, Anna Freud's clinical example of a patient who assumed a contemptuous attitude whenever observations about her symptoms were made proves enlightening. Analyzing the defense that manifested through hostility toward the analyst revealed a profoundly self-critical stance whenever the patient experienced emotions of tenderness, desire, or anxiety. Having interpreted the defense, subsequently, it allowed bringing to light the patient's identification with the hypercritical father.

As previously emphasized, Anna Freud places significant importance on analyzing defenses against affects. Since instincts are hypothetical constructs, Sandler suggests that speaking of desire rather than instinct is advantageous. This approach enables the consideration of the emotional aspect as a component of desire. Building on the idea that patients employ the same defenses to protect against emotions and instinctual impulses,

Anna Freud underscores the importance of observing how the patient defends against affects.

She points out that historically, defenses against emotions were not explicitly discussed; affects were regarded as accompaniments or derivatives of instincts. The prevailing assumption was that defenses were implicitly directed against instincts rather than affects. According to Anna Freud, individuals possess a limited repertoire of defenses that they can employ against both instincts and affects. However, illustrating defense mechanisms against emotions is much more accessible for the patient to grasp.

In the case of the aforementioned patient, Anna Freud asserts that rendering the contents conscious would have been impossible without initially analyzing the defenses against her emotions, manifested in ironic denigration. Commencing with the examination of these defenses enabled Anna Freud and her patient to unveil the historical origin of this defense: the patient's father, with whom she identified, desired his daughter to maintain strong self-control and ridiculed her whenever she expressed emotions more freely.

Anna Freud underscores the effectiveness of this technical approach, even when working with children, emphasizing the importance of observing when a child expresses an affect that might seem inappropriate to the situation, such as appearing happy in a circumstance typically associated with sadness. In these situations, the ego defensively intervenes by transforming the emotion, and the analysis of this transformation facilitates the awareness of the defense.

According to Anna Freud, when the analyst dismantles the defense, both the instinctual drive and the emotion can access consciousness. This, in turn, facilitates a more effective resolution to the conflict for the ego and the superego.

However, the decision to interpret defenses or not, according to Anna Freud, should depend on the motive for the defense. Returning to the beginning of the chapter, it is pertinent to highlight that, according to Anna Freud, three primary motivations drive defense: the anxiety of the superego, real anxiety, and anxiety caused by the potency of instincts.

Her technical guidelines prioritize the analysis of defenses as an effective intervention, especially in the first case, when the reason for defense is the anxiety of the superego. This is particularly impactful if the identifications contributing to the superego's formation become accessible during the analysis.

Interpreting defenses also demonstrates promise when they are motivated by real anxiety. However, according to Anna Freud, if defense serves to avoid pain or displeasure, the child should learn to endure greater amounts of displeasure without resorting to defensive mechanisms. In her view, this represents more a function of education than analysis. Nowadays, most psychoanalysts likely view this perspective as outdated, and this crucial point will be further explored in the following chapters.

When the defenses arise from the patient's fear of the potency of their instincts, Anna Freud warns that there is a risk of dismantling defensive measures without providing adequate support for the patient's ego. Although the analyst attempts to reassure patients by asserting that instinctual impulses are more controllable when brought into consciousness, this reassurance might prove illusory, particularly when the fear of the potency of instinctual impulses serves as the primary motivation for defense.

Anna Freud cautions that interpreting defenses has a dual effect: it can strengthen the ego by bringing unconscious instincts into consciousness, but it also carries the risk of weakening the ego by immobilizing defensive processes at the very moment they are exposed. This represents a crucial point in the theory of technique.

3 The Klein–Bion paradigm shift

Anna Maria Rosso

Core concepts in Melanie Klein's psychoanalytic theory

From her earliest works, Melanie Klein, though adhering to Freud's teachings, develops an original line of thought that leads her to a significant revision of the theory of drives, a new perspective on the nature of objects, and the formulation of her own general theory of development.

In Klein's theory, the object is no longer considered simply a means for drive satisfaction; rather, it becomes primarily another individual with whom the child establishes a relationship—both real and shaped by their unconscious phantasies—from the very beginning of life.

Using the innovative technique of play in child analysis, Klein initially sought to confirm Freud's theories, particularly focusing on children's inhibitions toward knowledge. She interpreted these inhibitions as resulting from the repression of sexual drives, driven by fears of punishment associated with castration anxiety (Klein, 1924). However, her observation of children's play soon allowed her to identify the early emergence of Oedipal phantasies and interests, accompanied by a much earlier and more severe development of the superego than Freud had originally proposed (Klein, 1928).

Observing the sometimes-violent nature of children's phantasies during play led Klein to reinterpret Freud's emphasis on the death drive's biological roots, favoring a more psychological perspective. While Freud (1920) arrived at his final reformulation of drive theory by identifying the death drive as opposed to the life drive, viewing it as a result of a biological tendency toward self-destruction, Klein focused on sadism. She viewed sadism as an expression of the death drive, linking it to the oral and anal stages of development, consistent with Freud's thinking, but understood it more specifically as a distinct psychological phenomenon, inherently tied to the infant's relationship with the mother from the earliest moments of life (Klein, 1932).

The projection of the child's own sadism onto the object is at the root of persecutory anxiety and the harshness of the early superego. From this perspective, the infant's psychic life is dominated by a drive to possess,

DOI: 10.4324/9781003536994-5

control, and destroy the mother's body (Klein, 1930). The central dynamic is no longer a conflict between the pursuit of pleasure and the fear of punishment but rather a struggle between destructive impulses and the fear of retaliation. Klein suggests that the Oedipal conflict itself originates in this phase of early sadism, as the destructive phantasies directed toward the parents and their sexual union generate the child's anxiety, leading them to project their hatred onto bad objects, perceived as cruel and persecutory largely due to their own projected sadism.

Klein (1935) argues that the child possesses an innate, unconscious awareness of the mother's existence and that projecting their own sadism is essential for survival. The child perceives the internal death instinct as if it were an external threat, experiencing it as a fear of dying that manifests as a sense of persecution, imagined as a relationship with an unpredictable and hostile object (Klein, 1946). This perception arises because the child tends to personify all their sensations, interpreting them as coming from either good or bad objects, depending on whether they are experienced as pleasant or unpleasant (Klein, 1935). In Klein's view, it is clear that drives and objects are deeply interconnected, as drives are inherently directed toward the object.

While in her early writings Klein focuses on the death instinct and persecutory anxiety, which largely result from the projection of the child's own hatred, she subsequently shifts her attention to depressive anxiety, where the child's feelings of love toward the object come to the forefront, accompanied by the fear of harming and losing it. In her 1935 work, *A Contribution to the Psychogenesis of Manic-Depressive States*, Klein describes how depressive anxiety emerges after the "paranoid position," characterized by a concern for the object's well-being. This form of anxiety reflects the child's love for the mother and gratitude for the care received, highlighting feelings of loss and guilt.

Starting in 1946, with her work *Notes on Some Schizoid Mechanisms*, Klein returned to examining the dynamics of paranoid functioning, taking a significant step toward a more mature synthesis of her ideas. During this time, she deepened her understanding of splitting as a defense mechanism and introduced the "revolutionary" concept of projective identification, which would become a cornerstone of her theory. Her understanding of sadism as a key aspect of the child's early dynamics paved the way for the concept of projective identification, as a means by which the child projects internal feelings of aggression onto external objects.

Ten years later, Klein further expanded her theoretical framework by focusing on the study of envy (1957). She defined envy as a form of innate aggression directed at objects perceived as good. The child, unable to tolerate that the object possesses positive qualities they themselves do not share, seeks to destroy those qualities. Although envy may have constitutional roots, it can be exacerbated by unmet needs, persistent anxiety, or instability in the maternal figure. This innate aggression contributes to the broader struggle between integration and fragmentation in human life, a central theme in the later phase of Klein's theory.

In the final phase of her theory, Klein describes human life as a continuous struggle between two opposing forces: on one side, integration, supported by love and the desire for reparation; on the other, fragmentation, driven by hatred and envy.

Maintaining a cohesive image of the object and the self—one that includes both positive and negative aspects—is a complex task. It requires confronting depressive anxiety and guilt, relinquishing phantasies of omnipotence, and accepting the limitations of love and the inherent ambivalence in relationships. When hatred takes the upper hand, it becomes difficult to sustain an integrated view of oneself and the object, leading to a regression into schizoparanoid mechanisms, where predominant splitting encourages disintegration and psychological impoverishment.

Klein's final vision of the human condition is that of an individual striving to preserve their own wholeness as well as that of the object, despite the suffering this may bring. This ongoing struggle stands in opposition to the tendency toward fragmentation caused by destructiveness and envy, yet it is precisely this effort that makes the search for internal balance and the coexistence of opposites possible.

Melanie Klein's perspective on anxiety and defenses

From her earliest writings, Melanie Klein engaged with a question already raised by Freud in 1926 regarding the existence of early defense mechanisms. Freud had hypothesized that, in the early stages of psychic development—prior to the clear differentiation of ego and id, and before the formation of the superego—the mind might rely on forms of defense that differ from those employed once these psychic structures are more fully established.

Klein's initial contributions to the study of defenses align closely with Freud's ideas, particularly regarding the role of projection as a defense mechanism against the death instinct. Initially, she concentrated on obsessive defenses, which she viewed as responses to sadism. However, she soon shifted her attention to primitive defenses, focusing on early, intense, and omnipotent projection.

From her analysis of Erna (1927) onward, Klein observed that the child's severe obsessive neurosis concealed an underlying paranoid state. She realized that obsessive defenses served to ease persecutory anxiety. As a result, she devoted less attention to neurotic defenses, such as repression, suggesting that these mechanisms act against libidinal impulses in later stages of development. In contrast, she believed that primitive defenses, being far more powerful, could eliminate parts of the mind. These defenses, according to Klein, played a dual role: shielding the individual from persecutory and depressive anxiety while also being essential for developing a sense of self and shaping personality.

Melanie Klein emphasized the crucial role of the transition, in psychic development, from a focus on anxiety for one's own survival to the ability to feel concern for others—a shift that involves assuming emotional responsibility and a desire to repair the emotional harm one may have caused. In her developmental theory, Klein chose to use the term "positions" rather than "phases" or "stages." A "position" refers to a mental state characterized by specific ways of relating to objects, distinct forms of anxiety, and particular defense mechanisms. Although these positions are part of a developmental process, they do not unfold in a strictly linear sequence: throughout life, primitive mental states can reemerge alongside more mature ones. Unlike phases or stages, which are typically seen as sequential steps to be overcome, positions are understood as mental states that can resurface at any point in life, creating continuous fluctuations.

All individuals naturally strive for growth and use defenses to manage anxiety, but this process is not uniform. At times, defenses remain rigid, obstructing development and trapping the individual in regressive or dysfunctional patterns; at other times, positive experiences can help to loosen these defenses, allowing for more effective management of anxiety.

Klein identified two fundamental mental positions: the schizoparanoid position and the depressive position. In the following paragraphs, I will focus specifically on the function of defenses within these positions.

Understanding defenses in the schizoparanoid position

The schizoparanoid position, as described by Melanie Klein (1946), represents a primitive mental state dominated by deep anxieties of annihilation and survival fears, manifested through the constant perception of external threats from persecutory forces. As mentioned earlier, such anxiety emerges from the outward projection of the child's own sadism, a representation of the death instinct.

While projection defends against the internal death instinct, it paradoxically generates persecutory anxiety. This anxiety, in turn, activates defenses based on splitting, allowing the child to keep experiences and representations of self and object rigidly separate. On one side is the ideal object, perceived as completely good and reassuring, while on the other, the persecutory object is experienced as threatening and dangerous. Similarly, the self-image oscillates between completely good or bad. Splitting simplifies the complexity of emotional experiences, reducing them to sharp contrasts such as "all or nothing" and "good or bad." The more intense the persecutory anxiety, the greater the use of splitting.

Experiences of deprivation amplify persecutory phantasies, heightening the sense of threat, while positive experiences bolster the ideal object, creating a sense of security. Gratification serves as a crucial buffer against feelings of persecution, whereas deprivation is perceived not just as a lack of pleasure, but as an existential threat, an imminent danger of annihilation.

Splitting helps maintain the separation between good and bad object representations, thus preserving the ideal object. To further secure the good object, idealization emerges as a natural extension of splitting, allowing the child to perceive the object as invulnerable. However, extreme idealization can distort internal and external reality, exaggerating the positive and denying the negative.

In her 1946 work *Notes on Some Schizoid Mechanisms*, Klein introduced the concept of projective identification, defining it as the effort to put parts of oneself in another as a means of managing anxiety. This process allows the child to externalize difficult emotions, managing them indirectly through the other. Negative parts of the self can be projected onto the object, identifying with these aspects to release the self or to attack and destroy the object. Conversely, positive parts can be projected to protect against internal threats or to idealize the external object.

Projection and introjection are at the core of the schizoparanoid position. The ego strives to absorb what is perceived as good and expel what is experienced as bad. However, positive aspects may be projected for safekeeping, while negative aspects may be introjected to keep them under control. These fluctuations can lead to varying perceptions: external threats appearing as persecutors or internal threats manifesting as hypochondriac fears.

When the emotional burden of persecution becomes too great, it can be magically denied. Segal (1964) describes this as a phantasy of having eradicated all persecutors or, alternatively, idealizing the bad object to the point of identifying with it. She observed this type of denial in schizoid patients who, despite having appeared to show only positive emotional states in childhood, clung to idealized negative objects in adulthood, unable to distinguish clearly between good and bad.

It is crucial to note, as Segal (1964) points out, that Klein did not depict an infant in a constant state of anxiety. Rather, she focused on how the infant goes through periods of anxiety, even if infrequent. The frequency and intensity with which a child deals with anxiety and the defenses they use to cope with it form the basis of future psychological development.

Although the ego is still fragile and poorly organized, its ability to defend itself during times of anxiety—even through primitive defenses—plays a key role in fostering psychological growth. From this perspective, the defenses used take on a positive dimension.

Despite being primitive, splitting has not only negative implications. It offers a first way of organizing the child's chaotic emotional experiences. Acting as a filter, it helps manage and structure the child's early perceptions, enabling them to differentiate themselves from the outside world and to discern between what is safe and what is threatening. As Segal (1964) suggests, persecutory anxiety lays the foundation for the ability to recognize and respond to real dangers. Idealization, on the other hand, fosters a sense of trust in the goodness of objects and one-self, facilitating positive relationships and the ability to believe in ideals, while projective identification serves as an early form of empathy. Thus, the defensive mechanisms of the schizoparanoid position, in addition to protecting the early self from anxiety, provide essential elements for development.

Developmental progression depends on the predominance of positive experiences over negative ones. When positive experiences are more fre-quent, the child develops confidence in the strength of the ideal object and vital instincts over persecutory objects and destructive impulses. This con-fidence allows the self to identify with the ideal object, thus reducing the use of extreme defenses. As persecutory anxiety subsides, the need for pro-jection and splitting also decreases. The ego becomes more confident in its own and others' goodness, improving its ability to handle aggression internally.

Conversely, if negative experiences dominate, the developmental path shifts. Environmental factors and intrinsic traits, such as levels of sadism and envy, play an important role. Klein (1957) elaborates on the role of envy, pointing out that it tends to destroy the goodness of the object, pre-venting the introjection of positive experiences. Intense envy can disturb the ability to distinguish between good and bad objects, thus blocking de-velopment. By aiming to attack destructively the source of gratification, it hinders the defensive process of splitting because the ideal object must be attacked rather than preserved.

Spoiling or devaluing the good object can function as a defense against envy, as can extreme idealization, although the latter is inherently unstable: the more idealized the object, the greater its potential to become a source of envy (Klein, 1957).

However, as Segal (1964) states, deep envy and the defenses used against it lead to despair, since the inability to recognize a good ideal object extin-guishes the hope of finding support, both externally, because of object envy, and internally, because of the lack of positive introjection.

Understanding defenses in the depressive position

In her 1935 work, *A Contribution to the Psychogenesis of Manic-Depressive States*, Melanie Klein introduces the concept of the depressive position, de-scribing its characteristic anxieties and defenses while moving beyond the idea of development as a sequence of distinct stages.

She emphasizes that a positive relationship with the mother and the ex-ternal world helps the child confront early paranoid anxieties. This support enables the child to develop a more realistic perception of the mother and the world, thus reducing the need for splitting and projection. Gradually, the mother is perceived as a single, whole person—recognized as the same individual who is loved when providing pleasant experiences and who is disliked when causing unpleasant ones. At this point, the child's ego, even while experiencing the conflict between love and hate, can maintain a stable emotional connection. This stability allows feelings of grief and sorrow over the perceived loss of the mother to emerge. Awareness of their capacity to harm what they love generates feelings of guilt, alongside a desire to make amends. The depressive conflict thus becomes a continuous struggle between destructive tendencies and reparative impulses. When efforts at reparation are successful, the child's hope is renewed; if not, the ego risks slipping into despair.

The depressive position marks a crucial point in development, representing a significant shift in perceiving reality. It enables a deeper connection with objective reality, as the child starts to recognize their inner life, acknowledging both their love and hatred. This awareness helps them better distinguish between their phantasies and the external world. Perceiving the mother as a whole person means that the fear of loss is experienced as a total loss. Previously, splitting allowed the unconscious phantasy of losing only the hated aspect of the mother. However, the newfound awareness of the mother's wholeness brings with it the anxiety of a complete loss. At the same time, as the child's ego becomes more integrated alongside their perception of the mother, they become aware of the ambivalence of their feelings and the emotional pain this conflict causes. This sense of loss, as Klein emphasizes, is reinforced particularly during times of separation from the mother, reaching its peak during weaning.

As the child experiences the object's goodness, paranoid anxieties diminish, and introjection becomes more intense. Klein notes that at this point, the child feels a strong need to internalize the good object to counter their fear of having harmed the object due to their cannibalistic impulses, as well as the anxiety about harboring persecutory objects within. This need to internalize, protect, and cherish the good object reaches its peak, driving a strong desire to repair any damage caused by their earlier sadistic impulses. However, excessive feelings of hatred and anxiety can lead to the perception of losing the loved object.

Klein emphasizes that the child may feel that not only their hatred but also their intense love contributes to the anxiety of having destroyed the object. At this point, the child's love and the unconscious desire to consume the object may overlap. In the depressive position, anxiety becomes less concerned with self-preservation—as it is in the earlier schizoparanoid position—and shifts instead toward the fear of losing the loved object and damaging the ego's sense of goodness, which is now closely bound up with the internalized object.

The fear of losing the real mother, intertwined with the fear of losing the internalized good object, can undermine the child's confidence in their ability to repair and restore the damaged object.

Klein also observes that the more the child perceives the object as split into good and bad parts, the stronger the need becomes to idealize it in an attempt to preserve the good object and reduce internal anxiety. She notes that some of her patients, who had distanced themselves from their mothers due to hatred or other mechanisms, idealized the mother, but only as an abstract image, disconnected from the real person. Klein suggests that this desire for perfection stems from the depressive anxiety of harboring a damaged internal object.

When too intense, depressive anxiety can defensively strengthen paranoid anxieties and their associated defenses. Klein reports observing in many of her patients an increase in paranoid suspicion as a defense against the depressive position.

Referring back to Freud's (1917) idea that one way to escape melancholy is through mania, Klein highlights that mania is closely linked to the defensive recourse to omnipotent denial of persecutors. She specifies that this primarily involves the denial of psychic reality, differentiating this defense from scotomization, which refers to the psychic process that can lead to denying and distancing oneself from external reality.

The hyperactivity characteristic of mania indicates, through its relentless defensive effort to dominate and control, both the attempt to hold onto internalized good objects and the need to deny the significance and dependence on the good object, as well as the presence of bad objects. By resorting to the defense of omnipotent denial, the individual seeks to control and dominate objects, not only to suppress their fear of them but also to "magically" restore the object, thus rejecting feelings of guilt. Omnipotence is inherent in unconscious phantasies of being able to destroy and revive objects, devour them without harm, destroy them without suffering, or internalize bad objects without being affected. The intense desire for objects is accompanied by a tendency to devalue their importance, serving as a defense against feelings of guilt and the anxiety associated with loss.

In her 1940 work *Mourning and Its Relation to Manic-Depressive States*, Klein further examines the specific defenses associated with the depressive position. She highlights that idealization, which plays a crucial role in the schizoparanoid position by maintaining an idealized object to counteract feelings of persecution, is also significant in the manic position. In this context, idealization is closely tied to denial, serving to preserve the perceived goodness of the object—not as a defense against persecutory anxiety, but rather to ward off the depressive anxiety of loss and guilt.

Alongside this, other key defenses include desire to dominate, triumph, and contempt. The desire to dominate serves as a means to conceal dependence. The child attempts to control the object, using it to fulfill their desires without ever openly acknowledging their reliance on it. This behavior reveals a contradiction: while striving for autonomy, the child keeps the object under their control as a form of support, thus maintaining a hidden dependence.

Triumph serves as another means of denying reality, this time targeting feelings of respect and value toward the object. By feeling superior and victorious, the individual avoids recognizing the object's importance. This mechanism is rooted in a belief in one's own omnipotence and invulnerability, functioning as a way to evade the fear of losing the beloved object. However, as Klein (1940) notes, the guilt that emerges from achieving success while others suffer can hinder the pursuit of success. This avoidance helps to mitigate the anxiety of potential retaliation from defeated objects and the painful guilt associated with having humiliated and harmed the loved object.

Finally, contempt serves as a defense mechanism against feelings of loss and guilt. By devaluing the object and viewing it as insignificant or inferior, the individual avoids taking responsibility for potential harm. In this way, contempt becomes a justification for repeated attacks, perpetuating the cycle of manic defenses.

Initially, the object is experienced with mixed feelings—both loved and attacked—leading to anxiety about loss and guilt. When this anxiety becomes overwhelming, manic defenses take over, resulting in attempts to control, devalue, and disdain the object. However, this approach does not resolve the underlying issue. The inability to engage in genuine reparation exacerbates the object's destruction, increasing the fear of retaliation from the object. Consequently, depressive anxiety intensifies into a deeper sense of threat and persecution. Good objects that were meant to be repaired and protected become perceived as persecutory, triggering stronger paranoid anxieties. This shift further reinforces both paranoid defenses, which aim to destroy the object, and manic defenses, which rely on omnipotent denial.

Even the act of reparation can serve a manic defensive function (Klein, 1937) when it is performed superficially and omnipotently, without genuinely acknowledging the guilt and pain tied to one's destructiveness. This form of reparation functions as a defense against the experience of guilt and loss. As Segal (1964) explains, it has three main characteristics: it targets distant objects, harmed by others rather than by the subject, and is directed at objects perceived as inferior and contemptible. These objects are not genuinely loved but are instead regarded—consciously or unconsciously—with disdain, seen as ungrateful and potentially threatening. Segal notes that individuals engaged in charitable work may sometimes view the recipients of their help as ungrateful, of little value, and even menacing. Such reparation is ultimately ineffective, providing no real relief, as the object remains, on some level, an object of contempt rather than one that is truly repaired.

Authentic reparation, however, is not a defense and allows for the resolution of the depressive position. It involves acknowledging one's psychic reality, recognizing the pain caused by destructive impulses, and undertaking genuine reparative actions toward the loved object. Unlike manic defenses, which evade psychic reality to avoid suffering, authentic reparation directly engages with emotions, transforming pain into an opportunity for growth. This process enables the individual to endure loss without being overwhelmed by hatred, fostering a belief that their love can truly repair what has been damaged.

Additionally, this process is accompanied by more accurate reality-testing, where the child becomes aware of the impact of their impulses and learns to relinquish omnipotent control, accepting others as they are.

During the elaboration of the depressive position, the ego is strengthened through the internalization of good objects, which become integrated into both the ego and the superego. This process significantly transforms relationships with others: the child starts to perceive people as complex, distinct individuals, developing the capacity to care for them and take responsibility for their own emotions and actions. This marks a crucial step in learning to manage feelings of guilt, representing a shift in how the child navigates relationships and emotions.

The superego also undergoes change. While it is characterized by a rigid division between idealized and persecutory objects in the schizoparanoid position, in the depressive position, it becomes more balanced and less punitive. Instead of merely punishing, it acts as an internal guide, encouraging reparation and supporting the child's desire to rebuild and protect what they love.

The mother's concrete response plays a vital role in this process. Her return after an absence and her care help the child reassess the power of their destructive impulses. The child begins to realize that their intense emotions do not control the presence or absence of the loved object. This understanding facilitates a shift toward a more realistic way of thinking, one that is less dominated by phantasies.

The elaboration of the depressive position also forms the basis for creativity and sublimation. As Segal (1964) notes, the desire to repair and rebuild the damaged object fuels a creative drive, expressed through symbolism and art. This drive arises from the need to transform loss into new meanings, turning pain into something positive.

While this process replaces the rigidity of the schizoparanoid position with a richer and more nuanced perspective, the depressive position is never fully overcome. The anxieties associated with guilt and loss can resurface at various stages of life, particularly when facing new challenges or losses, reactivating both manic and paranoid defenses. However, internalizing a good internal object helps individuals better cope with painful realities and the work of mourning, reestablish trust in the goodness of their internal world, and reinvest in other relationships.

Just as in the schizoparanoid position, both paranoid and manic defenses play a crucial role in the depressive position by supporting development.

They enable the still-fragile ego of the child to tolerate anxiety and achieve greater integration. This progression allows for a move away from extreme defenses, making it possible to adopt more mature strategies.

Klein's perspective on mature defenses

Klein made only limited observations on neurotic defenses, focusing primarily on obsessive defenses (Klein, 1927, 1931, 1935, 1940, 1945, 1957) and repression (Klein, 1930, 1952). However, with her conceptualization of the depressive position, Klein (1935, 1940) revised her views on obsessive defenses, particularly in relation to undoing, which she came to regard as a manic defense aligned with an omnipotent form of reparation.

While Klein had extensively addressed paranoid and manic defenses, she made relatively few references to mature defenses based on repression. Nonetheless, in one of her later writings (Klein, 1952), she presented an especially intriguing perspective on repression.

She had previously emphasized that repression differs from primitive defense mechanisms in that these more primitive defenses exert a forceful impact on psychic life, significantly affecting personality structure by excluding parts of the personality from conscious awareness (Klein, 1930). Repression and its associated defenses, however, involve only the affective and/or cognitive contents of the mind, sparing the psychic structure itself. Primitive defenses rooted in omnipotence alter, distort, and impoverish the ego, whereas repression enables the preservation of awareness and differentiation between internal and external reality (Hinshelwood, 1989).

Defenses rooted in primitive omnipotence tend to alter, distort, and impoverish the ego, whereas repression allows for the preservation of awareness and the differentiation between internal and external reality (Hinshelwood, 1989).

In her 1952 work, *Some Theoretical Conclusions Regarding the Emotional Life of the Infant*, Klein further noted that the extent of repression would be determined by the intensity of early splitting mechanisms: the more extensive and forceful these early mechanisms of splitting have been, the less permeable the boundaries between the unconscious and conscious mind will be. Specifically, she asserts:

> A further step in the development of instinctual inhibitions comes about when the ego can make use of repression. We have seen the ways in which the ego uses splitting during the paranoid-schizoid phase. The mechanism of splitting underlies repression (as is implied in Freud's concept); but in contrast to the earliest forms of splitting which lead to states of disintegration, repression does not normally result in a disintegration of the self. Since at this stage there is greater integration, within both the conscious and the unconscious parts of the mind, and since in repression the splitting

predominantly effects a division between conscious and unconscious, neither part of the self is exposed to the degree of disintegration which may arise in previous stages. However, the extent to which splitting processes are resorted to in the first few months of life vitally influences the use of repression at a later stage. For if early schizoid mechanisms and anxieties have not been sufficiently overcome, the result may be that instead of a fluid boundary between the conscious and unconscious, a rigid barrier between them arises; this indicates that repression is excessive and that, in consequence, development is disturbed.

(Klein, 1952, pp. 86–87)

Bion's transformative perspective

Bion's thinking broadened our understanding of defense mechanisms by moving beyond the intrapsychic dimension outlined by Freud and elaborated further by Klein. In particular, Bion proposed a conception of mental functioning deeply linked to the capacity of the psychic apparatus to transform raw emotional experience into thought, ascribing the most primitive and destructive defense mechanisms to failures in this function.

In his essay *Differentiation of the Psychotic from the Non-Psychotic Personalities*, Bion (1957) introduced the distinction between two dimensions of personality that coexist within every individual: a psychotic part and a non-psychotic part. The psychotic part, which is activated in the presence of intolerable anxiety, defends itself not so much through repression or denial, but through massive evacuations of emotional experience, attacks on significant links, and a profound confusion between reality and fantasy. These mechanisms not only temporarily protect the subject from psychological pain, but ultimately compromise the very possibility of thinking and relating to the internal and external world. In this context, thought is not simply inhibited: it is attacked and replaced by mental states that are hallucinatory, disorganized, or formally structured yet devoid of transformative value.

According to Bion, what characterizes the psychotic part of the personality is the minute splitting of the entire conscious part of internal and external reality and the subsequent expulsion of these fragments, derived from the splitting, into objects so that they can penetrate or engulf them.

The hyperactivity of the mechanisms of splitting and projective identification, used to free oneself from awareness of reality, precludes the development of verbal thought, on which awareness of psychic reality depends. Not only is primitive thought attacked, but so are all the links between the various thought processes, thus making access to symbol formation impossible. This condition, in Bion's view, makes it impossible to resort to repression, since the psychotic part of the personality

> has attempted to rid itself of the apparatus on which the psyche depends to carry out the repressions; the unconscious would seem to be replaced by the world of dream furniture.
>
> (Bion, 1957, p. 270)

In his subsequent work, *Attacks on Linking*, Bion (1959) further develops this theoretical perspective. Here, Bion describes the defensive mechanism of attacking links as a form of active destruction of the very function that allows connections to be created between thoughts, between emotions and representations, between the self and the object. When the link (affective, cognitive, or symbolic) becomes a source of distress, the mind may choose to attack it, dissolving its internal coherence and preventing any symbolic process. The link thus becomes a target of defense, with devastating consequences for the ability to contain and transform emotional experience.

However, in this paper, Bion, through the presentation and discussion of some clinical vignettes, conceptualizes a normal degree of projective identification which, associated with introjective identification, forms the basis for normal development. He reports on a patient whose insistent recourse to projective identification led him to hypothesize that he had not been able to make sufficient use of it in his life. Bion writes:

> Throughout the analysis, the patient resorted to projective identification with a persistence suggesting it was a mechanism of which he had never been able to avail himself sufficiently; the analysis afforded him an opportunity for the exercise of a mechanism of which he had been cheated.
>
> (Bion, 1959, p. 312)

and then,

> When the patient strove to rid himself of fears of death which were felt to be too powerful for his personality to contain, he split off his fears and put them into me, the idea apparently being that if they were allowed to repose there long enough they would undergo modification by my psyche and could then be safely re-introjected. On the occasion I have in mind, the patient had felt, probably for reasons similar to those I give in my fifth illustration, the probability clouds, that I evacuated them so quickly that the feelings were not modified, but had become more painful.
>
> (Bion, 1959, p. 312)

It is in this regard that Bion recounts how, over time, he came to understand that the patient's insistent recourse to projective identification should not be understood as an expression of primary aggression, but rather as a defensive reaction to the hostility perceived in the analyst's attitude.

This led Bion to reconsider the developmental function of projective identification in the early mother–infant relationship. He writes:

> My deduction was that in order to understand what the child wanted, the mother should have treated the infant's cry as more than a demand for her presence. From the infant's point of view, she should have taken into herself, and thus experienced, the fear that the child was dying. It was this fear that the child could not contain. He strove to split it off together with the part of the personality in which it lay and project it into the mother. An understanding mother is able to experience the feeling of dread that this baby was striving to deal with by projective identification, and yet retain a balanced outlook. This patient had had to deal with a mother who could not tolerate experiencing such feelings and reacted either by denying them ingress, or alternatively by becoming a prey to the anxiety which resulted from introjection of the infant's feelings. The latter reaction must, I think, have been rare: denial was dominant.
>
> (Bion, 1959, p. 313)

In this new and revolutionary perspective, the excessive and pathological use of projective identification would therefore depend not only on the child's innate destructiveness, but also on maternal failure. However, Bion also reiterates in this paper how much the child's hatred and envy of the mother's capacity can devour his psyche and hinder the possibility of internalizing good objects.

Projective identification is thus conceived as the process through which the child (and the patient) can come into contact with the mental states of the other and keep alive their curiosity about them. Projective identification allows them to externalize emotions that are too intense to be processed internally and that can only be observed and thought about if entrusted to another person with a psychic structure capable of containing them.

However, if this process is hindered—for example, by a mother/analyst who is unable or unwilling to receive and transform the emotional projections of the child/patient, or by a child/patient who, driven by envy or hostility, refuses to recognize this function in the other—the link is broken and this rupture seriously damages the ability to be curious, which is the fundamental driving force of learning and mental development, leading to a profound developmental arrest.

When it is no longer possible to entrust overwhelming emotions to another person, the emotional world becomes unbearable. The subject may then develop a destructive reaction directed not only toward emotions, but also toward the external reality that evokes them. Hatred extends to all emotional states, triggering a destructive dynamic that eventually involves perceptual functions and basic forms of thought that allow sensory experience to be linked to consciousness.

Bion concludes by emphasizing that, in such a psychic condition, emotion is perceived as too intense and threatening to be managed by a still immature mind. It is experienced as something that binds objects together, giving them a reality distinct from the self, and thus perceived as a threat to original narcissism.

The internal object—derived from a mother's breast which, being unable to contain and transform emotions, is internalized in a dysfunctional form—ends up being perceived as an element that amplifies, rather than calms, the emotions from which one should defend oneself. As a result, this gives rise to attacks on the emotional capacity to form links.

This dynamic hinders the formation of authentic emotional connections, favoring modes of thinking dominated by cold, impersonal associations, which may seem logically coherent but lack emotional warmth. The links that can endure are perverse, destructive, and devoid of vitality.

Bion further elaborates his thinking in two essays from 1962, *A Theory of Thinking* (Bion, 1962a) and *Learning from Experience* (Bion, 1962b), in which he presents his theory of thinking and introduces the concept of the alpha function. He distinguishes thoughts from the apparatus for thinking thoughts, specifying that, in his view, thinking is a development of the pressure of thoughts. The latter can be classified as preconceptions, conceptions, and finally concepts. The model of pre-conception is the child's innate disposition to expect the breast; when this expectation is fulfilled, conception occurs, which can then be defined as the outcome of an emotional experience of satisfaction.

According to Bion, it is the encounter of a preconception with a frustration that generates thought and the apparatus for thinking thoughts, but only on condition that the child has sufficient capacity to tolerate frustration. If, on the other hand, this capacity is insufficient, reality cannot be recognized or tolerated, and must instead be evacuated through projective identification: instead of the apparatus for thinking thoughts, the apparatus of projective identification develops in a hypertrophic manner.

Bion adds that, in cases where intolerance to frustration is not so pronounced as to resort to evacuation, but at the same time is not sufficient to tolerate reality, the path to omnipotence opens up, implying a retreat into omniscience, which precludes learning from experience through thinking and prevents the ability to distinguish between true and false.

Bion then introduces the concept of the alpha function, defining it as that which allows sensory data to be converted into alpha elements, elements that constitute the material for dream thoughts, allowing the ability to wake up and go to sleep, and thus to be in a state of consciousness or unconsciousness. The ability to be aware of oneself is understood by Bion as knowing oneself through one's experience of oneself, and this ability can develop if normal projective identification is possible in the mother–child relationship. In this narrow sense, the term consciousness refers to self-awareness.

In *Learning from Experience*, Bion (1962b) further clarifies his thinking by stating that the alpha function allows awareness of emotional experience, without which it is not possible to learn from experience.

> Alpha-function is needed for conscious thinking and reasoning and for the relegation of thinking to the unconscious when it is necessary to disencumber consciousness of the burden of thought by learning a skill. If there are only beta elements, which cannot be made unconscious, there can be no repression, suppression, or learning. This creates the impression that the patient is incapable of discrimination. He cannot be unaware of any single sensory stimulus: yet such hypersensitivity is not contact with reality.
>
> (Bion, 1962b, p. 8)

Bion goes further, observing that even love may interfere with the child's drive to satisfy the need for nourishment. This happens because love can be accompanied by overwhelming emotional intensity, is intertwined with envy and, above all, makes hatred possible, which without it could not exist. When emotions such as fear, hatred, and envy become too threatening, the subject may activate defenses so strong that they obliterate emotional awareness entirely. This process compromises interest in the truth and hinders the development of the alpha function, which is essential for transforming emotional experiences into thought.

According to Bion, the mind is thus required to perform a transformative function, converting unprocessed sensory and emotional impressions (beta elements) into thinkable content (alpha elements). Beta elements represent raw, undigested forms of experience that cannot be thought or symbolically represented. The alpha function has the task of transforming these elements into thoughts, rendering them accessible to dreaming, memory, and conscious thought. When this function is intact, the psychic apparatus can tolerate experience, metabolize it, and produce thought. When it is compromised, however, experience is evacuated as a raw element that cannot be symbolized, generating persecutory anxieties and radical defenses.

The failure of the alpha function perpetuates the use of primitive defenses, such as massive projection, splitting that cannot be metabolized, and evacuative projective identification. In this sense, defense no longer takes the form of repression or disavowal, but of a transformative failure: an inability of the mind to "think itself."

Emotion, when not transformed into thought, is instead expressed through the body, through behaviors, symptoms, or evacuated into the mind of another through extreme projections.

In *Elements of Psycho-Analysis*, Bion (1963) explores these processes in greater depth, introducing the theory of emotional links and the container-contained model. According to Bion, every thought arises from an emotional and cognitive link: love (L), hate (H), or desire to know (K). When these links become intolerable, they are attacked or evacuated, compromising the function of thought. The container (usually identified in the mother–child relationship or, in analysis, in the analyst's mind) has the function of receiving, containing, and transforming the subject's beta elements. The container-contained relationship is conceived as a dynamic of psychic exchange: if the container is able to transform raw elements into thinkable ones, the subject can reappropriate the experience and use it to grow mentally. If this does not happen, the link breaks down, and radical defenses emerge. The container-contained model is not only a theory of development, but also a clinical key to understanding psychotic and borderline defenses: when the container fails, either through absence or intrusiveness, the content remains untransformed, acting as an internal disturbance that the subject attempts to evacuate through extreme defensive modes. This model has had a profound impact on clinical practice, offering a tool for understanding experiences of unthinkability, internal chaos, and psychic emptiness.

In *Transformations* (Bion, 1965), the author takes a further theoretical step, distinguishing between truth-seeking versus defensive transformations. The former generate authentic thought, dreams, and symbolization; the latter operate to avoid anxiety, giving rise to distortions, hallucinations, or empty thoughts. Bion describes how the mind can transform experience not in order to understand it, but to deny it: an example of this mechanism is transformation in hallucinosis, where the beta element is not metabolized, but projected and perceived as external reality. Defensive transformations, therefore, not only deny content but also alter the very modes of thinking, producing a mental state in which thought is present only as formal imitation, emptied of its transformative and cognitive function. In serious pathologies, what is observed is not merely the presence of disturbing content, but above all the breakdown of the mental processes that make it possible to think such content.

Bion's thought has had a profound and lasting impact on contemporary psychoanalysis, profoundly influencing the theory and clinical practice of primitive mental functioning. His reformulation of defense as a failure of mental transformation has opened up new perspectives on the treatment of psychosis, borderline disorders, and forms of concrete or evacuative thinking. Overall, Bion redefined the concept of defense mechanism in a profoundly innovative way: no longer merely as the repression of unacceptable content, but as an attack or collapse of the mental function that makes thought itself possible. His ideas open up a new space of understanding for serious pathologies, particularly psychotic and borderline states, but also for all those functions in which mental activity becomes blocked, impoverished, or rigid.

His contribution remains fundamental to any psychoanalytic approach that seeks to understand not only what we defend ourselves against, but also what is prevented from coming into being within the mind. Many contemporary authors have taken up Bion's legacy, developing his insights in new directions. These developments will be explored in greater depth in Chapter 6, which will examine the main contemporary authors who have continued, transformed, and enriched Bion's thinking, helping to make it one of the richest sources of theoretical and clinical innovation in 21st-century psychoanalysis.

4 The British Independents' twist

Anna Maria Rosso

The British Independents, originally known as the *Middle Group*, emerged as a third group within the British Psychoanalytical Society (BPS) following the *Controversial Discussions* of the early 1940s. These theoretical debates revolved around a number of divergent views, with central disagreements arising between Anna Freud and Melanie Klein. The *Middle Group* was established with the introduction of a training protocol within the BPS that required candidates to undergo an initial supervision with either a Freudian or a Kleinian analyst, depending on their chosen affiliation, and a subsequent supervision with an analyst from the *Middle Group*. This group was distinctive in that its members did not fully align with either the Freudian or the Kleinian schools, although they shared certain theoretical and clinical perspectives with both.

As Rayner (1991) notes, the origins of the Middle Group can be traced back to the very foundation of the BPS by Ernest Jones in 1913. From the outset, the founders displayed a notable openness to diverse psychoanalytic ideas and welcomed psychoanalysts from other countries to London. In 1926, Melanie Klein relocated to London and soon began to challenge Anna Freud's theoretical positions, just as Anna Freud had recently published her work on child analysis. The Society was increasingly animated by debates surrounding Klein's contributions, and when Anna Freud herself moved to London in 1938, tensions between the two schools grew so intense that the unity of the BPS was at risk.

It was through the intervention of analysts who did not fully endorse either of the two dominant perspectives that a *Gentlemen's Agreement* was eventually reached, thus averting a split within the Society. This agreement formally recognized both the Freudian and Kleinian groups and introduced the training requirement involving Middle Group analysts, thereby establishing this third group within the BPS. Thereafter, the Middle Group became known as the *Independents*, advocating for the freedom to develop ideas autonomously and to incorporate clinically valuable contributions regardless of their theoretical origin.

The Independents comprise psychoanalysts who, while incorporating some Freudian and Kleinian insights, have each developed unique lines

DOI: 10.4324/9781003536994-6

of thought. As Rayner (1991) observes, the Independents are not united by a single theoretical framework but by a critical openness and respect for diverse ideas, which are rigorously tested in clinical practice rather than accepted dogmatically. They represent a heterogeneous, open group of analysts, each with a distinct perspective, yet united by their shared emphasis on the crucial role of the environment in a child's development.

In contrast to Freud's dualistic theory of life and death drives, and Klein's emphasis on the death instinct, the Independents take a different stance. While their views on the topic vary, they generally regard aggression as rooted in the instinct for survival, primarily viewing it as a response to environmental frustration.

The Independents argue that the quality of relationships and interactions with external objects plays a crucial role in shaping a child's psychic reality. The environment, in their view, does not merely serve to mitigate early drives and fantasies, as Klein suggested, but is rather a foundational element: it creates, activates, and shapes fantasies, anxieties, and defenses. Accordingly, the environment performs essential functions for the psyche, either facilitating or hindering development, either vitalizing mental life or, conversely, inhibiting or deactivating it, depending on the quality of responses provided to the child.

For the Independents, environmental responses can thus stimulate or stifle entire areas of psychic and emotional life. Parents, through their behavior, influence the child's ability to live, recognize, and address their inner reality, either activating or inhibiting specific innate resources and potential. This process can unfold constructively or dysfunctionally, through invasive or limiting dynamics that, in the Independents' view, often lie at the root of psychopathology. Specifically, intrusion or deprivation of fundamental experiences may impair the development of a healthy psyche.

While recognizing the centrality of unconscious phantasy, the Independents assign decisive importance to the environment's influence on fundamental needs for relatedness, security, recognition, and individuation. In this framework, each individual develops an internal reality in which drives and phantasies are not isolated but are shaped by the environmental support received in response to these essential needs.

In this chapter, I will consider the contributions of a selection of Independents who provided significant and original insights into the understanding of defenses: Michael Balint, Ronald Fairbairn, and Donald Winnicott.

Michael Balint

Balint, like Melanie Klein, was analyzed in Budapest by Ferenczi, with whom he maintained a profound theoretical and personal connection. In 1939, he relocated to London, where he refined and expanded his studies, focusing on the pivotal role of early mother–child relationships. He attributed central importance to relational deficiencies in the development of personality and the genesis of psychopathology.

While acknowledging the pursuit of pleasure as a primary motivation, he proposed that the quest for love is an equally fundamental and complementary drive. These two poles—the pursuit of pleasure and the pursuit of a relationship with the object—constitute, in Balint's view, two primary motivational forces (Balint, 1956).

Balint shared with the Independent psychoanalysts the notion that object relations are present from the very earliest stages of life and affirmed that a rudimentary relationship with the environment exists even during intrauterine life.

At this stage, the self and the environment are experienced as a single *"harmonious blend,"* devoid of any sense of differentiation. After birth, however, this fusion cannot be sustained, and the need to recreate it, even if only temporarily, becomes a crucial element in the relationship with the mother. Balint described this need as the quest to rediscover *primary love*, characterized by a relationship in which one partner can make unlimited demands, while the other responds unconditionally, without desires or interests of their own, ensuring a state of total and perfect harmony. In this context, the infant perceives the first object as entirely at their service, devoid of any autonomy (Balint, 1959).

A significant trauma during this phase can result in what Balint (1968) terms a *basic fault*, a sense of a compromised self that does not provoke resentment but generates profound anxiety. This fault arises from a discrepancy between the child's needs during the first two years of life and the quality of care received. The causes of this discrepancy can be congenital—such as when the child's needs are exceptionally intense—or environmental, as in cases of neglect, inadequate care, overprotection, or a lack of empathy (Balint, 1959). Such divergence leads to a state of deficiency whose consequences are only partially reversible.

In response to the subsequent traumatic discovery of the separate existence of objects, Balint identifies two primary defensive modes of adaptation: *ocnophilia* and *philobatism*.

The ocnophile attempts to alleviate the differentiation anxiety by clinging to objects, which are perceived as anchors of security in a threatening world. This need for attachment is intrinsically tied to the fear of abandonment, as objects, possessing their own autonomy, can escape the subject's control, exposing them to the risk of loss. The ocnophile perceives the world as composed of objects separated by empty spaces, which are inherently menacing. Fear arises whenever the ocnophile detaches from objects and subsides only upon re-establishing attachment.

To navigate this dynamic, the ocnophile resorts to magical thinking. They project themselves onto objects, convincing themselves that the more intensely they cling, the more securely the objects will hold them in return. Alternatively, they may introject the objects, creating the consolatory illusion that these objects are part of them and, therefore, incapable of abandoning them. However, these strategies only alter the individual's internal world, leaving the external reality unchanged and rendering them perpetually vulnerable to frustration.

The ocnophile's need for control leads to the idealization of objects as absolutely good and indispensable. This primitive and archaic mode of thinking fails to acknowledge objects as independent entities, as such recognition would reveal them as potential sources of abandonment.

The philobat, in contrast, addresses the trauma by accepting the autonomy of objects, yet adopts a fundamentally different relational mode. They avoid the risks associated with independent objects by seeking refuge in *friendly expanses*, which are perceived as safe and familiar. These spaces serve as an echo of the primordial harmony in which the philobat feels supported and protected. To sustain this state, the philobat takes an active approach: they develop skills that enable them to master difficult and dangerous situations, recreating the illusion of total control over the environment.

However, as Balint observes, the philobat's ultimate aim is not merely to master reality. Their higher objective is to achieve a level of competence so refined that it allows them to act effortlessly, with absolute naturalness. This process, which Balint terms "progression for the sake of progression," enables the philobat to return to a state of harmonious blend, akin to the experience of primary love. Once this mastery is achieved, the philobat experiences an illusion of omnipotence: the world transforms into an "enchanted realm," where every desire appears to be fulfilled effortlessly (Balint, 1959).

An illuminating example provided by Balint (1959) is that of a remarkably skilled juggler and acrobat, capable of stopping a ball, no matter from which direction it is thrown, precisely on the tip of his finger, as if by magic. In this state, the object is no longer perceived as separate but appears magically undifferentiated, integrated into a perfect harmony between the subject and the environment.

The philobat's trust in their *friendly expanses* reflects a behavior that is just as primitive as that of the ocnophile. The philobat firmly believes that their abilities are sufficient to face any risk, with the conviction that the world will not only yield to their mastery but will also create a "perfect understanding" between themselves and their surroundings. This omnipotent attitude constitutes a regression to the most archaic form of relationship with the world.

The price the philobat pays for this is the constant repetition of the original trauma, a form of traumatic neurosis. To regain the illusion of *friendly expanses* and to experience *thrill situations*, the philobat must inevitably step out of their zone of safety and repeatedly expose themselves to risks that echo the original trauma—risks that, at times, can be extreme.

Although opposite in their modalities, the ocnophile and the philobat share a common ambivalence toward objects. The ocnophile, despite clinging to objects, harbors suspicion and mistrust, perceiving them as potentially abandoning. The philobat, on the other hand, adopts an attitude of superiority and condescension, viewing objects as tools at their disposal. Paradoxically, both strategies risk undermining object relations: the ocnophile through suffocating attachment, and the philobat through a detachment that reduces objects to replaceable instruments.

Balint emphasizes that, when taken to extremes, both attitudes become pathological. The ocnophile lives in constant fear that objects of love may change or disappear, while the philobat remains detached, confident in their ability to either rediscover these objects unchanged or replace them with ease. More often, however, no individual is entirely ocnophile or philobat; these tendencies coexist in varying proportions. As Balint states:

> Both these attitudes are more or less pathological. Health is obviously not dependent on the ingredients, but on their proper combination in suitable proportions To repeat: both ocnophilia and philobatism are chronologically secondary to the state of primary love, both imply an ambivalent attitude to objects, and both types use denial to rid the mind of certain unacceptable aspects of reality. They are ingredients only to be used in various proportions by the mind when building up its habitual patterns and methods for dealing with the problems created by the world of objects.
>
> (Balint, 1955, p. 236)

Ronald Fairbairn

Ronald Fairbairn became a member of the BPS in 1938. Despite joining, he maintained a relatively isolated position within the Society, both due to geographical distance, as he lived and worked in Edinburgh, far from London, and because of his inclination toward independent development of ideas. A careful student of Freud and particularly interested in the work of Melanie Klein, Fairbairn formulated an original theory that established him as one of the most radical proponents of object relations psychoanalysis.

Understanding Fairbairn's thought proves challenging, as his work constructs a metapsychological framework that, while at times intricate, does not ultimately achieve a clear synthesis. As Kernberg (1980) notes, a concise yet effective summary of Fairbairn's thought can be found in a 1963 article in which Fairbairn schematically outlines the key points distinguishing his ideas from those of Freud and Melanie Klein: the ego is present from birth, the id does not exist, libido functions as an aspect of the ego, there is no death drive, and aggression is viewed as a reaction to frustration. From birth, the ego seeks an object, and libido, rather than following the pleasure principle, is directed toward reality, fulfilling the reality principle through the relationship with the mother. Despite the significant role ascribed to the real mother, Fairbairn, as Kernberg highlights, does not equate the intrapsychic with the interpersonal, as his focus remains specifically on the formation of object relations within the internal psychic world.

Schizoid factors in personality (Fairbairn, 1940) marked the initial area of Fairbairn's inquiry. It is important to note that he employs the term "splitting" differently from Klein: for him, the ego splits not so much due to the child's projected aggression onto the mother, as Klein proposed, but rather in response to the anxiety stemming from an unsatisfying primary relationship with the mother.

For Fairbairn, ego splitting does not imply a simple division between good and bad aspects but rather reflects a more complex structure. By this term, he refers to the process through which different parts of the ego emerge, each involved in a specific object relation. Although Fairbairn does not use the term "self," this concept of splitting implies the formation of various internal configurations within the individual.

In his work on schizoid factors in personality (Fairbairn, 1940), he emphasizes that ego splitting originates as a consequence of fixation during the early oral phase. The mouth is the first part of the body that the infant uses to establish intimate contact with the object; initially, during this phase, the infant merely sucks. Fairbairn describes this phase as "pre-ambivalent," as, in his view, the infant at this stage holds an exclusively libidinal disposition toward the object, and oral behavior represents the first means by which love is expressed.

The relationship with the mother during this phase is marked by experiences of "fullness" and "emptiness": when the infant is hungry, he feels empty; when satiated, he feels full, and he perceives the maternal breast in a similar manner—full before feeding and empty afterward. When deprived, the infant feels empty and projects this sense of lack onto the maternal breast. This deprivation intensifies his need to the point that he may interpret the empty breast as a consequence of his desire for satisfaction. The maternal breast, in its deprivational role, elicits profound anxiety in the infant, linked to the fear of having depleted or destroyed the libidinal object due to his own libidinal investment.

In Fairbairn's view, possessive and indifferent mothers, who do not allow the child to feel loved as a person, cause the child to regress to an early oral mode. At this stage, the mother is perceived not as a whole figure but merely as a "breast" (a partial object) rather than a mother with a breast (a whole object). Fairbairn describes the "worst mother" as one who views the child as her product rather than as a separate individual and, firmly resolved not to spoil her only child, prematurely and forcibly pushes him toward independence.

Regression to a primitive oral mode leads to a dynamic in which bodily contact replaces affective contact (partial object versus whole object), and bodily contents assume a predominant importance. The frustration of not feeling loved and of not seeing his own love appreciated leads the child to perceive the mother as a source of frustration, as if his mother regarded his own expressions of love as "bad." For the child, this scenario creates profound anxiety: it is as though his love itself has the power to destroy the mother's love. In response to this condition, the child defensively retains his love within himself.

In his 1940 work, Fairbairn clearly illustrates how defenses against the anxiety of "destroying love with love" are formed within the schizoid personality. He highlights the tendency in schizoid individuals to view libidinal objects as mere means to satisfy personal needs (a partial object relationship, seeing the mother as a "breast" rather than as a complete figure with a breast). This framework also leads to an overvaluation of mental contents, mirroring the overvaluation of bodily contents, as, on a deep level, an equivalence emerges between bodily and mental contents.

The schizoid individual consequently experiences difficulty in expressing emotions within relationships; if this tendency is pronounced, they defend against potential affective loss by eliminating affect itself and adopting an emotional detachment, causing others to perceive them as distant. This distance becomes necessary to safeguard the individual's internalized affective contents, which are perceived as dangerous.

To address relational difficulties in giving affection, schizoid individuals adopt various techniques. Among these are role-playing, often unconsciously adopting a social facade to establish connections, and exhibitionism, which can manifest as a preference for literary and artistic activities that enable self-expression without direct social engagement. Here, the defense consists in "giving without giving," replacing giving with "showing." However, this defensive strategy fails when the original anxiety associated with giving extends to the act of showing. For Fairbairn, giving equates to experiencing impoverishment and fearing a loss of self; he associates this anxiety with periods of creative sterility in artists.

Among other defenses employed by schizoid individuals, Fairbairn emphasizes the devaluation of one's own products as a mechanism to mitigate feelings of impoverishment, as seen, for example, in an artist who disparages their own work. Alternatively, there may be an overvaluation of one's own products, whereby they continue to be regarded as part of the self, similar to a mother who views her child as her possession, or an artist who considers their sold paintings as still belonging to them.

According to Fairbairn, intellectualization also plays a significant defensive role in schizoid individuals: the overvaluation of thought replaces affective expression, transforming affective issues into intellectual challenges. Libidinally invested, thought processes become the primary means of creative expression, and the world of thought takes the place of feelings; ideas thus substitute for emotions, and intellectual values replace affective values.

Fairbairn interprets this separation between thought and feeling as a splitting of the ego, which divides a more superficial, conscious part from a deeper part, where elements with high libidinal charge and sources of affectivity reside. According to Fairbairn, this split entails the removal of the deeper, highly libidinal part of the ego. In some cases, libidinal investment in thought processes may lead to the construction of elaborate intellectualized systems or to an attachment to a particular idea, which may be upheld with extreme conviction, as in the case of extremist political ideas. However, it is more common for schizoid individuals to observe the world with detachment and a sense of superiority.

According to Fairbairn, the tragedy of the schizoid individual lies in the difficulty, at varying levels, of loving and feeling loved. Fairbairn recounts the words of one of his patients, who told him, "Whatever you do, you must never like me" (Fairbairn, 1940, p. 26). If one's own love is experienced as "bad," then the love of others is also perceived in the same way. For the schizoid individual, what is painful is the feeling that his own love destroys those he loves. To protect himself from this threat, he develops a compulsion to hate and to be hated, while deeply longing to love and be loved. Fairbairn states,

> Like the troubadours (and perhaps dictators as well), he can only permit himself to love and be loved from a distance.
>
> (Fairbairn, 1940, p. 26)

The schizoid position, according to Fairbairn, originates from maternal failures in the relationship with the child during the early oral phase, whereas the depressive position arises from difficulties encountered in the later oral phase, which is considered ambivalent due to the alternation between sucking and biting. In this phase, the child may experience biting as destructive, but not his own love. The schizoid conflict involves loving without destroying through love itself, whereas the depressive conflict involves love and hate, specifically the fear of destroying through hatred (Fairbairn, 1941).

To control or prevent the loss of his love objects, the child internalizes them; this process, while protecting him from the anxiety of loss, hinders his progression toward adult dependency, as it implies a primary identification with the internalized bad objects.

It is important to clarify that Fairbairn uses the term "bad objects," already employed by Melanie Klein, while attributing to it a distinct and non-overlapping meaning. For Fairbairn, the bad object is not the malevolent object resulting from the child's projected hatred; rather, it corresponds to the frustrating object, one that fails to meet the child's need for intimacy.

The greater the frustration generated by the object, the stronger the child's drive to internalize it, thereby compromising their ability to detach from it. It is the emotional pain generated by the unavailability of the desired object that leads to the internalization of the frustrating object, so that the internalized object may serve as a compensatory substitute for the unsatisfying relationship with the actual external object. This process hinders separation from parents and limits the capacity to form emotional investments in new objects. Thus, unlike Klein, Fairbairn (1943) argues that internal objects are, by definition, psychopathological structures. Consequently, in Fairbairn's perspective, a particularly frustrating mother represents a significant obstacle for the child in the developmental progression from total dependence to mature dependence.

Fairbairn asserts that to defend the ego against conflicts originating in the oral phase, which may lead to schizoid states (if occurring in the early oral phase) or depressive states (if occurring in the later oral phase), the individual may employ nonspecific defensive techniques, including paranoid, obsessive, hysterical, and phobic modes. These defenses imply attempts to disidentify from the internalized bad object—a necessary condition, in Fairbairn's view, for the individual to progress from total dependency to mature dependency.

Through the paranoid defense, the bad object is expelled from the individual's psyche; in the obsessive defense, by contrast, a compromise is achieved between retaining and expelling the object, oscillating between holding on to and giving, between the acquisitive attitude typical of infantile dependency and the more giving attitude associated with mature dependency. With the hysterical defense, the love object is idealized to establish dependency on a more reassuring basis; in this case, the overvaluation of affective relationships compensates for rejection of the object. Finally, the phobic defense involves a constant oscillation between the desire to flee from the power of the object and submission to it, between distancing and returning, between separating from the object and regressive attraction toward identification with it.

The schizoid individual struggles between an extreme reluctance to abandon infantile dependency and a desperate desire to renounce it, oscillating between libidinal investment in external objects and a rapid withdrawal from them. They resort to paranoid, obsessive, hysterical, and phobic defensive techniques in attempts to break free from the state of infantile dependency.

According to Fairbairn, only if the individual is certain of being genuinely loved as a person by their parents and feels that their own love is truly accepted can they feel secure enough to invest in real external objects and gradually relinquish infantile dependency. In the absence of this assurance, the individual is unable to abandon dependency due to an overwhelming anxiety of separation, as relinquishing internalized bad infantile objects would mean forfeiting all hope of satisfying unmet needs.

Fairbairn's observations of schizoid individuals lead him to assert that primary identification with objects obstructs the transition from infantile dependency to mature dependency. The four defensive techniques represent attempts to rid oneself of internalized bad objects. Primary identification implies that if the object is bad, then the ego is also bad, and if the ego is bad, it contains bad objects. Bad objects are internalized both as a defensive means of control and due to the child's complete dependency, leaving them no alternative. Fairbairn (1943) acknowledges that no one passes through childhood without internalizing bad objects; these reside in all of us at deeper mental levels because they have been defensively repressed. For Fairbairn, repression essentially involves the removal of internalized bad objects, a defense activated not only because the relationship with the bad object is experienced as intolerable but also as shameful, due to primary identification with the object. The child would rather become bad themselves than view their parents as bad; thus, one motivation for becoming "bad" is to render their objects "good." Being in the presence of good objects can provide reassurance; however, the internalization of bad objects profoundly undermines one's sense of security. The repression of bad objects thus becomes a key defense mechanism, and if it proves insufficiently effective, the four psychopathological defensive techniques are then employed.

In 1943, Fairbairn describes an additional defense known as the moral defense, or guilt defense, which aids in repression through the introjection of good objects that assume the role of a super-ego. Fairbairn encapsulates this idea in the phrase:

It is better to be a sinner in a world ruled by God than to live in a world ruled by the Devil. A sinner in a world ruled by God may be bad; but there is always a certain sense of security to be derived from the fact that the world around is good—'God's in His heaven—All's right with the world!

(1943, pp. 65–66)

The nature and strength of defenses is one of the three critical factors identified by Fairbairn in determining the degree of psychopathology; the other factors are the precocity of bad object internalization, the "badness" level of these objects, and the depth of the ego's identification with them.

Later, in 1944, Fairbairn expands his conceptualization of ego splitting, distinguishing between internalized bad objects as either exciting or rejecting objects. He hypothesizes that an unsatisfactory relationship with the mother encompasses both experiences of hope and broken promises, leading to the internalization of the exciting object, as well as experiences of rejection, which result in the internalization of the rejecting object.

The exciting object is associated with a libidinal ego, which remains attached to and identified with this object, constantly seeking gratifying relationships, yet ultimately destined to be disappointed. On the other hand, the rejecting object is linked to an antilibidinal ego, or "internal saboteur" (Fairbairn, 1944, 1951), which impedes the desire for contact with others.

Conversely, positive and gratifying experiences actually lived with the mother give rise to an ideal object, which relates to that part of the original ego Fairbairn terms the "central ego." This part of the ego remains available to establish real relationships with the external world. Initially conceived as a unified whole, the ego thus becomes divided into three parts: libidinal, antilibidinal, and central. This division results from both the unsatisfactory experiences with the mother and the subsequent defensive strategy of internalization to control the object and prevent its loss (Fairbairn, 1944).

At this point, Fairbairn (1944, 1951) revises his earlier theory and defines the internalization of the ideal object as the "moral defense." In this framework, the central ego commits itself to the ideals represented by the ideal object, with the expectation that achieving these ideals will lead to genuine relational contact. In doing so, the central ego distances itself from the internal exciting and rejecting objects, allowing for a deeper investment in relationships with real people.

The central ego, identified with the gratifying ideal object, thus becomes a defense against the hatred that the antilibidinal ego directs toward the libidinal ego for its naive hopes and toward the libidinal object for its exciting but deceptive promises. Ego splitting, therefore, is realized not only through the repression of internalized object relations with the exciting and rejecting objects but also through the repression of those parts of the ego associated with these relationships.

According to Fairbairn, attachment to internalized bad objects explains the self-destructive tendency inherent in all psychopathological conditions. This tendency strongly hinders the establishment of satisfying interpersonal relationships, leading the individual to seek unsatisfying love objects or to behave in ways that provoke rejection. The inability to do without the parent drives the child to form a masochistic relationship with an unsatisfactory parent, as a defense aimed at preserving the hope that the "exciting" parent may one day fulfill their promises. Without this defense, the child would be faced with the unbearable anxiety of being completely alone.

In summary, Fairbairn's original contribution, considered in its entirety, offers a new perspective for conceptualizing the defenses of internalization, repression, and splitting. While he employs the same terms introduced by Klein, he uses them to describe profoundly different psychic processes. Specifically, the term "splitting" refers to the formation of three distinct representations of the self, which are in conflict with one another, each associated with a specific and separate representation of the object. Within this theoretical framework, repression is primarily understood as the removal of parts of the self that are identified with bad objects. Furthermore, in his study of schizoid factors in personality, it is noteworthy that Fairbairn not only addresses specific defenses, such as withdrawal and intellectualization, but also outlines a global defensive organization that permeates the entire personality structure.

Donald Winnicott

Donald Winnicott, who underwent extensive analysis by James Strachey and later by Joan Riviere, and was supervised by Melanie Klein in the late 1930s, is widely acknowledged as the most prominent figure among the Independent psychoanalysts. While he positioned his work within the framework of Freudian and Kleinian theories, Winnicott developed an original perspective within the field of object relations theory. It was only in his later writings (Winnicott, 1962a, 1968) that he explicitly highlighted the divergences between his views and Freud's drive theory, as well as Klein's conceptualizations.

At the heart of Winnicott's theoretical contributions lies an exploration of the relationship between the child and the environment, with a particular focus on the environmental factors that either facilitate or impede the child's developmental trajectory. His dual training as a pediatrician and psychoanalyst afforded him a unique vantage point for observing the tangible dynamics between parents and children, allowing him to focus particularly on the needs for intimate contact and differentiation. His central concern was to understand how a child becomes a person—specifically, how a distinctive and stable personality emerges over time.

Winnicott proposed that the child initially experiences a state of unintegration, achieving integration through maternal functions that involve recognizing and supporting the child's emotional experiences (Winnicott, 1962b).

According to Winnicott (1956), during the final months of pregnancy, mothers develop a mental state known as primary maternal preoccupation. This heightened sensitivity enables them to accurately identify their child's emotional experiences and respond to their needs. Such immediate and appropriate responses allow the infant to experience the illusion of having created what they require, although these provisions are actually the result of maternal care. This illusion of omnipotence, experienced during the early months of life, constitutes, in Winnicott's view, an essential foundation for healthy development and the formation of the "true Self" (Winnicott, 1953). However, when the mother fails to adequately mirror the child's experience, the child's capacity for self-recognition and integration may be compromised (Winnicott, 1971).

Winnicott (1958) further emphasizes the significance of the moment when the mother, attuned to her child's needs, allows them to experience being alone in a state of well-being, free from intrusion. This experience, termed the capacity to be alone in the presence of the mother, enables the child to connect with a healthy state of unintegration, from which their needs can emerge spontaneously.

Over time, primary maternal preoccupation gradually diminishes, adjusting to the child's evolving needs and facilitating a progressive disillusionment from omnipotence, resulting from less "perfect" maternal responses. A "good enough" mother, who progressively reduces her adaptation in accordance with the child's capacity for frustration, fosters the child's ability to tolerate absence. Conversely, a perfectly adapted mother would hinder the child's development toward separateness and individuation. The frustration arising from the disillusionment of omnipotence becomes tolerable at this stage of development, supported by the physiological drive toward separateness (Winnicott, 1960a).

Within the realm of omnipotence, the child engages with a subjective object—an object that they create and perceive as being under their control. Over the course of development, the child gradually gains access to the objective object, an entity of external reality that is distinct and independent. To navigate this transition and manage the associated anxiety, Winnicott (1963a) identifies a third dimension, referred to as the intermediate reality or potential space: an area situated between the world of subjective objects and that of objective objects.

This transitional area encompasses tangible objects to which the child creatively assigns symbolic meaning, such as a blanket or a stuffed toy. These transitional objects, imbued with emotional significance, allow the child to dwell in a space that is neither entirely subjective nor wholly governed by the constraints of external reality. This space, which later evolves into play as the child matures, forms the foundation for the adult capacity to appreciate music, art, literature, and to engage in free and creative thinking. Access to this dimension, with its lifelong implications, hinges on the experience of the area of omnipotent illusion within the early relationship with the mother (Winnicott, 1953).

The progression toward separateness also entails the child's capacity to "use the object" (Winnicott, 1969), expressing their needs with the natural intensity and ruthlessness characteristic of their spontaneity. If the object withstands these expressions without resorting to retaliation or abandoning its function, the child can solidify their sense of self, integrating their aggression as a vital and legitimate expression of their authenticity. The maternal ability to tolerate the child's voracious attacks during moments of heightened excitement and hunger, without punitive reactions, along with her enduring presence as the environmental mother, enables the child to integrate two distinct maternal representations: the object-mother and the environmental-mother. This integration supports the development of the capacity to care for the mother, and eventually for others, nurtured by the maternal acceptance of the child's spontaneous reparative gestures (Winnicott, 1963b).

Regarding defenses, Winnicott (1960b) asserts that the mechanisms protecting against anxiety linked to instinctual drives or the loss of the object presuppose the existence of an autonomous Self, a stable configuration of the Ego, and possibly a personal body image. However, in the earliest stages of life, anxiety does not manifest as fear of separation or castration but as a profound fear of total annihilation. In the initial stage of development, Winnicott (1962b) urges us not to view the infant merely as a hungry individual whose drives can be satisfied or frustrated. Instead, he describes the infant as an immature being, perpetually exposed to the threat of unthinkable anxiety. This extreme anxiety is managed by an essential maternal function, which consists of the mother's capacity to empathize with the infant and intuitively meet their fundamental needs.

This perspective differs from that of Melanie Klein, who explored the early stages of development and primitive defenses with a primary focus on the infant's internal mechanisms. While Klein emphasized the internal psychic processes of the child, Winnicott placed greater importance on maternal care and the defenses that arise in response to environmental failures. He argued that, although Klein's contributions are foundational, a complete understanding also requires an analysis of the role of the environment and its shortcomings, which lie at the heart of his theoretical framework.

A central concept in Winnicott's theory is the true Self, understood as the capacity to experience a sense of continuity in existence and to develop a unique psychic reality and bodily schema at one's own pace. When maternal care is inadequate, the development of the true Self is compromised. Instead of existing spontaneously, the child is compelled to react to environmental stimuli.

From a developmental perspective, the Self begins as a potential within the infant. This potential can only mature in a sufficiently supportive environment. When nurtured, the Self evolves into an integrated structure, capable of distinguishing between what belongs to the individual's subjective experience (Me) and what exists outside of it (Not-me). In an optimal context, this process culminates in the formation of a complete Self, able to maintain a clear distinction between the individual's subjective core and external reality.

An individual can develop an authentic sense of Self only when they are allowed to *be*, free from excessive pressures imposed by the environment. Such pressures, often caused by deprivation or intrusion, force the child to react rather than exist. Winnicott (1949) illustrates this dynamic with the image of a bubble: just as a bubble deforms under external pressure, so too does the Self adapt to environmental demands, especially when the environment fails to adequately meet the child's needs.

Threats to the true Self generate profound anxiety, against which the child develops defenses. In this context, the false Self serves a protective function, concealing and safeguarding the true Self. Winnicott (1960a) conceptualizes the false Self as existing along a continuum. At one extreme, the true Self is entirely hidden, while at the other, the false Self operates as a functional adaptation, enabling the individual to navigate social contexts. In this balanced state, the false Self protects the true Self, allowing the individual to avoid excessive vulnerability.

In the most severe cases, the true Self fails to develop, as environmental intrusions or deprivations compel the individual to conform rigidly to external demands. At intermediate levels, the true Self remains dormant, while the false Self operates as a provisional defense, holding space until more favorable conditions allow the true Self to emerge. This dynamic is frequently observed in analysis, where the false Self prompts patients to seek treatment and to test the analyst's dependability before allowing the true Self to reveal itself.

Winnicott cautions that, in extreme cases, the false Self may become so rigidly entrenched that it precludes any possibility of growth. Such a deeply ingrained defensive structure can make it exceedingly difficult for the analyst to discern the presence of a false personality in the initial stages of treatment. The challenge is especially pronounced when the false Self manifests in intellectually gifted individuals, whose cognitive sophistication serves to mask the underlying rigidity of their defensive organization.

In these circumstances, the intellect assumes the role of the false Self's operational hub, leading to a dissociation between mental activity and psychosomatic experience. Intellectual endeavors are deployed as a means of escape from embodied existence. Winnicott describes such individuals as those who, despite considerable academic or professional achievements, feel an increasing sense of estrangement from their inner selves as their external successes mount. In some cases, they may even sabotage their accomplishments, bewildering those around them, who are left unable to comprehend the underlying motives of such self-destructive behavior.

According to Winnicott, the false Self originates from the mother's inability to sustain the infant's illusion of omnipotence during the early months of life. This deficiency manifests in the failure to recognize the infant's spontaneous gestures and in the mother's tendency to impose her own actions, thereby compelling the child to adapt. Instead of being seen and accepted for who they truly are, the infant conforms to a distorted image reflected by the mother, leading to the development of a false Self. Although the individual may appear authentic to others, they are unable to experience genuine inner vitality and are often overwhelmed by a painful sense of futility.

Winnicott emphasizes that the development of extreme forms of the false Self is not solely the result of the absence of a consistently "good enough" mother. Rather, it is the experience of an unpredictable and inconsistent mother—at times nurturing, at other times rejecting—that fosters the formation of a rigid false Self. In such cases, the child constructs this defensive structure as a means of shielding themselves from the confusion created by an unstable environment.

Only when the true Self has been recognized and supported during the early stages of life can the individual clearly differentiate internal reality from external reality. Under these conditions, the false Self can serve a protective role without overshadowing the true Self. Winnicott illustrates this distinction with the example of the actor. An actor who remains in touch with their true Self can be authentic both on and off the stage. By contrast, an actor who depends on the applause of the audience loses their sense of self once they step away from the spotlight.

When the false Self does not supplant the true Self but merely acts as its protector, the individual retains access to the intermediate area of illusion. This state allows for the use of symbols and the full enjoyment of cultural experiences, enabling a life that is both creative and authentic.

Winnicott (1963a) emphasizes that, in a healthy individual, there exists a profound core of personality that remains entirely separate from the realm of objective objects. This intimate element, which must be protected, engages solely with subjective objects and remains the foundational source of authenticity and a sense of reality for the individual, while preserving the capacity to temporarily dwell within the intermediate area of experience, where creativity can flourish. Conversely, when the false Self develops in place of the true Self, the individual loses the ability to derive pleasure from cultural experiences. Instead, they become trapped in an unrelenting search for external stimuli and pressures, which enable them to react. In such circumstances, reacting becomes a substitute for existing: it is through reaction to external stimuli that the individual perceives a semblance of existence.

In an earlier work, *Mind and its Relation to the Psyche-Soma* (1949), Winnicott had already observed how a discontinuous maternal presence could provoke hyperactivity in mental functioning. In these cases, intellectual activity develops excessively, taking on roles that would ordinarily belong to the external environment. This form of adaptation, however, reinforces dependence on the mother and results in only an apparent personal growth, one rooted in compliance rather than genuine development.

As development progresses, this dynamic can evolve into a difficulty in recognizing one's own need for dependence. Instead, the individual tends to identify with the role of caregiver, replicating learned relational patterns. A person who has internalized such experiences may appear highly skilled in supporting others, demonstrating a remarkable ability to adapt to the needs of the mother or anyone in a dependent position. However, closer examination can reveal the underlying falsity of their personality, exposing a lack of authenticity.

Winnicott cautions against the risks posed by this dynamic, particularly when evaluating candidates for professions such as psychiatry or psychiatric social work. All psychoanalysts are familiar with the challenges of identifying these traits during the selection of candidates for psychoanalytic training, where a false personality may be masked by an appearance of competence.

5 Insight into defenses in North American psychoanalysis

Anna Maria Rosso

North American psychoanalysis has undergone a profound evolution over time, shaped both by its Freudian roots and the theoretical contributions of European psychoanalysts who emigrated to the United States. Beginning in the 1940s, ego psychology—championed by Heinz Hartmann, Ernst Kris, and Rudolph Loewenstein—emerged as the dominant paradigm, emphasizing the adaptive functions of the ego and its role in mediating interactions with external reality. In the 1970s, groundbreaking contributions such as Heinz Kohut's self-psychology shifted the focus from instinctual conflict to the cohesion of the self, introducing concepts such as empathic attunement and the centrality of self-objects. Concurrently, Otto Kernberg proposed an integration of ego psychology and object relations theory, offering a dynamic understanding of borderline and narcissistic personality structures, with particular attention to processes of splitting and idealization.

These theoretical advancements have steered North American psychoanalysis toward an increasing interest in the interplay between intrapsychic dynamics and environmental interactions, fostering a plurality of approaches ranging from ego psychology to interpersonalism and relational psychoanalysis. This chapter focuses on the analysis of three pivotal figures who, from distinct perspectives, have advanced our understanding of the concept of defense: Heinz Hartmann, with his emphasis on ego autonomy and the conflict-free sphere; Otto Kernberg, who illuminated the role of splitting and primitive defense mechanisms in borderline psychopathology; and Heinz Kohut, who redefined the concept of defense by integrating it into his self-psychology framework, highlighting its adaptive significance in maintaining self-cohesion.

Heinz Hartmann and ego psychology

Heinz Hartmann, trained in Vienna and personally invited by Freud to join the Vienna Psychoanalytic Society in 1922, relocated to New York in 1941, two years after the publication of his seminal work *Ego Psychology and the Problem of Adaptation*. In the United States, he became one of the founders

DOI: 10.4324/9781003536994-7

of the New York Psychoanalytic Institute, establishing himself as a pivotal and innovative figure on the international psychoanalytic stage.

In his theoretical framework, Hartmann places reality at the core of his model, focusing on the elements that enable human beings to adapt and thrive within their environments. While remaining anchored to Freud's instinctual structural model, Hartmann expands the scope of psychoanalysis by shifting its emphasis from psychopathology to a general psychoanalytic psychology that also encompasses normal psychic processes (Hartmann, 1951). From this perspective, he proposes that the ego does not emerge from the id solely as a reaction to frustrations but that both derive from an initially undifferentiated matrix. Functions such as perception, memory, and motor activity develop autonomously and later integrate into the ego, enabling its independent operation within a "conflict-free sphere" (Hartmann, 1939).

Certain ego functions thus operate outside the realm of psychic conflict, exerting significant influence as autonomous factors. These functions play a critical role in shaping the defensive mechanisms adopted by the individual and their outcomes (Hartmann & Kris, 1946).

In this context, defense mechanisms are not confined to regulating unacceptable drives but also assume a constructive role in addressing the challenges posed by reality. Hartmann highlights the adaptive function of these mechanisms, illustrating, for example, how the use of fantasy can serve not only to evade instinctual conflicts but also to facilitate moments of introspection and insight that secondary-process thinking alone might not achieve. Similarly, mechanisms such as reaction formation extend beyond the management of unacceptable impulses, contributing to the development of more socially appropriate interpersonal relationships.

Within this theoretical framework, defenses respond to both intrapsychic pressures and the adaptive demands imposed by the social environment. Mastery of reality, enabled in part by learning processes, inherently involves a degree of instinctual satisfaction, and these learning processes form the indispensable foundation for the development of defenses against danger (Hartmann, Kris, & Loewenstein, 1946).

Hartmann conceptualizes the ego as the psychic organ responsible for adaptation to the environment, with its primary objective being the maintenance of homeostasis and control. He argues that the ego does not derive solely from the id but possesses an autonomous primary energy of constitutional origin, which supports both its original autonomous functions and those that develop secondarily in response to conflict (Hartmann, 1955). This autonomy enables the ego to ensure effective environmental adaptation, provided the environment remains sufficiently predictable (Hartmann, 1939).

While remaining faithful to the classical instinctual model and regarding the object as merely one of several factors influencing child development, Hartmann also explored the role of the mother–child relationship in shaping certain defense mechanisms. He hypothesized that specific defenses could be activated by particular conflicts present in the mother (Hartmann, Kris, & Loewenstein, 1951).

However, Hartmann's most significant contribution lies in his revision of the economic perspective. He proposed that the ego, in addition to desexualizing libido as Freud described, is also capable of neutralizing aggressive drives (Hartmann, Kris, & Loewenstein, 1949). Neutralized aggressive energy can be redirected to support defensive counter-investments, thereby reducing instinctual demands. While Freud assigned a predominant role to libidinal investment, Hartmann emphasized the neutralization of aggressive impulses, considering it fundamental to adaptation. This process, in turn, fosters healthier object relations and helps to prevent the emergence of psychosomatic disorders.

According to Hartmann (1950), the failure to neutralize aggressive drives compromises the ego's defensive capacity, increasing the risk of dysfunction. The ongoing process of neutralization, independent of the intensity of instinctual demands, strengthens the ego, enhancing both its defensive and adaptive functions.

Moreover, the ego's ability to accumulate deinstinctualized energy and its orientation toward environmental adaptation assign a central role to reality. Within this theoretical framework, defense mechanisms can also be shaped by the demands of reality, independently of intrapsychic conflict.

Otto Kernberg: toward the integration of ego psychology and object relations theory

Kernberg, born in Vienna, moved to Chile at the age of 11 due to Nazi persecution. There, he completed his studies in medicine and psychiatry and underwent psychoanalytic training at the Chilean Psychoanalytic Association. In 1951, he relocated to the United States, joining the Menninger Clinic in Kansas to further his training. Later, he settled in New York, where he built a distinguished academic and clinical career at New York Presbyterian Hospital and Cornell University Medical College. Drawing from his Kleinian training and his extensive experience in ego psychology, Kernberg developed a remarkable integration of object relations theory and ego psychology.

In his theoretical framework, Kernberg assigns a central role to affects, proposing that representations of the self and object are interconnected through affective states, which are organized into libidinal and aggressive drives within the context of object relations. While adhering to the structural model of the psyche, Kernberg expands it by hypothesizing that the quality of the id, ego, and superego structures is shaped by the affects associated with lived experiences of gratification or frustration. Object relations, therefore, are conceptualized as a configuration comprising the self, the object, and the dominant affect governing their interaction.

According to Kernberg, libidinal drives emerge from pleasurable experiences, whereas aggressive drives arise from unpleasant ones, with both retaining their roles as primary motivational forces. Psychic development is characterized by the internalization of units of object relations—each composed of the self, the object, and the affect—along with the defenses mobilized against them. The structure of the ego, shaped by these relational units, organizes the drives (Kernberg, 1976).

In Kernberg's conceptualization, drives are psychic phenomena derived from the interplay of emotional experiences and interactions with objects, whether real or internal. Libido and aggression, far from being mere biological impulses, are contingent upon the quality of object relations, which can amplify or diminish their intensity. This perspective introduces a novel understanding of psychic conflict and defenses. Psychic conflicts are no longer viewed as simple tensions between somatically rooted drives and the psychic agencies of the id, ego, and superego; instead, they are understood as reflections of internalized object relations. Similarly, defenses are not directed against isolated drives but against units of object relations, which, in Kernberg's view, constitute the unconscious, reinterpreted not merely as the repressed part of the mind.

Regarding defenses, Kernberg largely adopts Klein's conceptualization, emphasizing the structuring role of splitting in early life. However, unlike Klein, he hypothesizes that it is only around the third year of life that split representations of self and object, both good and bad, begin to integrate gradually, leading to the formation of whole representations of the self and object. At this stage, according to Kernberg (2004), repression can replace splitting as the primary defense mechanism. It is the integration of these representations that enables the neutralization of drives, already identified by Hartmann as the principal source of energy available to the ego for defensive operations grounded in repression. It is precisely at this point, Kernberg (1976) posits, that the dynamic unconscious begins to take shape. At this stage of development, Kernberg considers Freud's tripartite structural model to become fully applicable. He further emphasizes that interactions with the environment play a decisive role in the formation of the superego and its subsequent integration with the ego. This integration, once incorporated into the personality, contributes to shaping the identity of the ego. Positive interactions with real objects are crucial in consolidating the achieved sense of identity (Kernberg, 1976, 1982).

Kernberg is also one of the most prominent psychoanalysts in developing a psychodynamic diagnostic classification. His aim is to distinguish between patients who can benefit from classical psychoanalytic treatment and those who require a different approach, which he terms expressive psychotherapy (Kernberg, 1986).

Kernberg identifies three main categories of pathology: neurotic pathology, severe character pathology, and an intermediate group, each differentiated by their predominant defense mechanisms—repression, splitting, and a co-existence of the two.

In the intermediate group, he includes passive-aggressive, sadomasochistic, and some infantile and narcissistic personalities. Splitting, by contrast, is viewed as the central defense mechanism in individuals with borderline personality organization, as well as in antisocial and narcissistic personalities, characterized by highly polarized representations of self and object.

Following Freud's approach, which linked specific defenses to different neuroses, Kernberg (1986) identifies habitual defense patterns that characterize distinct personality types.

Devaluation, omnipotence, and withdrawal are hallmark defenses in the psychological functioning of individuals with narcissistic personality disorder. However, Kernberg (1986) posits that pathological narcissism should be understood along a continuum of severity. In the most severe cases, these defenses dominate mental functioning and serve to protect the individual from an underlying borderline organization, characterized by low distress tolerance and poor impulse control. The defenses of devaluation, omnipotent control, and withdrawal also serve to shield the individual from envy, which fuels intense feelings of inferiority that the grandiose self was constructed to counteract. For such individuals, object idealization functions as a projection of the grandiose self. The failure to develop a healthy and reasonably benevolent superego leaves these individuals vulnerable to attacks from a sadistic and malevolent superego. To defend against this, they frequently resort to projecting malevolence onto others, a mechanism that fosters paranoid traits.

Unlike Melanie Klein, Kernberg (1986) hypothesizes that envy originates from a rejecting primary relationship, which gives rise to feelings of hatred and envy. From this perspective, grandiosity represents the best means the child, relying on particular capacities, has found to sustain themselves. It becomes a tool for provoking envy in others in an attempt to rid themselves of it but undermines the capacity to rely on others, forcing the child to rely grandiosely on themselves alone.

In individuals with borderline personality organization, the pervasive use of splitting weakens the ego to the extent that it compromises the ability to regulate impulses and emotions. This vulnerability is further exacerbated by the particular intensity of destructive impulses, which may be either innate or the result of traumatic experiences. However, it is precisely the intensity of these destructive impulses that necessitates the use of splitting as a defensive mechanism to protect the positive representations of self and object.

The defense of primitive idealization emerges as a corollary of splitting. It allows the individual to sustain the phantasy of an omnipotent and grandiose object with which they can identify. Kernberg (1975) distinguishes between two forms of idealization: primitive and subsequent. Primitive idealization functions to shield the individual from threatening representations and lacks a direct connection to aggression. In contrast, subsequent idealization arises from the need to defend against aggressive feelings, playing a more complex role in intrapsychic dynamics.

According to Kernberg, projective identification is characterized by a lack of differentiation between self and object, manifesting in the feeling of empathizing with the projected object while maintaining a sense of control over it. Unlike simple projection, which renders the external world excessively threatening, projective identification introduces a semblance of control over the projected object, thereby mitigating the associated anxiety.

The weakness of the ego, resulting from the extensive defensive reliance on splitting, inhibits the resolution of conflicts at the intrapsychic level. Omnipotence, on the other hand, serves as a defense against persecutory anxiety, while devaluation protects against fear of the object, providing a measure of emotional stability within the context of a fragile ego.

The analysis of defenses occupies a central role in Kernberg's psychoanalytic model of nosology (1976, 2004). This model, as will be explored in the following chapter, was further systematized in the *Psychodynamic Diagnostic Manual* (PDM; Alliance of Psychoanalytic Organization, 2006) and its second edition, the *Psychodynamic Diagnostic Manual-2* (PDM-2; Lingiardi & McWilliams, 2017).

In Kernberg's theoretical framework, splitting and its associated defensive mechanisms—such as projective identification, denial, primitive idealization, omnipotent control, and devaluation—characterize the psychotic personality organization, serving a dual function. On the one hand, they preserve internalized idealized object relations by separating them from persecutory ones, thus protecting the former and safeguarding the capacity to depend on good objects. On the other hand, they compensate for the loss of reality testing, a compromise that hinders the differentiation between self and non-self, as well as between intrapsychic stimuli and external reality.

These same primitive defenses rooted in splitting are also characteristic of borderline personality organization, where, however, reality testing is generally preserved (Kernberg, 2004). The borderline structure, extensively studied by Kernberg, becomes consolidated and exacerbated in the presence of predominantly negative experiences, owing to the action of splitting and projection mechanisms. These defenses create a vicious cycle: the defensive reliance on idealization, aimed at preserving the good object, impedes the integration of split representations.

Furthermore, projective identification—through which destructiveness is systematically attributed to others—along with omnipotent control and devaluation, hinders the development of positive relationships while simultaneously fueling interpersonal conflict (Kernberg, 2018). This theoretical formulation highlights how primitive defenses undermine not only relational dynamics but also the process of intrapsychic integration, thereby reinforcing personality fragmentation.

Heinz Kohut and self psychology

Heinz Kohut, born in Vienna, emigrated to the United States in 1940 due to Nazi persecution, shortly after completing his medical studies. In the United States, he pursued psychoanalytic training at the Chicago Psychoanalytic Institute, where he began developing his original theoretical contributions to psychoanalysis.

Starting in the early 1970s (Kohut, 1971), Kohut published a series of works focusing on the concept of the self as the central core of the individual. He defined the self as "a center of initiative and a recipient of impressions" (Kohut, 1977), attributing to it functions that, in the instinctual structural model, were previously assigned to the id, ego, and superego. This approach marked a significant shift, moving the focus from instinctual dynamics to the cohesion of the self as the foundational element of personality.

According to Kohut, the self is formed and consolidated through interactions with empathic parents capable of mirroring the child's emotional states and responding to their needs. These parents serve as self-objects, which the child perceives not as separate entities but as extensions of their own self. Self-objects fulfill two fundamental functions: providing the child with admiration for their abilities and allowing them to idealize the parents, experiencing a sense of fusion. These processes contribute to giving the child a sense of both perfection and being part of the parent.

The parent's ability to mirror the child and their willingness to be idealized are critical for the development of the self. Mirroring facilitates the formation of the grandiose self, which evolves into realistic ambitions, while the libidinal investment in the idealized parental imago allows for its internalization as the ego ideal. This ego ideal, later incorporated into the superego, supports a narcissistic investment that enables the individual to derive satisfaction from themselves without relying on external approval.

Over time, through the inevitable, gradual, and tolerable empathic failures of parents, the idealized images of the self and self-objects become progressively more realistic. This process, which Kohut terms "transmuting internalization," facilitates the formation of a cohesive self, structured around two primary poles: on one side, healthy ambition and self-assurance, derived from the experience of empathic and affirming mirroring; on the other, the internalization of ideals and values, resulting from the ability to idealize the parental imago. Normal development thus leads to robust self-esteem and a balanced sense of self-love.

In contrast, if the child does not experience adequate empathic mirroring or lacks the opportunity to idealize the self-object, a fragile self-structure develops, marked by a defective sense of self and a significant impairment in the capacity to sustain stable self-esteem. Kohut (1971) emphasizes that in cases of severe narcissistic trauma, the grandiose self is neither diminished nor integrated into the adult personality but instead remains intact, continuing to pursue archaic goals. Similarly, if the parent fails to meet the child's need to be admired, the idealized parental imago remains unchanged, leaving the individual with a persistent need for an archaic self-object to maintain their narcissistic equilibrium.

This condition can also arise in response to the loss of or prolonged separation from the idealized parent. Under such circumstances, the child is unable to withdraw their idealizing investments from the parent, perceive them progressively in a more realistic light, and reinvest these energies into the construction of the self. Kohut, in this regard, cites the fantasies of an idealized father often observed in individuals who had lost their fathers during wartime. He emphasizes that the actual absence of the idealized parent prevents the child from gradually recognizing their realistic limitations, thus explaining the persistence of idealization.

In such cases, according to Kohut, the idealized parental imago becomes split and/or repressed, remaining in an archaic form. This prevents the transformation of the fantasy, its integration into the reality-ego, and the formation of an idealized superego. This deficiency fosters a constant need for an idealized self-object, upon whose support and approval the individual continues to depend.

Defenses may also be activated against the reemergence of the need for mirroring and idealization of the self-object, particularly when such needs have been traumatically frustrated. Depending on the psychic location of the defenses, this can result in vertical splitting—manifested by an alternation between feelings of grandiosity, which deny the need for approval, and feelings of emptiness and low self-esteem—or horizontal splitting, characterized by emotional detachment from objects from whom narcissistic support might otherwise be sought.

Kohut identified the mother's ability to function as a self-object—through empathic mirroring responses that allow the child to express even their grandiosity—as the cornerstone for the development of a solid and cohesive self. For the consolidation of the nuclear self, it is essential that the child can construct an idealized parental image, which, through a process of transmuting internalization (Kohut & Wolf, 1978), enables the development of ideals, ambitions, and the capacity to utilize their talents and resources.

Kohut agrees with Freud (1914) in recognizing an initial phase of primary narcissism, in which the self is libidinally invested. However, he places particular emphasis on the stage in which, through normal maternal failures, the child moves beyond primary narcissism and becomes aware of their dependence on the external object. At this stage, the child develops a grandiose self to defend against the perception of their own vulnerability and relies on the external object to satisfy the need for admiration and approval. When the external object meets this need, it supports the child's self, enabling them to idealize the parental imago and invest it libidinally, generating feelings of well-being.

Over time, Kohut progressively distanced himself from the classical drive model, reinterpreting Oedipal conflict through the lens of self-psychology (Kohut, 1977, 1984). In his view, the primary motivation of the individual is the attainment of self-cohesion, and the principal anxiety is the fear of imperfection and a lack of cohesion and continuity. The development of the grandiose self, according to Kohut, is a normal, transitory developmental phase, while the Oedipal complex represents the outcome of a vulnerable self that has not received the support of an adequate self-object. For Kohut, while the drive for love and self-assertion is innate, aggressive drives emerge only in response to unempathic caregiving. If parents respond empathically to both the child's feelings of love for the parent of the opposite sex and their desire to assert themselves against the parent of the same sex—without reacting with hostility or seduction—the child's sense of self is strengthened. However, when the self is fragile, feelings of affection and the desire for assertion transform into greed and hostility. In this emotional context, Kohut (1977) suggests that castration anxiety conceals a deeper fear: the disintegration of the self.

In the theoretical framework of self-psychology, idealization assumes a pivotal role that extends beyond its classification as a mere defense mechanism. During development, grandiosity and idealization fulfill an essential structuring function for the cohesion of the self. Once integrated into the grandiose self and the idealized parental imago, these elements can gradually be relinquished, fostering the development of self-assurance, realistic ambitions, and values imbued with libidinal investment. However, when self-objects fail to support the development of a sufficiently cohesive self, grandiosity and idealization persist in a defensive capacity, aimed at protecting the self's vulnerability. Under such conditions, the need for self-objects capable of enabling idealization becomes indispensable for sustaining the fragile self and shielding against the profound anxiety of losing the sense of self-cohesion.

The less the child's grandiose-exhibitionistic self is neutralized through empathic parental responses and the less the idealization of the parental imago is facilitated, the weaker the development of a solid sense of identity. Consequently, the defensive need to protect the vulnerable self through idealizing defenses persists, limiting the capacity to develop realistic ambitions. In the absence of adequate integration, grandiosity and the need for external approval crystallize into rigid and dysfunctional defensive patterns.

In light of these considerations, Kohut (1984) questions the indispensability of the traditional psychoanalytic focus on defenses and the role the concept of "defense" occupies in psychoanalytic theory. He observes that while the classical analyst seeks to identify well-defined "mechanisms," the self-psychologist addresses the entire personality in all its complexity. In his later writings, published posthumously, Kohut critiques classical theory, asserting that while it is effective when applied to isolated processes of psychic life, it is inadequate for understanding the totality of human personality and its development along the temporal axis of life.

Kohut prefers the term "defensiveness" over "defensive mechanisms," viewing it as a psychologically valid attempt at adaptation. For him, defense is not merely a response to instinctual drives but an activity in service of psychological survival. His focus is on the condition of the self—its position in time, its past, and its future. Rarely does he consider the patient in terms of instinctual desires and defenses, interpreting defense instead as an effort to preserve that part of the nuclear self which, though fragile and precariously structured, has been built despite significant deficits in early self-objects.

Furthermore, Kohut argues that idealization is not merely a defense but also a psychological process with a constructive role in mature object relations. When combined with object libido, it becomes an essential source of energy for creative activities. Through this perspective, Kohut reshaped the study of defenses, shifting the focus from instinctual conflict to the protection of the self. He offered a more empathic and relational view of defenses, emphasizing their role in regulating self-esteem and managing the self's vulnerabilities. This perspective opened new theoretical and clinical horizons, enriching the understanding of personality development and therapeutic practice.

6 Does the concept of defense still hold water in psychoanalysis?

Notes from the current psychoanalytic literature

Anna Maria Rosso

The concept of defense has been a foundational pillar of psychoanalytic theory and clinical practice since Freud first introduced it as a psychic mechanism for managing drive-related pressures. Over time, the concept has evolved, acquiring different meanings across historical periods and theoretical schools. Questioning its continued relevance today entails a dual task: first, retracing its historical and conceptual development; second, assessing its current role in psychoanalytic thought and clinical work.

While the preceding chapters traced the evolution of the concept across major theoretical models, this chapter turns to selected contributions from contemporary literature.

Far from being obsolete, the concept of defense today stands as a dynamic, multidimensional construct—capable of bridging diverse epistemological perspectives and offering a potent interpretive lens for understanding psychic functioning. This remains true even as contemporary psychoanalysis tends to focus more on non-neurotic clinical structures.

In a kind of counterpoint to this prevailing trend, the chapter begins by revisiting repression—the defense mechanism perhaps most neglected in current discourse—before exploring the distinction between repression and splitting, and concluding with a discussion of projective identification, arguably the most extensively theorized defense in recent psychoanalytic literature.

Repression: a neglected defense today?

The return of repression: Akhtar and the Freudian legacy

Akhtar (2020) argues that the contemporary neglect of repression stems both from a diminished engagement with Freudian metapsychology and from the clinical and theoretical emphasis of recent decades on treating patients with more primitive mental states. These factors, he suggests, have contributed to the mistaken assumption that repression operates exclusively in neurotic forms of psychopathology.

DOI: 10.4324/9781003536994-8

In response, Akhtar offers a careful reconsideration of Freud's 1915 essay on repression, underscoring several aspects that remain clinically relevant, particularly in relation to technique. Drawing on various studies (Cohen & Kinston, 1984; Frank, 1969; Frank & Muslin, 1967; Kinston & Cohen, 1986, 1988) that explore the distinction between "primal repression" and "repression proper" (Freud, 1900, 1915b, 1926), he highlights Freud's shift in 1926, when the origin of primal repression was linked to the displeasure generated by hyperstimulation in an immature mental apparatus. Associated with preverbal stages of development, primal repression becomes an "unrememberable and unforgettable" substratum (Frank, 1969, p. 48) that can be accessed only through nonverbal channels (Kinston & Cohen, 1986, p. 338).

On this basis, Akhtar proposes that analysts can recognize primal repression only through empathic attunement to bodily communication, and that reconstruction—rather than interpretation—is the preferred technical approach. Interpretation, he argues, should be reserved for the later, verbally represented material of proper repression.

Akhtar also revisits Freud's notion that successful repression coincides with the banishment of incompatible content from consciousness, while failure entails the return of the repressed. As Freud warned, what is banished may "proliferate in the dark" (1915, p. 149), threatening to implode or explode. Yet Akhtar suggests that the return of the repressed may also mark the success of repression, particularly when expressed in creative form. Poetry, for instance, may function as a

> de-repressing venture, a bridge between the nonverbal and the verbal, between the instinctual and the phonetic … that has the potential of deepening self-knowledge in its creator.
>
> (Akhtar, 2020, pp. 248–249)

Technically, this implies that the analyst should remain patient and avoid premature interpretation. In a compelling footnote, Akhtar further speculates that Freud's 1915 reference to psychic implosion may anticipate Bion's (1959) later concept of *attacks on linking*.

Akhtar (2020) asserts the ubiquity of repression, extending from normal psychological functioning to neurotic and severe psychopathological conditions. He argues that the widely accepted contrast between repression and splitting—originally proposed by Melanie Klein (1946) and later reiterated by Kernberg (1970) in his tripartite model of neurotic, borderline, and psychotic levels of functioning—has resulted in a "water-tight compartmentalization" (p. 252) that does not withstand scrutiny.

This observation carries significant technical implications: acknowledging the coexistence of repression and splitting in all patients expands the analyst's capacity to employ confrontation, interpretation, or reconstruction, as clinically appropriate.

Akhtar further cautions against viewing repression solely as a defense against instinctual drives. Echoing Freud's (1916) discussion of criminals from a sense of guilt, he emphasizes that repression may also be directed against superego demands. Moreover, repression can not only inhibit instinctual expression but at times facilitate its discharge.

He therefore urges analysts to recognize both the pervasiveness and the continuing relevance of repression in clinical practice and theoretical reflection.

Broadening the concept: Eagle and the notion of a repressive style

Alongside the renewed interest in classical formulations of repression, several authors have proposed theoretical extensions that, while provocative, raise concerns about the conceptual coherence of the term itself.

Among them, Eagle (2000a, 2000b) has written extensively on repression, offering a number of noteworthy theoretical observations. One such point involves a key elaboration: the ego may defend itself against instinctual impulses independently of the socializing processes that constrain sexual drive expression.

Recalling that both Freud (1923, 1926) and Anna Freud (1936) emphasized how the sheer intensity of a stimulus can itself threaten ego stability, Eagle argues that the perception of threat—and thus the need to activate defense—depends on the ego's strength.

According to this view, individuals with fragile egos may be especially vulnerable to being overwhelmed by intense affect or arousal, potentially resulting in massive repression. Yet precisely because such repression is difficult to sustain and taxing on the psychic apparatus, it becomes more prone to failure and the return of the repressed. From this perspective, repression would target not only wishful phantasies and punishment-related representations, but also—if emotional intensity itself is perceived as threatening—the very experience of emotion and its activating conditions.

The failure of repression, therefore, may manifest not only as the return of unacceptable content, but also—as is perhaps more salient in some individuals—as the overwhelming impact of emotional intensity and arousal itself.

This line of reasoning leads Eagle to significantly broaden the scope of repression beyond its Freudian origins. In a later paper (Eagle, 2000b), this expansive approach becomes even more evident, culminating in the proposal of a *repressive style*—a personality dimension marked by a chronic tendency to exclude distressing mental content from conscious awareness.

Conceived in these terms, the notion of a repressive style has become the focus of empirical research in psychology, as evidenced by the wide-ranging review of studies presented by Eagle.

Collectively, these studies suggest that individuals with a repressive style exhibit elevated thresholds for detecting emotionally taboo material, display impairments in forming aggressive concepts, and show lower risk for depression and suicide. At the same time, however, they tend to present with elevated blood pressure and increased susceptibility to physical illness.

Eagle's substantial broadening of the concept ultimately leads him to propose replacing the term *repression* with *avoidant defenses*, explicitly linking it to attachment theory. This move represents a marked departure from the core of Freud's original formulation.

While these developments are undoubtedly thought-provoking, they call for critical scrutiny regarding their theoretical implications. Expanding the concept of repression to encompass an entire defensive style—conceived as a stable personality trait—risks undermining its metapsychological specificity. In Freud's view, repression is a discrete defense mechanism, operating unconsciously and dynamically to exclude unacceptable mental representations from awareness.

Subsuming broad and observable forms of cognitive avoidance under the rubric of repression risks diluting its conceptual precision and blurring the boundaries between repression and other, qualitatively distinct psychic processes.

Preserving conceptual specificity: contemporary clarifications

In today's increasingly pluralistic psychoanalytic landscape, conceptual clarity and terminological precision are more vital than ever. This concern animates a study by Hinshelwood (2008), who compares repression and splitting through a close semantic analysis. Returning to Freud's 1915 text, he underscores that the defining feature of repression is the generation of substitute representations that mask repressed ideas, allowing them to emerge in dreams and symptoms as symbolic expressions, thus displacing direct drive gratification.

In earlier notes (Hinshelwood, 2006), Melanie Klein described repression proper as the ego's capacity to separate mental contents, safeguarding "good" thoughts by removing "bad" ones from consciousness. In more primitive psychic states, however, thoughts are not merely separated but annihilated and expelled altogether. While repression allows for masked or symbolic formations and merely removes conflict from conscious awareness, splitting compromises ego structure itself, impairs its functions, and leads to structural deficiency.

Brook (1992) had already observed that, in repression, repressed and unrepressed contents reside in distinct psychic systems. That is, the repressed is assigned to the unconscious, while unrepressed material remains available to consciousness. These two systems possess different spatial, functional, and qualitative properties. In contrast, in splitting, separated mental contents are not necessarily divided along conscious–unconscious lines; both poles of the split may exist simultaneously at both levels.

Savvopoulos, Manolopoulos, and Beratis (2011) highlight several defining features of repression in Freud's original theory (1900, 1915a, 1915b): it presupposes the emergence of the secondary process, the consolidation of the conscious/unconscious distinction, and the development of verbal representation; it is also linked to situations in which drive gratification is experienced as more painful than pleasurable. Similarly, for Winnicott (1959, 1961), repression becomes available only when ego structure is sufficiently consolidated—alongside the capacity for symbolization and access to the transitional space.

These classical formulations remain crucial for preserving the conceptual specificity of repression. Without them, the term risks becoming diluted—used, as Eagle (2000b) appears to suggest, to describe any defensive condition in which individuals avoid emotional truth due to insufficient psychological resources. Such an extension blurs the boundary between repression and conceptually distinct functions, such as failed containment and a compromised alpha-function (see Chapter 3). The Freudian notion of repression, rooted in metapsychology, should not be conflated with these broader—though theoretically distinct and no less significant—conceptual frameworks.

Multiple meanings of splitting: conceptual mapping and clinical relevance

Blass (2015) cautions against the conceptual ambiguity surrounding the term *splitting*, identifying four distinct meanings in contemporary psychoanalytic discourse: splitting as dissociation, as disavowal, as a division of representations, and as a division of the mind. Although all four usages can be traced back to Freud, each has developed along different theoretical trajectories. What follows is a synthesis of Blass's nuanced examination, which aims to disentangle these overlapping meanings and to clarify their clinical and theoretical implications.

Splitting as dissociation

In discussing *splitting as dissociation*, Blass (2015) notes that Freud (1893–1895) first introduced the concept of splitting in his studies on hysteria, describing mental states in which a portion of consciousness separates from ordinary awareness. Freud employed terms such as *Spaltung* and *Abspaltung* to characterize dissociative phenomena, referring to "double consciousness" and psychic groupings split off from the ego and organized around incompatible contents.

This psychic configuration, which underlies the structure of hysteria, is associated with the presence of traumatic experiences—even when relatively mild. Freud emphasized that what is repressed in such cases is not merely isolated ideas, but entire psychic organizations that remain partially accessible to consciousness (Breuer & Freud, 1893). Initially, this form of splitting is not clearly distinguished from repression and is instead understood as an effect of defense. It does not imply a multiplicity of selves, but rather a shift in libidinal investment from a conscious to an unconscious sector of the mind.

Although Freud later moved away from the dissociative model, it was taken up and further developed by Ferenczi (1932), who linked it to early trauma—particularly premature sexualization.

Kohut (1971) reintroduced and reformulated the concept, distinguishing between *horizontal splitting*—which separates the conscious from the unconscious via repression—and *vertical splitting*, which refers to the coexistence of distinct and compartmentalized psychic structures. The latter is characteristic of narcissistic pathology, where individuals oscillate between grandiosity and vulnerability. Kohut attributes this form of splitting to relational trauma, particularly failures in early parental mirroring of the child's narcissistic needs. He further conceptualizes vertical splitting as a form of disavowal, though he cautions that it must be differentiated from Freudian disavowal, which refers to a distinct form of psychic division.

Splitting as disavowal

Freud's conceptualization of splitting as the outcome of disavowal—introduced in several writings from the 1920s (1924a, 1927), revisited in the *Outline of Psychoanalysis* (1938a), and elaborated further in *The Splitting of the Ego in the Process of Defense* (1938b)—is carefully examined by Blass (2015), who foregrounds its theoretical distinctiveness.

In this formulation, the ego is confronted with a psychically intolerable reality. The paradigmatic example is the child's reaction to the discovery of the anatomical absence of the penis in girls, experienced as a threat of castration.

In response, the child disavows the perceived reality and creates a fetish as a symbolic substitute, thereby preserving the illusion that the girl possesses a penis and allowing masturbatory activity to continue unimpeded by castration anxiety.

This process is not reducible to repression or denial in the ordinary sense, but rather constitutes an instance of disavowal (*Verleugnung*). Freud explains that in disavowal, reality is accurately perceived but simultaneously rejected on both emotional and cognitive levels. The ego adopts two contradictory positions: one that acknowledges reality, and another that, under the influence of instinctual drives, retreats from it. These opposing positions coexist without mutual influence, producing a genuine splitting of the ego.

Freud is careful to differentiate this type of splitting from both the psychotic split and the one produced by repression. While repression targets instinctual wishes at the level of the id, disavowal involves a division within the ego itself and is directed against external reality. Had the boy responded to the castration threat through repression, he would have suppressed his sexual phantasies and renounced masturbation.

Moreover, unlike dissociative splitting, where trauma fragments the ego, disavowal entails a deliberate act by the ego to divide itself in order to avoid repression and its consequences. In dissociation, the split is imposed by the impact of reality; in disavowal, the ego splits reality itself in order to make it bearable.

Freud also stresses that disavowal does not result in the formation of distinct psychic groupings, as seen in dissociation, but in the coexistence of two conflicting attitudes toward the same fact. On these grounds, Blass (2015) concludes that disavowal cannot be assimilated to repression or dissociation and must be regarded as a distinct defensive mechanism.

Splitting of representations and Kernberg's representation model

Two additional forms of splitting—those involving mental representations and the structure of the mind—can be linked to concepts Freud developed during the elaboration of the structural model. In *Instincts and Their Vicissitudes* (1915a), *The Ego and the Id* (1923), and *Negation* (1925), Freud describes a dynamic in which the ego maintains pleasure equilibrium by introjecting positively valenced aspects and projecting negatively valenced ones. This defensive configuration enables the ego to internalize sources of gratification while externalizing sources of displeasure, resulting in a perception of the external world as hostile—precisely because it contains the disavowed aspects of the ego itself.

This form of splitting, while not systematically elaborated by Freud, is identified by Blass (2015) as conceptually and clinically significant. According to his reading, it differs from other types of splitting in at least three ways: it constitutes a normal phase of psychic development; it operates through projection and introjection rather than repression or dissociation; and it pertains to the internal representation of self and object, rather than to the personality as a whole or to external reality.

Additional support for this conceptual distinction comes from Freud's broader metapsychological writings, in which tensions between internal objects are frequently described without recourse to the term *splitting*. For example, the coexistence of love and hate toward the same object—as in the Oedipus complex or transference—reflects ambivalence rather than structural division. Similarly, Freud's conception of the ego as composed of multiple and sometimes conflicting identifications, such as in *Mourning and Melancholia*, implies a form of inner division, but not one that amounts to psychic splitting in the technical sense.

What Blass refers to as *splitting of representations* involves a process by which a single object is experienced as if it were two separate entities. In this configuration, contradictory qualities—such as love and hate or gratification and frustration—are dissociated and assigned to distinct internal images, with no recognition that they belong to the same psychic reality.

This dynamic can affect both the self and the object and, while typical of early developmental stages, its persistence into adulthood is associated with psychopathology.

In Blass's view, this form of splitting synthesizes two central ideas in Freudian theory: the division of positive and negative aspects of the object, and the notion that internal objects are mental representations shaped by processes of identification and internalization. From this perspective, splitting concerns the way in which the ego organizes and regulates internalized object representations.

To articulate the clinical implications of this model, Blass draws on Otto Kernberg's representational theory of splitting, grounded in early affective development. Kernberg (1967, 2001) suggests that emotionally intense interactions—particularly those involving pleasure in the early maternal relationship—produce undifferentiated "all-good" representations of self and object, while traumatic or painful experiences give rise to "all-bad" representations.

At early stages, these polarized images remain unintegrated and unconscious, whereas less emotionally charged interactions are processed at conscious or preconscious levels and play a more adaptive role. In this framework, splitting serves a protective function by containing anxiety and preserving idealized representations. However, when the integration of opposing representations fails—or when there is regression to this primitive mode—a fragmented psychic structure may emerge, as in borderline pathology. This is reflected in the tendency to oscillate rapidly between idealized and persecutory object representations, destabilizing both emotional life and the analytic relationship.

Kernberg emphasizes the analytic task of interpreting how patients enact split internalized object relations, often shifting between complementary roles. By bringing these unconscious dynamics into awareness, the analytic process fosters the integration of dissociated representations—between self and object, and between idealized and persecutory images.

Within Kernberg's framework, splitting is considered an archaic defense. Initially a passive consequence of ego immaturity, it can later become an active mechanism through which the ego deliberately separates positive and negative introjections. The trajectory of this process is shaped not only by the quality of early caregiver relationships but also by intrapsychic factors, such as intense frustration and the resulting aggression—particularly during the oral phase of development.

Kleinian splitting: internal objects, unconscious phantasy, and the death drive

A distinction is warranted, as emphasized in the analysis by Blass (2015), between Kernberg's conception of splitting and that of Melanie Klein, despite their frequent comparison. While both perspectives draw on Freudian assumptions—particularly the early division between internalized good and bad elements—their underlying conceptual frameworks diverge.

In Klein's model, splitting involves not only mental representations but also the internal object as a psychic entity, as well as the ego itself. Rather than referring to mental images of objects, Klein conceptualizes the object as a real presence in the psyche, capable of being fragmented. The division of the object implies a corresponding division of the ego, such that the split does not simply occur between representations, but marks an actual rupture within the psychic structure. As Blass (2015) notes, Klein described the process of splitting in terms of a division of both ego and object into "good" and "bad" components, with consequences that extend beyond representation.

This distinction is further clarified by Hanna Segal (1964, a key interpreter of Kleinian theory, who explains that the ego projects outward the part of itself infused with the death instinct—often onto the mother's breast—thus transforming the breast into a persecutory object. The terror associated with internal destructiveness is thereby externalized, creating a sense of threat and persecution. When the bad object is experienced as fragmented into multiple hostile parts, the ego is faced with a proliferation of persecutors. Conversely, libidinal aspects may be projected onto the object to create an idealized figure of protection and security. In this way, the infant's first object—the breast—is immediately divided into opposing figures: one good and nurturing, the other bad and threatening.

Crucially, this split is not driven by an inability to tolerate conflicting representations of the same object, but by internal pressure exerted by destructive instinctual forces. What is divided, in this view, are not symbolic images, but concrete psychic elements of the ego and the internal object. The internalized object is not a separate mental content but an integral part of the ego itself. Consequently, in unconscious phantasy, when a part of the self attacks an internal maternal object, the ego is simultaneously injured, with direct consequences for psychic organization.

Klein makes this explicit in her seminal 1946 paper, *Notes on Some Schizoid Mechanisms*, where she states that the ego cannot divide an object—internal or external—without also dividing itself. The internal experience of the object in phantasy thus has structural consequences: the more sadistically fragmented the incorporation of the object, the more the ego fractures in response to these internalized destructive elements. Although these are movements of the child's unconscious phantasy, they have tangible effects, fragmenting affect, internal relations, and even thought processes.

Although both Kernberg and Klein posit a division between good and bad elements, the nature and implications of this split are fundamentally different. In Klein's framework, splitting is not merely the result of conflicting identifications or representational dissociation; it arises from instinctual aggression and generates complex unconscious relationships with internal objects.

The psychic consequences may include self-destructive attacks on the ego, on mental functions, and on internal objects themselves. One of Klein's illustrative examples involves a patient who, fearing that his analyst might perceive him as hostile, defensively split off and suppressed parts of his ego that he associated with danger. In his unconscious phantasy, this defensive maneuver equated to the destruction of a portion of his own personality.

Such a conception has clear implications for psychoanalytic technique. The therapeutic task is not simply to integrate split representations, but to recognize and interpret the splitting dynamics as they emerge in the transference and shape the patient's experience of the analytic relationship. Blass (2015) underscores that Klein's model remains grounded in Freudian theory—not only in the dynamics of introjection and projection, but also in Freud's conception of the ego-superego relation in melancholia and his dual-drive theory. In this light, splitting is viewed as a structural and internally generated phenomenon, rather than a consequence of environmental failure or ego immaturity.

Ultimately, for Klein, splitting is a drive-based process—an internal event that engages the whole psychic architecture. While potentially destructive, it also carries adaptive value: it allows the infantile psyche to manage uncontainable anxieties and to establish the basic structures of mental life, including the capacity to distinguish between good and bad and to form judgments. As Rosenfeld (1971) also observed, splitting in early life serves as a normal defense, protecting both ego and object from the death instinct. It retains its function until love and trust in good internal objects are sufficiently consolidated (Klein, 1935).

Ontological implications of splitting: the psyche as internally divided

The various theories of splitting, as emphasized in Blass's (2015) analysis, reflect autonomous and often irreconcilable theoretical trajectories.

Kernberg's representational model, for instance, does not derive from Freudian reflections on disavowal, and conflating these frameworks—an increasingly common trend in the literature—has contributed to considerable conceptual ambiguity. Freudian ideas evolved in divergent directions: the dissociative model developed in the work of Ferenczi and Kohut, while considerations on the division of the object gave rise to both Kleinian and Kernbergian theories. Despite certain shared premises, these remain fundamentally distinct approaches.

Beyond their theoretical formulations, these models also differ in their implicit anthropology. The dissociative view presupposes a unified subjectivity disrupted by traumatic external events. Disavowal implies an unconscious wish to turn away from reality while still acknowledging it on some level. The representational model, by contrast, traces internal conflict to the mind's early incapacity to reconcile opposing aspects of experience—a difficulty later compounded by aggression. Yet this perspective tends to conceptualize internal division in cognitive and functional terms, often without fully accounting for its psychic meaning.

The Kleinian model departs significantly from this stance, positing that psychic fracture is intrinsic to the human condition. Splitting is not something that happens *to* the mind but something the mind actively performs in response to both internal aggression and the need to preserve the good object. It arises from the conflict between libidinal and destructive drives and defines the psyche as structurally divided, animated by forces that do not always achieve integration.

Reflecting on this ontological division, Blass argues, inevitably brings the question of aggression into focus. If one assumes a fundamentally cohesive human subject, then aggression appears as an external intrusion. If, however, psychic fragmentation is viewed as original, then aggression emerges from within. This distinction reshapes our very understanding of psychic danger. A unified mind cannot truly fear destruction, since no separate part would remain to suffer it. A divided mind, by contrast, allows for one part to attack another—rendering the experience of internal devastation plausible.

From a clinical standpoint, exploring the different modalities of splitting enhances the analyst's capacity to grasp psychic complexity and to formulate interventions that go beyond standard interpretive strategies. Rather than asking simply what a patient is defending against, it becomes relevant to ask how the defense is structured. Is reality being denied to avoid repression, or are parts of the self being eliminated to protect a vulnerable internal object? When a patient appears to disregard certain aspects of reality, one must consider whether this reflects a process of conscious denial, or the psychic absence of a part of the mind—potentially as a consequence of trauma or its aftermath.

Structural and pathological splitting: Sechaud's perspective

The question of whether splitting plays a structuring or pathogenic role has long been debated. Revisiting this duality, Sechaud (2015) returns to Freud's writings from 1932 and 1938. In the earlier of these texts, Freud conceives of splitting as a process essential to psychic differentiation: it is precisely through the division of the ego that the superego comes into being. The differentiation among psychic agencies, while not entirely impermeable, permits the operation of repression and the emergence of substitute formations, thanks to the partial permeability of the barriers that enables the transformation of drive derivatives.

When such processes of differentiation break down, more severe forms of splitting can arise, particularly in non-neurotic psychic organizations. What emerges is not a dynamic conflict but a structural rupture within the ego—one that compromises cohesion and severs its parts in ways that may become irreversible. In this context, splitting takes the form of a radical and unconscious operation, whose aim is the total avoidance of conflict.

In contrast to everyday speech, where feeling "split" often connotes a conscious awareness of inner conflict, true splitting, as theorized here, is unconscious. The ego holds two incompatible contents without registering their contradiction, maintaining them on separate tracks without integration.

This condition stems from profoundly unconscious defensive processes—such as denial, rejection, foreclosure, disavowal, and negative hallucination—whose function is to shield the ego from situations in which the stimulus barrier risks being overwhelmed, whether by excessive internal drive pressure or by intense or impoverished environmental inputs.

Such defenses are mobilized in response to traumatic experiences as Freud came to define them after 1920: events that flood the psychic apparatus and prevent the transformation of excitation into weakly cathected mental representations. Under these conditions, the ego may fragment. A portion of it may withdraw and become inaccessible, thinking and connecting functions may collapse, projective mechanisms intensify, and the internal object may be split into persecutory and idealized components.

Drawing also on Bayle's (1996) contributions, Sechaud proposes a distinction between functional, transient forms of splitting—which protect narcissism by averting contact with emotionally disruptive representations—and deeper, structural forms, which originate in defenses against failures in symbolization and subjectivation rooted in narcissistic emptiness. In the absence of symbolizing processes that enable representation and thought, splitting functions as a protective defense against annihilation anxiety.

Thus, splitting reveals a dual nature. It can be structuring when it contributes to the delineation of internal and external boundaries, facilitates repression, and supports the ego's mediating function between inner reality and external demands. Yet when this structuring capacity fails, the ego becomes vulnerable to unprocessed stimuli from both internal and external sources, risking collapse into the drive toward Nirvana—regression to a state of zero excitation.

According to Sechaud (2015), psychoanalytic treatment, understood in Winnicottian terms as an encounter between two psyches within a potential space, is seen as the condition under which what had remained frozen may come to life. Through this encounter, a psychic apparatus capable of differentiation and symbolization can begin to take form.

Ultimately, examining the divergent conceptions of splitting underscores the impossibility of reducing the notion to a single explanatory model. Each theoretical tradition ascribes different origins, functions, and clinical expressions to the phenomenon. For the analyst, the challenge is not to select one model over another, but to discern—in each clinical situation—the prevailing psychic configuration, and to tailor the intervention accordingly, in a way that respects subjective complexity.

Projective identification: from primitive defense to intersubjective transformation

Projective identification refers to a particular unconscious and omnipotent phantasy that functions as a defense against primitive anxieties. The mechanism integrates Kleinian notions of splitting, projection, and early forms of identification.

In her 1946 paper *Notes on Some Schizoid Mechanisms*, Melanie Klein describes a process whereby the child projects both bad and good parts of the self onto the mother. In the former case—considered by Klein the prototype of an aggressive object relation—the aim is to harm, possess, and control the object. In the latter, it is the loving aspects of the self that are projected.

It is only in the 1952 version of this paper that she explicitly names the process *projective identification*. The mechanism involves separating aspects of the self from the rest of the personality and projecting them into an object, typically the mother's breast or the mother herself. The object is then perceived as if it genuinely contains these projected elements, with the subject forming a partial or total identification with it.

In its original formulation, projective identification is understood as an intrapsychic phenomenon, occurring entirely within the subject's mind and independent of the actual involvement of the external object.

However, subsequent clinical observations (Joseph, 1985, 1987; Ogden, 1992; Rosenfeld, 1971; Sandler & Sandler, 1978) demonstrated that patients often attempt to induce in others—particularly the analyst—thoughts, feelings, or behaviors that mirror the projected material, thereby enlisting the external object in unconscious enactments that serve to manage psychic distress.

Bion (1959, 1962a, 1962b), in his work on containment (discussed in Chapter 3), highlights the essential role of the mother—and by extension, the analyst—in receiving and metabolizing the infant's projections. This transformative capacity allows the child to endure emotional experience and eventually to think about it. The process breaks down when the maternal figure cannot accommodate the projected elements within her own mental space, or when she responds with counter-projection, returning to the child unprocessed or hostile content—whether originating from the mother herself or attributed to the child.

For Betty Joseph (2012), projective identification is rooted in an unconscious phantasy of undoing separation and avoiding psychic pain by merging with the object. Although the process often generates persecutory and claustrophobic anxieties, it provides temporary protection from feelings of envy, rage, dependence, admiration, and the fear of loss.

The refusal to recognize the boundary between self and object, also described by Rosenfeld (1964) and further developed by Sodré (2012), underscores the interdependence of projection, introjection, and manic defenses. Sodré shows how these mechanisms, taken to an extreme, can lead to a breakdown of identity. As she writes:

> The sense of identity derives simultaneously from the differentiation of the self from its objects and from various forms of identification with different aspects of objects. All object relations depend on the ability to remain oneself while at the same time having the ability to temporarily identify with the other's point of view. Every meaningful exchange between two people involves a complex process of projections, introjections, and identifications.
>
> (pp. 131–132)

Within this framework, not only can projective identification be pathological, but introjective identification may also become so, especially when the underlying phantasy involves internal possession of the object rather than a recognition of its separateness. To illustrate this dynamic, Sodré recalls a Portuguese expression—*"think you have the king in your belly"*—used to describe someone who, having "eaten" the king, imagines themselves superior even to him. This phrase captures the manic dimension of a process in which the self triumphs over the object, appropriating its power.

Projective identification: from defense to interpersonal process

Initially conceptualized as a defensive phantasy aimed at managing primitive anxieties, projective identification has undergone a significant transformation in contemporary psychoanalytic thought.

Increasingly, it is understood as an inherently interpersonal process that plays a central role in shaping the affective and relational dynamics of the analytic relationship.

This reconceptualization is particularly evident in contemporary Kleinian and post-Kleinian frameworks, where projective identification is closely linked to countertransference. It is regarded as a key mechanism through which the patient unconsciously influences the analyst's emotional experience—transmitting unmentalized states that cannot be communicated directly.

Joseph (2012) emphasizes that projective identification always involves a form of unconscious communication, even when its primary function is defensive. Rosenfeld (1971), working with psychotic patients, deepened the clinical understanding of this mechanism by highlighting its multiple functions: communicative, evacuative, defensive (particularly against envy and aggression), and parasitic. He described extreme forms of projective identification in which the patient becomes convinced that they live entirely within the analyst, obliterating psychic boundaries.

Building on these insights, Joseph (1987) illustrated how patients may draw the analyst into enactments that function as intricate defensive structures designed to maintain a precarious psychic balance. Similarly, Sandler (1990) showed how patients unconsciously assign roles to the analyst that reflect internal object relations—transforming the analytic space into a stage for enacting unprocessed relational patterns.

Feldman (2009) extended this line of thinking by asking what kind of internal work the analyst must do in order to register and metabolize aspects of the patient's experience that remain inaccessible to verbal elaboration.

These developments in clinical theory have paralleled an important shift in how countertransference is understood. The analyst's affective responses are no longer seen merely as distortions stemming from unresolved personal conflicts, but as privileged channels through which elements of the patient's unconscious may emerge. Joseph underscores the importance of the analyst's capacity to receive these projections, to reflect on them without being overtaken by enactment, and to return them in a form that fosters meaning and integration.

Feldman (2009) offers a nuanced distinction between two broad modalities of projective identification: one in which the patient entrusts the analyst with intolerable, unmentalized contents in the hope that they will be contained and transformed; and another, more evacuative form, where the goal is to rid the self of psychic material that cannot be symbolized. In the latter case, interpretive efforts by the analyst may be experienced as intrusive or even persecutory, especially when the patient is unconsciously seeking not understanding but repetition of internal object relations that remain inaccessible to thought. Under these conditions, the shift from action to reflection may provoke hostility or lead to a defensive withdrawal.

In this broader view, projective identification is not only a means of discharging anxiety or transmitting non-verbal states, but also a form of interpersonal pressure—a mechanism by which the patient attempts to shape or compel the analyst's emotional and behavioral response. The analyst may feel subtly or overtly coerced into occupying a particular role, speaking or acting in ways that mirror the projected content.

Theoretical developments over recent decades have deepened our understanding of the forms and functions of projective identification. Spillius (2012) observes that contemporary Kleinian thought increasingly treats projection and projective identification as part of a continuum, and places greater emphasis on the dialectic between projective and introjective identification. She identifies distinct subtypes with specific clinical implications: the *evocative* form, in which the subject unconsciously elicits a particular response from the object; and the *attributive* or *acquisitive* forms, described by Britton (2000), where aspects of the self are either projected onto the object or the subject unconsciously phantasizes about acquiring attributes believed to belong to the object.

These distinctions open up new perspectives on related psychoanalytic concepts, including projective counter-identification (Grinberg, 1979), the shared analytic field (Baranger, Baranger, Rogers, & Churcher, 2008), and its further developments in contemporary field theory (Ferro & Civitarese, 2015).

For a comprehensive account of projective identification, the reader is referred to the volume edited by Spillius and O'Shaughnessy (2012), which compiles foundational texts by Klein and Bion alongside contributions from psychoanalysts across the globe. While a detailed exploration of these perspectives exceeds the scope of this chapter, some of the most significant conceptual reformulations—particularly those proposed by Grotstein and Ogden—will be briefly considered in the final section.

Intersubjective and ontological perspectives

Drawing on Kleinian and Bionian foundations, both Ogden and Grotstein reconceptualize projective identification as a transformative process grounded in intersubjectivity and psychic development.

In one of his most influential essays, Ogden (1979) outlines a threefold understanding of projective identification: (a) as an intrapsychic defense, (b) as an interpersonal strategy, and (c) as a co-constructed experience.

While the first two dimensions elaborate on ideas already implicit in Klein and Bion, the third introduces a significant shift by locating projective identification at the core of the analytic intersubjective field. Here, it is no longer merely a mechanism used by one subject to influence another, but a dynamic process in which the analyst is called to undergo, metabolize, and give shape to complex affective communication.

This conception is further articulated in Ogden's notion of the analytic third (1994), a psychic space that emerges from the interaction between patient and analyst but is reducible to neither. Within this intersubjective matrix, projective identification functions as a vector for the co-creation of meaning—what Ogden (1992) evocatively calls a "dream for two." The boundaries between self and other are temporarily suspended to allow for the emergence of new psychic configurations. The analyst, with their own subjectivity and limitations, is not a passive recipient of projections but an active participant in the process itself.

In his later work, Ogden (1997, 2016) shifts the emphasis from structural models to the lived, phenomenological experience of the analytic encounter. Projective identification is reimagined as a poetic form of unconscious communication, an aesthetic gesture as much as a psychic one, operating through affective, sensory, and symbolic channels.

In this expanded framework, the analyst is no longer merely a container of the patient's projected states but a co-author of the emotional experience that takes shape in the session.

Such a perspective profoundly alters the epistemological status of projective identification. It is no longer simply a phenomenon to be interpreted, but an experiential event to be inhabited, a space of psychic co-belonging. Interpretation, while still necessary, becomes secondary to the analyst's capacity to remain immersed in the shared field and to engage with it—through presence, reverie, and embodied attunement.

James Grotstein developed a metapsychology of projective identification that stands out for its speculative depth and structural complexity. Deeply influenced by Bion's thought, his perspective is nonetheless more explicitly oriented toward questions of subjectivity, psychic continuity, and transcendence. Projective identification, in Grotstein's view, is not merely a defensive maneuver or a primitive form of communication; it is an ontological, almost metaphysical experience that reaches into the foundational layers of the Self.

He describes it as an ontological-experiential process through which the nascent self seeks recognition and containment—an existential appeal directed toward the other. Rather than simply expelling intolerable content, the subject uses projective identification to establish contact with the other in an attempt to come into being. What is projected are not only disturbing emotions but also primary fragments of the self, accompanied by an implicit plea that the other—typically the analyst—bear witness to one's existence. This original psychic language, through which the unformed self-attempts to assert its existence and continuity, was first formulated by Grotstein (1981).

At this level, projective identification is less about manipulating the other than about inducing an experience of self *in* the other, with the hope that it will be returned as a reflection capable of grounding identity. It is, in Grotstein's terms, both a creative and a desperate act—rooted in the need to be thought of, to exist in the mind of another.

Building on Bion's conceptual framework, Grotstein introduces the notion of *projective transidentification* (Grotstein, 2000), a term that denotes a shift from evacuative projection toward a more integrated form of relational being. In this process, the subject not only projects parts of themselves into the other but simultaneously experiences those aspects as present in the other—creating a shared psychic identity that transcends the initial split.

Projective transidentification thus entails not the evacuation of internal states but their transformation through relational mirroring. It constitutes an ontological metamorphosis, in which the Other becomes a co-constitutive presence within the Self. This experience unfolds in what Grotstein calls a space of *psychic inter-existence*—an intermediate domain where subjectivities intersect, overlap, and co-create meaning.

At the heart of this model is Grotstein's conception of the Self as plural, polyphonic, and multidimensional—a constellation of internal and external subjectivities that interpenetrate and reflect one another. In this view, both projective identification and its transformation into projective transidentification are forms of unconscious communication between internalized and externalized others. Each subject is conceived as carrying within themselves the psychic imprint of the other.

Grotstein (2007) ties this conceptualization to a post-Bionian revision of the notion of *reverie*. In this expanded formulation, reverie is not merely a container for raw anxiety but a space that receives and holds the subject's longing to exist as a complex, shared being. Transidentificatory projection becomes a means not of psychic evacuation, but of forging an ontological bond—one grounded in mutual mirroring and psychic co-belonging.

The heuristic utility of defense mechanisms in empirical research in psychoanalysis

7 Exploring the defenses in outcome research in psychoanalysis

Anna Maria Rosso

The trajectory of outcome research in psychoanalysis mirrors the progressive refinement of clinical investigative frameworks, underscoring a heightened focus on empirical substantiation. Wallerstein (2005) presents an exhaustive analysis delineating four successive waves of studies, charting the discipline's gradual ascent toward empirical recognition. This synthesis not only encapsulates the advancements in assessing the efficacy of psychoanalytic interventions but also foregrounds the methodological complexities that have accompanied the field's pursuit of scientific validation. Wallerstein delineates four discrete eras, each marked by distinct methodological paradigms that trace the evolution of evaluative instruments and the growing recognition of empirical benchmarks as pivotal to substantiating psychoanalytic efficacy. His analysis traverses the spectrum from the retrospective, descriptively driven inquiries of the initial generation to contemporary investigations grounded in stringent protocols and standardized frameworks, offering a thorough exposition of the progressive maturation of outcome research in psychoanalysis.

The inaugural generation of studies, spanning from 1917 to 1968, encompasses methodologically rudimentary investigations, predominantly reliant on retrospective surveys wherein analysts appraised the therapeutic outcomes of their patients. Nevertheless, these inquiries are hampered by the absence of clearly articulated diagnostic parameters, criteria for treatability, and standardized definitions of analytic success (e.g., Coriat, 1917; Hamburg et al., 1967; Knight, 1941).

In delineating the second generation, Wallerstein identifies some seminal studies originating in North America, three of which are affiliated with the psychoanalytic institutes of Boston, Columbia, and New York. These large-scale investigations, conducted on extensive patient cohorts (Bachrach, Weber, & Solomon, 1985; Erle & Goldberg, 1979, 1984; Knapp, Levin, McCarter, Wermer, & Zetzel, 1960; Sashin, Eldred, & Van Amerongen, 1975; Weber, Solomon, & Bachrach, 1985), are further enriched by intensive single-case studies and complemented by some European initiatives (Fonagy & Target, 1994, 1996; Leuzinger-Bohleber, Stuhr, Ruger, & Beutel, 2003).

DOI: 10.4324/9781003536994-10

This phase is distinguished by its prospective orientation and the re-fined articulation of therapeutic outcome criteria, encompassing dimen-sions such as symptom alleviation, mitigation of subjective distress, occupational efficacy, sexual fulfillment, the quality of interpersonal dynamics, and the capacity for introspective insight. These facets were systematically evaluated through rating scales administered at pre- and post-treatment intervals.

A pivotal methodological advancement emerged from the study at the Columbia Psychoanalytic Centre, which introduced a critical distinction between criteria designed to appraise clinical outcomes and those intended to gauge the maturation of the psychoanalytic process itself. A hallmark of this investigation lay in the incorporation of independent evaluators—external to the therapeutic dyad—ensuring heightened objectivity in the assessment of treatment outcomes. Simultaneously, intensive single-case studies engaged patients who, upon concluding their analysis, partook in weekly follow-up sessions led by analysts distinct from their original thera-pists (Pfeffer, 1959, 1961, 1963). However, Wallerstein underscores a pivotal limitation inherent to this second generation—namely, the absence of pro-longed follow-up assessments to ascertain the durability and stability of the observed therapeutic gains over time.

The third generational wave of studies (Kantrowitz, Katz, Paolitto, Sashin, & Solomon, 1987; Wallerstein, 1986) confronts this shortcoming by embracing more sophisticated methodological frameworks. Despite its temporal overlap with the second generation, this phase is characterized by the deployment of rigorously structured research designs, extending the investigative scope to encompass not only therapeutic endpoints but also the intricate processes that underpin them. This evolution is marked by the utilization of longitudinal studies and operationalized evaluative criteria, reflecting a decisive shift toward methodological precision.

In contrast, fourth-generation studies pivot toward the development of instruments designed to probe structural transformations within person-ality, transcending the confines of symptom reduction or enhancements in overall well-being. Wallerstein (2005) underscores that psychoanalysis endeavors to catalyze profound shifts in the architecture of personality—transformations that elude detection through tools constrained to meas-uring discrete behavioral markers (e.g., occupational absences, somatic complaints). From this perspective, Wallerstein outlines several person-ality assessment scales related to personality organization and structural change (cf. DeWitt, Milbrath, & Simon, 2018), which require the recording and transcription of multiple therapy sessions or the conduction of semi-structured interviews. This process entails rigorous training and a signifi-cant time commitment across the phases of administration, transcription, and coding.

It is noteworthy, however, that none of the instruments referenced by Wallerstein explicitly address defensive functioning—an indispensable dimension in the evaluation of personality organization. This lacuna is accentuated by the advent of the Psychodynamic Diagnostic Manual-2 (PDM-2; Lingiardi & McWilliams, 2017), a diagnostic framework oriented toward appraising the holistic functioning of personality, extending beyond the mere identification of psychopathological symptoms. The PDM-2 integrates the evaluation of defensive functioning within both Axis P, which interrogates personality structure and pattern, and Axis M, dedicated to the appraisal of overall mental functioning.

The Defense Mechanism Rating Scales (DMRS; Perry, 1990), alongside its subsequent Q-sort adaptation (DMRS-Q; Di Giuseppe, Perry, Petraglia, Janzen, & Lingiardi, 2014), is delineated in the PDM-2 (Lingiardi & McWilliams, 2017) as the gold standard for the empirical assessment of defense mechanisms.

The DMRS represents a pivotal innovation by operationalizing the observation of defense mechanisms through meticulous analysis of therapy sessions. This methodological advancement has enabled the longitudinal monitoring of intrapsychic shifts throughout treatment, facilitating correlations between defensive functioning and clinical outcomes, thereby cultivating a more dynamic interface between empirical research and psychotherapeutic praxis.

Nonetheless, despite the methodological strides afforded by the DMRS, several constraints continue to impede its widespread application in psychoanalytic contexts. The method's pronounced sensitivity to the nuances of individual sessions, the substantial temporal investment demanded for coding, and the requisite use of audio or video recordings constitute formidable barriers, curtailing the broader integration of the DMRS within psychoanalytic research.

This chapter delves into the evolving trajectory of research on defensive functioning within outcome studies of psychodynamic psychotherapies and psychoanalytic treatments, illuminating the strengths and limitations inherent to the DMRS. Building upon these considerations, complementary instruments—most notably the Rorschach—will be advanced as potential adjuncts to refine the evaluation of defensive functioning, fostering a more intricate and integrative perspective on the psychoanalytic process and its therapeutic outcomes.

The Defense Mechanism Rating Scales

The development of instruments aimed at assessing defensive functioning with robust psychometric properties—encompassing both reliability and validity—presents a formidable challenge for researchers. This complexity is rooted in the intrinsic nature of the construct, defined by the unconscious operation of defense mechanisms and the susceptibility to countertransference bias when evaluations are conducted by the treating therapist.

Such obstacles preclude the viability of self-report instruments (Perry & Ianni, 1998), notwithstanding the existence of measures like the Defense Mechanism Inventory (DMI) by Gleser and Ihilevich (1969) and the Defense Style Questionnaire (DSQ) by Bond, Gardner, Christian, and Sigal (1983). As a result, current methodologies predominantly favor instruments necessitating assessment by independent raters. Foremost among these is the Defense Mechanism Rating Scales (DMRS), developed by Perry in 1990, which continues to represent the most extensively utilized tool in the field.

The DMRS is anchored in Vaillant's (1976, 1986) hierarchical model of defenses, encompassing 30 distinct defense mechanisms stratified across seven hierarchical tiers, ascending in adaptiveness. Positioned at the least adaptive pole are defenses linked to behavioral enactments, such as acting out, passive aggression, and help-rejecting complaining. The subsequent tier pertains to major image-distorting defenses, exemplified by the splitting of self and object representations and projective identification. The third level encompasses disavowal defenses, including denial, rationalization, projection, and autistic fantasy. This is succeeded by minor image-distorting defenses, which comprise idealization, devaluation of self and object, and omnipotence.

Neurotic defenses—such as repression, dissociation, reaction formation, and displacement—occupy the fifth tier. The sixth tier is characterized by obsessive defenses, including isolation of affect, intellectualization, and undoing. At the apex of the hierarchy reside the highly adaptive defense mechanisms, encompassing affiliation, altruism, anticipation, humor, self-assertion, self-observation, sublimation, and suppression.

The application of the DMRS involves the meticulous analysis of verbatim transcripts derived from audio-recorded and video-recorded therapy sessions, adhering closely to the coding protocols delineated in the reference manual. For each defense mechanism, the manual furnishes a precise definition, comprehensive descriptive criteria, differential diagnostic guidelines, and a rating scale illustrated with exemplars, enabling coders to discern the absence, probable utilization, or definitive enactment of the defense.

Throughout the coding process, defenses are identifiable at the precise juncture of their emergence, permitting a sequential analysis of their manifestation in response to therapist interventions—an aspect that will be elaborated in subsequent sections. Upon completion of the coding procedure, three distinct types of scores are generated: one reflecting the specific deployment of each defense mechanism, another indexing the hierarchical tier of defenses employed, and a composite score encapsulating overall defensive functioning, referred to as the Overall Defensive Functioning (ODF).

The capacity to sequentially discern and analyze defenses constitutes a principal advantage of the DMRS over alternative observer-rated assessment instruments. In contrast to these tools, which yield predominantly qualitative or semi-quantitative appraisals of entire sessions, the DMRS facilitates a more granular and dynamic evaluation of defensive functioning, affording a richer, more intricate portrayal of the therapeutic process.

Attaining proficiency in DMRS coding necessitates the completion of a specialized training program, as the coding procedure itself demands several hours per session transcript (Perry & Henry, 2004).

The substantial temporal investment required has, in recent years, prompted Di Giuseppe and colleagues (2014) to devise a Q-sort adaptation, designated as the DMRS-Q. This version comprises 150 items, with five items corresponding to each defense mechanism, which are allocated across seven forced-choice categories. These categories span from 1 (irrelevant and non-representative of the individual) to 7 (highly characteristic of the individual), reflecting the intensity and frequency with which the mechanisms are employed.

The coding procedure is accessible via the online platform at https://webapp.dmrs-q.com, facilitating the computation of three core scores: individual defense mechanism scores, scores for each hierarchical defensive level, and the ODF score. Additionally, the platform generates a qualitative report, termed the Defensive Profile Narrative (DPN). In comparison to the original DMRS, the DMRS-Q markedly enhances procedural efficiency, curtailing the required coding time to approximately 30 minutes per subject.

While the DMRS-Q does not mandate specialized training to attain satisfactory reliability, a comprehensive examination of the manual (Di Giuseppe & Perry, 2021) and a nuanced grasp of the hierarchical defense model—alongside the functions inherent to each level and the distinguishing features of individual defense mechanisms—remain indispensable. In DMRS-Q coding, the clinician's inferential judgment assumes a more prominent role compared to the traditional DMRS, as the Q-sort version circumvents the direct analysis of verbatim session transcripts.

An initial investigation by Di Giuseppe and colleagues (2014) yielded promising outcomes, revealing high concordance between the DMRS and DMRS-Q with respect to the overall ODF score, as well as substantial alignment in scores across individual defensive tiers. Subsequent studies have substantiated these results, reporting commendable inter-rater reliability (Békés et al., 2021) and demonstrating robust convergent and discriminant validity (Tanzilli et al., 2021).

Studies on treatment outcomes in clinical populations

The advent of the DMRS has facilitated a breadth of research endeavors aimed at investigating the trajectory of defensive functioning over the course of psychotherapeutic treatments. This section will examine a selection of these outcome studies, with particular emphasis on psycho-analytic psychotherapies and intensive psychoanalytic interventions.

Broadly speaking, the extant literature (e.g., Akkerman, Lewin, & Carr, 1999; Despland, de Roten, Despars, Stigler, & Perry, 2001; Drapeau, De Roten, Perry, & Despland, 2003; Hersoug, Sexton, & Høglend, 2002; Kramer, Despland, Michel, Drapeau, & de Roten, 2010; Perry, 2001; Perry, Beck, Constantinides, & Foley, 2009; Perry & Bond, 2012; Roy, Perry, Luborsky, & Banon, 20095862156201231233232256) underscores statistically significant enhancements in ODF across psychoanalytic psychotherapies—spanning both short-term and long-term modalities—delivered at varying frequencies, from weekly sessions to more intensive formats.

Høglend and Perry (1998) identified initial ODF scores as significant predictors of favorable therapeutic outcomes in a cohort of patients diagnosed with depression, exhibiting greater prognostic utility than scores derived from the Global Assessment of Functioning (GAF). Moreover, shifts in defensive functioning were found to manifest more swiftly in patients with depression relative to those with personality disorders, where defensive maturation appeared to unfold at a more measured pace (Perry et al., 2009). Enhancements in defensive functioning were further correlated with reduced dropout rates and increased session frequency (Perry, 2001), fostering more favorable treatment trajectories both throughout therapy and at 12-month follow-up evaluations (de Roten et al., 2021).

Perry and Bond's (2012) investigation further disclosed that the presence of multiple Axis I disorders, alongside a history of sexual abuse and violence, was associated with more attenuated shifts in defense mechanisms. Notably, defensive modifications within the initial two and a half years of therapy demonstrated a strong correlation with marked improvements observed at five-year follow-ups, as reflected in external indices of overall psychological functioning and symptomatology. By contrast, factors such as age, gender, social class, Axis II diagnoses, and GAF scores did not emerge as significant predictors of therapeutic change.

It is worth noting that, among the studies referenced, only one (Roy et al., 2009) focused on patients undergoing intensive psychoanalytic treatment, whereas the remaining investigations were conducted within the context of psychodynamic psychotherapies, typically characterized by weekly sessions. Roy et al.'s (2009) study encompassed a cohort of 17 patients who engaged in an average of 623 sessions (range: 141–1,162), all of whom were diagnosed with mood or personality disorders and participated in psychoanalysis at a frequency of four sessions per week. The findings indicated a statistically significant enhancement in ODF, with mean scores rising from 4.95 to 5.10. This improvement coincided with an increased reliance on mature defenses, while neurotic defenses exhibited stability throughout the treatment period.

A recent, methodologically rigorous investigation by Lindfors et al. (2019) explored a substantial cohort of patients undergoing intensive psychoanalytic treatment. However, direct comparisons with prior research are limited, as this study employed a self-report instrument—the 88-item DSQ (Andrews, Pollock, & Stewart, 1989)—to evaluate defensive functioning. The study juxtaposed 128 patients who engaged in psychoanalytic psychotherapy at a frequency of two to three sessions per week (averaging 232 sessions) with 41 patients who underwent psychoanalysis at four sessions per week (averaging 646 sessions), with assessments conducted at a ten-year follow-up post-therapy. Findings revealed significant divergences in self-reported defense mechanisms during the initial two years following treatment, though these distinctions were no longer evident at the ten-year follow-up.

While this study is marked by a significant methodological limitation arising from its reliance on a self-report instrument—which, by its very nature, cannot accurately capture unconscious defense mechanisms—research employing the DMRS is likewise constrained by notable challenges. The considerable investment required to attain reliability as a coder, the extensive time demanded for session coding, and the prerequisite of audio and/or video recordings constitute substantial impediments. In particular, session recordings may provoke resistance from therapists and are not invariably appropriate to propose to patients.

Consequently, studies employing the DMRS are often characterized by small sample sizes and a restricted number of sessions per patient. Moreover, patient cohorts in these investigations tend to exhibit diagnostic heterogeneity, and most research designs omit the inclusion of control groups, thereby constraining the generalizability of the results.

These methodological constraints underscore the pressing need for the development of assessment instruments and procedures that preserve rigorous standards of reliability and validity, while simultaneously alleviating impediments to research—such as the evaluative burden placed on coders and the logistical complexities inherent in the collection of clinical material.

Drapeau et al. (2003) identified an even more salient issue in their analysis of the four-session Brief Psychodynamic Investigation (BPI; Gillieron, 1989), conducted with a cohort of 61 outpatients diagnosed with mood and anxiety disorders.

The BPI constitutes a structured psychodynamic assessment modality designed to unfold across four sessions, with the objective of formulating a therapeutic plan tailored to address the patient's immediate crisis. This process is anchored in an initial dynamic interpretation that undergoes progressive elaboration. The principal aims of the BPI encompass the articulation of a diagnosis that synthesizes psychodynamic and psychiatric dimensions, the collection of data to inform subsequent therapeutic interventions, and the cultivation of an early therapeutic alliance.

In the initial session, the therapist advances a preliminary interpretation grounded in an assessment of the patient's pre-transference dynamics and the identification of core relational conflicts. The second and third sessions are devoted to the iterative refinement and expansion of this initial hypothesis, while the fourth session functions as a synthesis, providing an opportunity for therapist and patient to reflect on the emergent material and deliberate on prospective therapeutic interventions or avenues for future support.

Interestingly—and somewhat unexpectedly—the ODF score recorded during the fourth session was markedly higher than in the preceding sessions. Recognizing the improbability that four sessions could engender structural shifts in patients, the authors posited that these variations were attributable to the therapeutic context, indicative of transient state changes rather than substantive and enduring trait transformations.

The analysis of session transcripts indicated a decline in the use of mature defenses between the first and second sessions, followed by a subsequent increase during the fourth session, ultimately reverting to baseline levels. In parallel, obsessive defenses demonstrated a notable escalation, driven predominantly by heightened reliance on intellectualization. Conversely, narcissistic defenses—such as idealization and devaluation—underwent a pronounced reduction. No significant variations were detected across the remaining tiers of defensive functioning.

These findings indicate that the shifts in defensive mechanisms observed throughout the BPI are intricately linked to the therapeutic process, rather than signifying enduring structural modifications. Such fluctuations appear to be transient, shaped by the contextual framework and the relational dynamic cultivated with the therapist. The reduction in narcissistic defenses, coupled with the rise in obsessive defenses, was interpreted by the authors as a byproduct of the alleviation of distress experienced by patients.

The initial sessions appear to activate two core narcissistic dimensions: on the one hand, the acute crisis that precipitated the request for assistance; on the other, the vulnerability arising from the acknowledgment of one's inability to navigate difficulties autonomously.

The therapist's supportive presence mitigates anxiety and concerns related to self-esteem, attenuating fears of judgment or rejection. This engenders a heightened sense of security and diminishes the perceived threat embedded within the therapeutic encounter. The fourth session, in particular, assumes a stabilizing function, characterized by a structured analysis of the crisis and increased therapist engagement—contrasting with the first session, which unfolds in a more fluid, non-directive manner through the patient's free associations. The observed elevation in intellectualization during the concluding session likely reflects the patient's effort to cognitively assimilate the experience and construct a coherent narrative surrounding the crisis.

This study raises critical questions regarding the validity of employing the DMRS as a structural outcome measure in the evaluation of defense mechanisms, particularly when the analysis is confined to a limited number of sessions. Perry (2001) had previously observed that the stability of defenses, assessed on a weekly basis over five consecutive sessions, was low concerning the total number of defenses identified, moderate with respect to ODF, and highly variable across the seven hierarchical defensive levels. Perry concluded that defense mechanisms exhibit considerable short-term fluctuation, with a tendency to achieve greater stability over extended periods.

Single-case studies

The analysis of session transcripts, combined with the development of psychometrically robust assessment tools such as the DMRS, has facilitated the exploration of unconscious dimensions of patient functioning and the implicit elements of the therapeutic process. This methodological progress has paved the way for the adoption of systematic research frameworks applied to single-case studies, which are categorized within the fourth-generation micro-analytical investigations in empirical research (Lingiardi, Gazzillo, & Waldron, 2010).

All of the single-case studies reviewed (Di Giuseppe et al., 2014; Lingiardi et al., 2010; Perry, 2001; Perry et al., 2009; Perry & Bond, 2017; Perry, Petraglia, Olson, Presniak, & Metzger, 2012; Presniak, Olson, Porcerelli, & Dauphin, 2010) reported an increase in the utilization of mature defenses, coupled with a corresponding reduction in immature defenses over the course of treatment.

Two of these investigations (Lingiardi et al., 2010; Presniak et al., 2010) focused on intensive psychoanalytic interventions, conducted at a frequency of three to four sessions per week.

While these studies retain an exploratory nature and do not lend themselves to definitive or generalizable conclusions, the employment of rigorous methodologies and validated instruments facilitates clinically meaningful observations, generating new hypotheses and insights that merit further examination in subsequent research endeavors.

Micro-analytical research, grounded in the meticulous observation of session transcripts—some of which are recorded throughout the entire treatment process—has shown that incremental improvements in defensive functioning within individual sessions serve as predictors of long-term enhancements in ODF (Perry & Bond, 2017). Additionally, it has been observed that defensive levels tend to improve progressively, in accordance with the hierarchical structure of defenses, with rates of change varying significantly across individuals, underscoring the specificity and singularity of the therapeutic process.

Other notable findings indicate that enhancements in defensive functioning correlate with symptom reduction and improved social functioning

(Perry et al., 2009, 2012). Moreover, as defensive levels ascend, a reduction in the variability of defense mechanisms employed is observed, suggesting an increased capacity to withstand stressful situations (Perry et al., 2012).

Factors that may hinder the elevation of defensive functioning include the presence of personality disorders—particularly borderline personality disorder (BPD)—high levels of comorbidity within the former Axis I of the DSM, prolonged disorder duration, early onset, and a higher frequency of episodes.

Shifts in defensive functioning tend to occur more rapidly in brief treatments and in episodic disorders, such as major depression. In these instances, improvements are more likely to manifest during the interval between depressive episodes and their remission, rather than in subsequent phases (Perry et al., 2009). These findings appear to corroborate the observations made by Drapeau et al. (2003), who emphasized the transient character of improvements in ODF, positing that such enhancements do not necessarily signify profound structural changes.

Shifts in defensive functioning and therapist interventions

The analysis of defensive functioning and its interplay with therapeutic interventions is facilitated through the audio and video recording of sessions, followed by verbatim transcription. This method not only permits real-time observation of the patient's defensive functioning during sessions, but also enables the exploration of the relationship between therapist interventions and patient responses. To this end, several studies have utilized the Psychodynamic Intervention Rating Scales (PIRS; Cooper & Bond, 1992).

The PIRS is a structured, observer-based instrument developed to identify therapist interventions by analyzing session transcripts. It employs a manual that defines and provides examples of ten distinct types of interventions commonly applied in psychodynamic therapies. These include acknowledgments, work-enhancing strategies, contractual arrangements, questions, associations, support strategies, reflections, clarifications, defense interpretations, and transference interpretations. These interventions are further categorized into three functional domains: therapy-defining interventions, supportive interventions, and interpretive interventions.

Each intervention is rated on a five-point scale, reflecting the depth of the intervention and the degree of linkage established. In the case of defense interpretations, ratings range from one to five, with progressively higher levels of complexity—from a simple identification of defensive techniques aimed at diminishing emotional impact to a detailed articulation of the defensive process, its purpose, and its connection to past relational dynamics.

In applying the PIRS, the analyst identifies the initiation and conclusion of each intervention, determines its type, and assigns a depth rating based on the scale provided. The raw data are then expressed as a proportion of the total interventions conducted during the session. To derive an overall measure of the session, interventions are summed by category and divided by the total number of interventions, yielding a percentage score.

The combined use of the DMRS and PIRS in session transcripts has shown that the therapist's ability to accurately assess the patient's defensive level—and to effectively balance supportive and interpretive interventions—serves as a key predictor of the quality of the therapeutic alliance (Despland et al., 2001). Perry et al. (2012) found that the accuracy of interpretations correlates directly with significant improvements in defensive functioning, both within individual sessions and across the longer term.

In a study involving predominantly psychoanalysts (20 out of 22), it was observed that defense interpretations occurred more frequently than transference interpretations. The frequency of such interventions increased during the early phases of therapy, becoming more profound as treatment advanced. These interventions were linked to a reduction in immature defenses by the conclusion of the therapeutic process (Hersoug, Bøgwald, & Høglend, 2005).

Interpretive interventions have been shown to foster overall improvements in defensive functioning, while clarification and supportive strategies have played a pivotal role in stabilizing the therapeutic alliance and facilitating the exploration of internal conflicts, without triggering excessive defensive reactions in patients (Perry & Bond, 2017).

Further research by Bhatia et al. (2016) emphasized that therapists tend to direct their interpretations toward the defenses most frequently utilized by the patient. This observation aligns with Greenson's (1967) concept of preeminence, which asserts that the most prominent and enduring defenses are those most closely linked to the patient's psychopathology, reflecting their character structure. Consequently, therapists tend to focus on these defenses, even if the patient occasionally manifests more mature or more primitive defenses than their usual defensive level.

A recent study conducted by Drapeau, Stelmaszczyk, Baucom, Henry, and Hébert (2018) examined two patients undergoing intensive psychoanalytic treatment, comparing the therapeutic trajectories of one patient with a positive outcome and another with a negative outcome. The first patient completed 811 sessions over five years and seven months, while the second participated in 702 sessions over four years and five months. The analysis focused on 20 sessions for the first case and 16 for the second.

In the case with a positive outcome, the therapist predominantly employed supportive interventions, followed by interpretive interventions. Conversely, the case with a negative outcome exhibited a sustained reliance on supportive interventions, often in contexts marked by low levels of emotional engagement from the patient.

In the positive outcome case, interpretive interventions were linked to heightened emotional engagement and a temporary reduction in the maturity of the patient's defenses. Conversely, supportive interventions had the opposite effect, fostering greater emotional stability and facilitating the use of more mature defenses.

The findings of this study underscore the pivotal role of interpretive interventions in psychoanalytic treatment, while also emphasizing the need for their careful and measured application to prevent unnecessarily intensifying the patient's defensiveness. The efficacy of interpretations appears to be amplified when preceded by supportive interventions, whereas excessive reliance on supportive measures may be counterproductive.

Defense interpretations were found to increase the patient's emotional engagement by bringing unconscious conflicts to the surface, thereby eliciting intense affective responses. However, this process may temporarily diminish defensive maturity, owing to heightened anxiety and the need to manage complex emotions. Consequently, the study highlights the importance of a balanced therapeutic approach—one that both supports the patient during transformative phases, helps navigate vulnerable moments, and fosters steady progress in defensive functioning.

Critical reflections and final observations

The development of the DMRS has catalyzed a wealth of studies, which collectively affirm the role of defensive functioning as a crucial predictor of therapeutic outcome. This body of research has also provided empirical validation for clinical insights that have long been suspected: interpretive interventions targeting the patient's defenses are effective when they are content-appropriate, timely, and integrated within a therapeutic relationship marked by a strong alliance and optimal emotional engagement.

However, the application of the DMRS necessitates considerable time and effort, which limits the feasibility of conducting studies involving large sample sizes. Consequently, much of the extant literature is based on naturalistic studies with small, clinically heterogeneous samples, often lacking control groups. Moreover, these studies frequently do not account for the influence of confounding variables, such as concurrent treatments alongside psychotherapy, thereby introducing potential methodological constraints.

The reviewed literature highlights several unresolved issues. First, the causal relationship between improvements in defensive functioning and broader psychological functioning warrants further exploration. Second, there remain lingering questions about the inherent limitations of the DMRS, particularly in its application to large-scale clinical and research settings. Finally, there is a pressing need to explore future research directions aimed at developing methodologies capable of overcoming current challenges and deepening our understanding of the role defensive functioning plays in therapeutic change processes.

The relationship between improvements in defensive functioning
and psychological well-being

While naturalistic studies provide valuable insights, they do not permit the establishment of direct causal relationships. Although the majority of the research reviewed here posits that changes in defensive functioning serve as a key mediator in symptom reduction and overall psychological improvement, clinical experience and contemporary post-Kleinian psychoanalytic theory offer an alternative perspective. From this viewpoint, changes in defensive functioning are regarded more as a reliable indicator of therapeutic efficacy, rather than a direct mediator of change.

If one accepts the notion that defense mechanisms reflect the activity of unconscious phantasies in response to conflictual object relations (Grotstein, 2009), their transformation signals profound structural modifications without necessarily serving as the cause of these changes. Within this conceptual framework, the idea that the analyst's intervention on the patient's defenses is essential for promoting improvements in defensive functioning—thereby leading to symptom reduction and enhanced psychological adaptation—risks oversimplifying and reductively framing the psychoanalytic process.

Beyond methodological and instrumental considerations, it is essential to reflect on the theoretical implications of defensive change, as they highlight significant shifts in the contemporary psychoanalytic paradigm. With the shift from epistemological to ontological psychoanalysis (see Ogden, 2019), the primary goal no longer resides solely in making the unconscious conscious, as per the classical assumption that symptoms stem from the repression of psychic content. Instead, the analyst's focus transitions to facilitating the emergence of a more authentic mode of existence for the patient, supporting the reorganization of the self.

The emphasis is placed on the patient's relational dynamics, with particular focus on the analyst's ability to provide containment that fosters the development of an internal emotional apparatus capable of processing experience. Within this theoretical framework, the analytic goal is reframed as facilitating the patient's experience of being, supporting the construction of a more cohesive and grounded sense of self—one capable of engaging with life more authentically.

The improvement in defensive functioning and the reduction in the use of primitive defenses do not simply indicate the resolution of conflicts or an increase in awareness; rather, they signify a deeper transformation in the patient's way of being. This transformation is facilitated by a therapeutic experience that enhances the patient's ability to contain and metabolize emotions.

The studies reviewed in this chapter often attribute therapeutic success primarily to the interpretive interventions of the therapist concerning the patient's defenses. However, from a broader standpoint, consistent with contemporary psychoanalytic thought, it can be argued that the efficacy of treatment is deeply influenced by the quality of the analytic relationship itself. It is the therapist's capacity to emotionally attune to the patient, recognize and contain their affective experience, and facilitate its transformation that truly catalyzes change.

In this framework, improvements in defensive functioning are not the mechanism of change per se, but rather serve as a visible marker of a more complex and profound process rooted in the therapeutic relationship. This process reflects the patient's evolving capacity to contain and process emotional experience, underscoring the transformative potential of analytic work when rooted in attuned, empathetic engagement.

The limitations of the DMRS

Despite the considerable contribution of the DMRS to enhancing our understanding of defensive functioning, several limitations merit careful consideration. Beyond the significant time commitment required for its application—which inherently restricts the number of sessions that can be analyzed, thus limiting the ability to assess a sufficient number of consecutive encounters—additional critical concerns have emerged.

Lingiardi (2023) observes that three decades of experience with the DMRS within his research group have led to insights suggesting the potential value of a critical and constructive revision of certain aspects of the scale. Among the areas identified for reconsideration are the first, third, and fifth levels of the scale, as well as specific challenges encountered when coding the splitting of object representation.

The first level, referred to as the action level, encompasses heterogeneous defenses that vary both in mechanism and severity (such as acting out, passive aggression, and hypochondriasis), prompting questions about the conceptual coherence of this grouping. At the third level, denial defenses include rationalization alongside negation and projection, even though rationalization is typically classified as a neurotic defense, which raises the possibility that it might be more appropriately placed at a higher level. Similarly, the fifth level, which includes repression, reaction formation, and displacement, also contains dissociation—despite its complex nature and wide range of intensity.

In this context, Lingiardi suggests distinguishing between minor dissociation, which could be classified among neurotic defenses, and major dissociation, which aligns more closely with borderline defenses.

Regarding the splitting of object representation, Lingiardi points out that identifying this mechanism can be particularly challenging within the confines of a single session. The emergence of both polarized aspects of the same object may not manifest during a single encounter, complicating the accurate coding of this defense.

De Roten et al. (2021) suggest further enhancing the scale by introducing a Level 0 dedicated to psychotic defense mechanisms, in line with the recommendations of Constantinides and Beck (2010). This level could encompass mechanisms such as psychotic denial, autistic withdrawal, distortion, delusional projection, fragmentation, and concretization. The identification of psychotic defenses may be possible even in individuals who do not exhibit overt psychotic symptoms, and their detection could provide insight into more profoundly impaired psychological functioning.

Another crucial issue pertains to the sensitivity of the DMRS to the therapeutic context, which complicates the differentiation between stable trait conditions and transient fluctuations. Drapeau et al. (2003) demonstrated that the assessment of defense mechanisms, based on session transcripts, may reflect temporary variations tied to the therapeutic process rather than the patient's underlying structural functioning. Decreases in ODF scores have been observed during the initial years of treatment (Perry, 2001), at the commencement of therapy, and in the periods immediately preceding the conclusion of the analytic work (Presniak et al., 2010). These findings support the hypothesis that the DMRS may capture temporary states, emphasizing short-term changes rather than stable structural shifts.

Overall, while recognizing the value of the DMRS as an assessment tool, these reflections underscore the need for further development and refinement. The aim is to enhance the instrument's capacity to distinguish between transient modifications and enduring changes, thereby offering a more accurate and reliable representation of defensive functioning across various clinical contexts.

Bhatia et al. (2016) highlight a limitation of the ODF score in terms of clinical utility, noting that it represents an average of the defenses employed by the patient during the session. While this approach is useful for assessing general trends, it may fail to accurately capture the patient's predominant defensive functioning. A more focused analysis of the most frequently employed defenses, as opposed to relying solely on a composite average, could provide a more precise and clinically relevant measure of the patient's psychological functioning.

It is crucial to emphasize that relying solely on statistical changes in the ODF score can be misleading. Although all the studies reviewed report statistically significant improvements in ODF scores throughout treatment, only one single-case study (Perry et al., 2009) documents a patient who, after over 13 years of therapy, achieved an ODF score exceeding 5.64—the threshold associated with the level of defensive functioning classified as healthy-neurotic.

In all other studies, despite observed increases in ODF scores, these improvements never reached the threshold associated with defensive functioning typical of individuals with a healthy-neurotic personality organization. This discrepancy suggests that, while progress in defensive functioning is apparent, it does not always lead to a reorganization of the patient's personality structure.

Taken together, these findings raise crucial questions about the nature and limitations of measuring defensive functioning, highlighting the necessity of complementing quantitative analysis with a more qualitative and contextually sensitive clinical assessment. Such an approach is vital for capturing the subtleties of the therapeutic process and the patient's individual growth.

Future research directions

Among all the studies utilizing the DMRS to assess defensive functioning, only four (Drapeau et al., 2018; Lingiardi et al., 2010; Presniak et al., 2010; Roy et al., 2009) have specifically focused on psychoanalytic treatments. Of these, three are single-case studies, while only one (Roy et al., 2009)—despite significant methodological limitations—examined a larger sample, though limited to 17 patients.

Further evidence of psychoanalysts' limited engagement with the DMRS comes from a bibliographic analysis conducted in December 2024. A search using the term "Defensive Mechanism Rating Scales" as a keyword yielded 183 results in the PsycInfo database. In contrast, the Psychoanalytic Electronic Publishing (PEP) database returned only 11 studies, with just 5 involving empirical research.

This reluctance may, in part, reflect the well-documented resistance within the psychoanalytic community toward empirical research (e.g., Blechner, 2009; Busch & Milrod, 2010; Chiesa, 2010). However, it is equally plausible that specific features of the DMRS contribute to this hesitancy. Foremost among these is the tool's reliance on audio or video recordings of sessions—an approach often perceived as potentially intrusive to the analytic relationship. Moreover, the DMRS is based on a hierarchical model that may not fully align with established psychoanalytic theoretical frameworks.

Another significant limitation of the DMRS lies in its sensitivity to the specific context of individual sessions, which reflects transient state conditions rather than stable trait expressions. This raises concerns regarding the instrument's capacity to provide an accurate and enduring depiction of the patient's defensive organization. Furthermore, the time required for coding constrains the number of sessions that can be analyzed, thereby limiting the ability to obtain a more comprehensive and representative understanding of the patient's structural functioning.

The recent introduction of the Q-sort version, the DMRS-Q (Di Giuseppe et al., 2014), aims to reduce the time commitment required for its application. However, the DMRS-Q necessitates a thorough understanding of the patient, requiring its completion either by the treating therapist or by a clinician who has conducted multiple interviews with the patient.

This dual approach, while practical, introduces its own set of challenges. When the scale is completed by the treating analyst, the assessment may lack the necessary independence, potentially introducing biases that undermine the reliability of the data. On the other hand, if a different clinician conducts the interviews, it may impose a considerable time burden on the patient, which could reduce their willingness to participate, particularly in long-term treatments. Additionally, the establishment of a new relationship with the researcher could disrupt the ongoing analytic relationship, introducing further complexities to the therapeutic process.

These considerations highlight the methodological challenges inherent in the use of the DMRS within psychoanalytic contexts, pointing to the necessity for further adaptations to increase the instrument's compatibility with clinical practice and the specific demands of psychoanalytic research.

Given the limitations of both the DMRS and DMRS-Q, it becomes imperative to explore alternative tools for assessing defensive functioning. Excluding self-report measures, for the reasons previously outlined, and observer-rated instruments, which present significant application challenges, defensive functioning can be evaluated through performance-based tests such as the Rorschach and the Thematic Apperception Test (TAT).

Although the Defense Mechanism Manual (DMM; Cramer, 1991) may be applied to the TAT, its scope is significantly limited, as it identifies only three defense mechanisms—denial, projection, and identification. In contrast, the Rorschach offers a broader array of options through three distinct scales: the Lerner Defense Scale (LDS; Lerner & Lerner, 1980), the Rorschach Defense Scales (RDS; Cooper & Arnow, 1986), and the Comprehensive Rorschach Defense Scale (CRDS; Gacono & Rosso, in this volume).

As these three scales will be examined in detail in the forthcoming chapters, the aim here is to emphasize why the Rorschach is particularly well-suited for use by psychoanalysts.

First and foremost, the Rorschach was developed by a psychoanalyst and has, over time, been extensively researched and applied by clinicians with psychoanalytic and psychodynamic orientations (e.g., Lerner, 1998; Meloy, Acklin, Gacono, & Murray, 1997; Rapaport, Gill, & Schafer, 1946; Schafer, 1954). Exner's work (2003) further reinforced the reliability and validity of the Rorschach interpretation, establishing the Rorschach Comprehensive System (CS) as a diagnostic instrument with robust empirical support (Mihura, Meyer, Dumitrascu, & Bombel, 2013).

Recently, the CS has been updated to incorporate the latest empirical findings (Exner, Fontan, & Andronikof, 2022), ensuring its continued clinical relevance and its capacity to yield meaningful data in the assessment of psychological functioning. Additionally, it now includes supplementary scales (Smith, Weinberger-Katzav, & Fontan, 2022), which are particularly effective for evaluating psychodynamic constructs, further expanding its applicability and reinforcing its versatility in the analysis of defensive functioning.

These characteristics, coupled with its rich psychoanalytic tradition and solid empirical foundation, establish the Rorschach as a valuable tool for examining defense mechanisms and the deeper psychological functioning of patients, exhibiting a sensitivity that aligns seamlessly with psychoanalytic clinical practice.

The Rorschach not only enables the assessment of defensive functioning but also offers profound insights into thought processes, affective organization, self-representation, and interpersonal dynamics. For these reasons, the Rorschach is recommended for nomothetic research within psychoanalysis (Bornstein, 2007) and is likely to engage the interest of psychoanalysts eager to master its administration, scoring, and interpretative techniques, thereby integrating it into their research endeavors. For psychoanalysts already trained in the Rorschach, a few hours of work can provide a wealth of information regarding the patient's psychological functioning. Notably, scoring the CRDS, as detailed in Chapter 10 of this volume, typically takes approximately 30 minutes for an average response protocol.

A significant concern in research on the process and outcomes of psychoanalytic treatment pertains to the reluctance of psychoanalysts to employ assessment tools that may intrude upon the analytic relationship. In this regard, the Rorschach offers the distinct advantage of being administered outside the analytic context. For example, it can be presented to individuals seeking consultation at a psychoanalytic center for the purpose of obtaining a referral to an analyst for treatment. In such instances, participation in the research may be facilitated by the analyst conducting the initial consultation, without direct involvement of the treating analyst.

The analyst conducting the initial consultation is able to formulate a diagnosis at the outset of treatment based on psychodynamic criteria, such as those outlined in the PDM-2 (Lingiardi & McWilliams, 2017), thereby overcoming the limitations of the categorical diagnostic approach outlined in the DSM-5-TR (APA, 2022).

Furthermore, the analyst may make use of the Psychodiagnostic Chart-2 (PDC-2; Gordon & Bornstein, 2018), a complementary instrument that provides indicative scores reflecting the patient's level of personality organization and mental functioning.

The PDC-2 operationalizes complex psychodynamic constructs, transforming them into measurable variables amenable to statistical analysis. This methodology facilitates the integration of clinical evaluation with empirical measures, enabling correlations with data derived from the Rorschach, and contributing to a more nuanced and scientifically grounded understanding of the patient.

For patients who agree to participate in research, the commitment required is minimal, typically limited to periodic meetings—generally once a year—for test administration and, if desired, a follow-up feedback session to discuss the results.

This approach allows the research to proceed independently of the treating analyst, thereby preserving the integrity of the analytic relationship. The analysand has the option to disclose or withhold information regarding their participation from their analyst. Should the analysand choose to introduce this matter into the analytic space, it may itself serve as a topic for reflection and clinical exploration.

Thus, the consultation center can conduct research autonomously, minimizing its impact on ongoing analysis and ensuring a clear functional separation between clinical practice and research activities.

8 Historical developments of assessing defenses on the Rorschach

Jason M. Smith and Carl B. Gacono

Defensive operations are involved in the ego's struggles with painful ideas, affects, and impulses (A. Freud, 1936). They manage, modulate, and maintain, and, in some cases, operate to prevent the ego from being overwhelmed by impulse. Their importance was captured during an interchange in *The Big Chill*, where Jeff Goldblum's character stated "Don't knock rationalization; where would we be without it? I don't know anyone who could get through the day without two or three juicy rationalizations. They're more important than sex."

Defenses have held a central position in psychoanalytic theory since Freud's 1893 introduction of the concept of "hysterical phenomena." Defense mechanisms, such as repression, prevent the recall or re-experiencing of a traumatic reality, thereby avoiding painful affect. Other defenses have their own corresponding functions. Freud identified several defense mechanisms, including regression, repression, reaction formation, isolation, undoing, projection, introjection, turning against the self, and reversal. These mechanisms were later systematically organized by Anna Freud (1936), who underscored that sublimation, while already present in Freud's earlier writings, should be considered the tenth mechanism. However, she placed sublimation within the domain of normal functioning, rather than within the study of neurosis, thereby distinguishing it from the other defense mechanisms.

In contrast to A. Freud's articulation of higher-level defenses (repression the central defense), Melanie Klein's (1946) observations of children lead to the identification of primitive defenses. For these splitting supported by denial, rather than repression, serves as the dominant mechanism (Kernberg, 1975). As noted by Lerner (1998),

> Kernberg proposed two overall levels of defensive organization. At the lower level, primitive dissociation or splitting is the crucial defense, bolstered by the related defenses of denial, primitive idealization, primitive devaluation, and projective identification. At the

DOI: 10.4324/9781003536994-11

higher level of defensive organization, repression supplants splitting as the major defense and is accompanied by the related defensive operations of intellectualization rationalization, undoing, and higher forms of projection and denial.

(p. 37)

A reliance on splitting, abnormal in adults, becomes evident in contradictory and alternating ego states most evident in borderline and other severe personality disorders (Acklin, 1997; Kernberg, 1975; Lerner, 1998).

Primitive defenses coincide with a person's part object orientation—an inability to integrate both good and bad objects. They can be understood within the developmental process of separation-individuation (Mahler, 1971). This process begins at the earliest signs of the infant's differentiation (hatching) from a symbiotic fusion with the mother and culminates in an early sense of self, individual identity, and object constancy (Mahler, Pine, & Bergman, 1975). From an object relations perspective, defenses not only protect the ego from overwhelming sensations but are considered a natural part of the developmental process (separation-individuation).

Concurrent to this process, movement occurs from the paranoid-schizoid to the depressive position (Klein, 1957). Having reached the depressive position, others are experienced as whole and separate objects (Hd to H in Rorschach coding). Good and bad qualities can be experienced simultaneously, and there is the capacity to mourn, grieve, and experience guilt, reflecting either neurotic or normal functioning.

While the Rorschach is not primarily a "projective or analytic technique" (Acklin, 1994; Exner, 2003; Rorschach, 1921/1942), it is ideally suited for examining defenses and object relations. Frequently, defense responses contain face validity. It is not a stretch to associate idealization with "a Godlike figure" (H), devaluation with "a deformed hunchback," or projective identification with "a monster with a huge club coming toward me." Aspects of the examinee–examiner relationship also reveal defense processes (Cooper, Perry, & Arnow, 1988; Schachtel, 1966). As noted by Schafer (1954), "defense operations may be expressed in various aspects of the Rorschach record. These aspects may be divided into three categories: scores, themes, and test attitudes" (p. 164). A familiarity with how the defense process manifests through the Rorschach assessment provides the examiner with additional insight into the patient's personality functioning (Acklin, 1997).

Rorschach assessment of defenses: traditional measures

The relationship between impulse and defense is understood, whereby, *minus* and unusual form suggests impulses that override defense (Schafer, 1954). Responses absent such disruptions reveal intact defenses. Examining poor form and severe cognitive slippage responses, informs dynamic issues which impact real-world behavior. One psychotic, psychopathic, serial killer produced several Mp-responses (Hd and Sx) in an otherwise intact but constricted record. These responses speak to delusions (sadistic; involved in eviscerating victims), issues related to the impulse (several AgC responses, etc.), and how impulses affect cognitive functioning.

The scoring sequence also reveals patterns of regression, recovery, and the dynamic issues surrounding the interplay between defense and impulse. For example, a patient overwhelmed by the color (affect) on Card VIII may produce *minus* form responses or produce one followed by several adequate form responses; the latter suggests resiliency (ability to recover). Other Rorschach indices suggest what caused regression, and/or what aided recovery. A Wv response (- or no form) followed by a Dd (*o* form) and popular suggests after initially being overwhelmed, the patient recovers by narrowing the focus and using a conventional reference. Resiliency can be inferred by recovery on the Rorschach's final responses (Card X) compared to those who end the task with *minus* responses and/or containing cognitive slippage.

The Holt system

Holt (1977) was one of the first Rorschach defense coding systems. Holt's system contained four sets of variables: content indices of primary process, formal indices of primary process, indices of control and defense, and overall ratings. Primary process indices were separated into libidinal and aggressive content. These were categorized into Level 1 (more primitive) and Level 2 (more socially acceptable) scores based on the extent to which primitive drive dominated the percept. Aggressive Content, for example, was divided into Level 1 (murderous/sadomasochistic aggression) and Level 2 (socially tolerated hostility/aggression).

Holt identified five defense categories: (1) remoteness; (2) context: (3) postponing strategies; (4) miscellaneous (elements of denial [negation, minimization, repudiation]; (5) overtness. Like isolation or intellectualization, remoteness involved distancing from an unacceptable impulse (e.g., looking down on a sex scene from a helicopter). Context involved creating a setting that makes the percept more acceptable (couching responses within cultural, aesthetic, intellectual, and humorous contexts; e.g., "animal being killed ... in a cartoon"). Postponing strategies contained delay and blocking, (e.g., I don't know what it is). Holt's miscellaneous category captured many Freudian defenses (rationalization, vagueness, projection, obsessional, isolation, avoidance, evasiveness, and impotence). The final category, overtness, delineated four types of aggression: overtness in behavior, verbal overtness, experiential overtness, and potential overtness (Lerner, 1998). Coding rated defense demand (if it was socially acceptable and how it emerged/communicated), defense effectiveness (effective in reducing anxiety), and formulating an adaptive regression score.

The Rorschach Index of Repressive Style

Levine and Spivack (1964) devised the Rorschach Index of Repressive Style (RIRS) to operationalize repression—a process inhibiting ideational processes, affecting ideas on the border between unconscious and preconscious. The RIRS measured a "repressive style" which was defined as "a consistent characteristic of an individual that is manifested in vague unelaborated language which is lacking in integration and flow" (p. 14; see Shapiro, 1965).

The RIRS scored responses on seven dimensions; (1) specificity; (2) elaboration; (3) impulse responses; (4) presence of primary thinking; (5) self-references; (6) presence of movement; (7) associative flow (Lerner, 1998). The extent to which responses were impersonal, lacked movement, reflected vague and unelaborated thinking, were unintegrated, and revealed an absence of associative flow indicated the degree of repressivity. Specific, detailed, logical, and reality bound responses suggested less repressive functioning.

While Holt's system and the RIRS generated a considerable amount of research, they proved too cumbersome for clinical application (Lerner, 1998). Additionally, "interest has shifted away from drive theory and structural theory and toward object-relations theory and self-psychology" (Lerner, 1998, p. 268), setting the stage for the Lerner Defense Scales (LDS, Lerner & Lerner, 1980) and the Rorschach Defense Scales (RDS, Cooper & Arnow, 1986).

Rorschach assessment of defenses: recent measures

Since the 1980s, two Rorschach defense scoring systems have been developed. These are the LDS (Lerner & Lerner, 1980) and the Cooper et al. (1988) RDS.

The Lerner Defense Scale (LDS)

Lerner and Lerner (1980; Lerner, 1998204205) integrated developments in psychoanalytic object relations theory with Rorschach defense research. They developed five variables (splitting, denial, devaluation, idealization, and projective identification) designed to assess the defenses mostly used by borderline persons. Devaluation, idealization, and denial were scored on continuums of severity ranging from 1–5 (idealization and devaluation) and 1–3 (denial). Level 1 scores represented the most mature presentation of the defense. Within these categories only responses containing an entire human figure, either static or in movement (H response) are analyzed. Two exceptions include the coding for splitting, which can involve two responses, and for projective identification which could use human detail responses.

Studies with the LDS were able to discriminate borderline persons from neurotic ones. Borderline persons produced significantly more splitting, projective identification, lower-level devaluation, and lower-level denial (Lerner, 1998; Lerner & Lerner, 1980; Rosso, Airaldi, & Camoirano, 2021). Splitting and projective identification were particularly robust as they were only produced by the borderline participants (Lerner, 1998; Lerner & Lerner, 1980). High level denial and high level devaluation were produced more frequently by neurotic persons (Lerner, 1998; Rosso et al., 2021). Idealization occurred more frequently in the neurotic group. Borderline participants were more likely to depreciate others. Unlike borderline subjects, when neurotics would use low-level denial or idealization it was accompanied by manifestations of high-level denial. The LDS also differentiated between inpatient borderline and schizophrenic persons; borderline persons produced more splitting and four of five scale measures of devaluation. Projective Identification was also found exclusively in the borderline group (Lerner, Sugarman, & Gaughran, 1981). Collins (1983) replicated these latter findings.

Multiple findings have supported the adaptive functions of idealization. A comparison of bulimic anorexics, anorexic ballet students, non-anorexic ballet students, and normal controls found the anorexic groups and anorexic ballet students used splitting and devaluation more often than the non-anorexic ballet students and normal controls. Idealization was produced more in the control group and the least in the bulimic anorexics (Van der Keshet, 1988). Gacono's (1988, 1990) study of psychopathic and non-psychopathic ASPD offenders also found a prevalence of low levels of denial and devaluation coupled with an absence of idealization.

The strength of the LDS rests on considerable research which links Rorschach human content directly to multiple areas of personality functioning (Blatt, Brenneis, Schimek, & Glick, 1976; Blatt & Lerner, 1983; Cooper & Arnow, 1984292844). The LDS' reliance on human representation, however, is a liability when assessing populations with reduced M and H (Collins, 1983; Gacono, 1988; Gacono & Meloy, 1994; Gacono, Meloy, & Berg, 1992). Of note, one researcher (Collins, 1983) expanded the LDS to include animal percepts and found that this modification increased the differentiation between borderlines and schizophrenics with splitting but not as much with projective identification.

Rorschach Defense Scales (RDS; Cooper & Arnow, *1986)*

The RDS (Cooper & Arnow, 1986) utilized human and non-human Rorschach content as well as aspects of the examinee–examiner relationship in assessing defense mechanisms (see also Schafer, 1954). The scoring system included 15 defenses grouped by level of personality organization (neurotic, borderline, psychotic; Cooper & Arnow, 1986; Cooper et al., 1988). Currently, it is a supplemental scale in the Exner Comprehensive System-Revised (CS-R; Exner, Fontan, & Andronikof, 2022; Smith & Gacono, 2022; Smith, Weinberger-Katzav, & Fontan, 2022).

The RDS categorizes many aspects of content, including specific imagery, verbal and affective articulation of percepts and comments about oneself or aspects of the testing situation (e.g., remarks or questions about the blots, the examiner, or the procedure). Specifically, Cooper and Arnow (1986) stated,

> Lerner and Lerner (1980) … restrict their analysis to percepts that include human figures, static or in motion … we find this circumscription unduly limiting for interpreting protocols in which there is a relative or absolute absence of human figures. More important, however, borderline defenses are more profitably examined with a broader data base regardless of the number of human responses.
>
> (p. 144)

The following discusses each definition of the 15 defenses (see Smith & Gacono, 2022 for an extensive description/manual on how to score the RDS).

Neurotic:

1 Repression (REP) is the primary defense mechanism in neurotic and normal personality organization. It operates unconsciously to keep libidinal or aggressive impulses out of awareness.
2 Intellectualization (INT) involves the substitution of logic, knowledge, and objectivity for feelings and impulses.
3 Isolation (ISO) involves the separation of affect from experience (i.e., where a person separates emotion from an idea).
4 Higher-level denial (HLD) involves an attempt to reduce or to minimize the impact of painful or conflict-laden perceptions through disavowal of its cognitive and affective significance.
5 Pollyannish denial (POD) involves "persistent efforts through selective perception, minimization, and use of fantasy to be conscious of only cheerful, optimistic, benevolent, pretty, untroubled, and/or otherwise positive aspects of experience, relationships, and behavior" (Schafer, 1954, p. 234).
6 Rationalization (RAT) occurs when justifications are used to make unacceptable ideas, feelings, or behavior more tolerable.
7 Reaction formation (REF) refers to an unconscious replacement or overemphasis on attitudes and impulses that are the opposite of particularly threatening, unconscious ones (Schafer, 1954).

Borderline:

8 Splitting (SPL) is the fundamental defense in borderline personality organization. It occurs when oppositely toned feelings and urges toward the object or the self are kept separate because if these feelings were experienced simultaneously toward the object or the self, unbearable affects such as guilt or anxiety would result.
9 Devaluation (DEV) refers to a tendency to depreciate, tarnish, or lessen the importance of one's inner and outer objects.

10 Primitive Idealization (PMI) involves a denial of unwanted characteristics of an object and then an enhancement of the object by projecting
one's own libido or omnipotence onto it.
11 Projection (PRO) occurs when objectionable feelings or experiences of a
person are unrealistically seen in the other rather than recognizing them
in oneself.
12 Projective Identification (PJI) involves the projection of good or bad self-
representations into an object for the purpose of either safeguarding a
vulnerable self-representation by placing it in another object, or for the
purpose of harming or controlling the object.
13 Omnipotence (OMP) is defined as where the person denies their feelings of powerlessness and worthlessness by making claims of unrealis-
tic powers or exaggerated self-worth.

Psychotic:

14 Hypomanic Denial (HYD) involves an extreme maneuver to avoid the
recognition or experience of emotional pain.
15 Massive or bland denial (MSD) is a severe form of denial involving significant distortions of reality to the point that a segment of subjective
experience or the external world is not integrated with the rest of the
experience.

RDS inter-rater reliability to be fair to excellent (0.45–1.00; see Smith &
Gacono, 2022 for an extensive discussion on RDS and LDS reliability and
validity; also Rosso, Gacono, Camoirano, & Smith, submitted). In terms
of validity, concurrent validity has been found between the RDS and LDS
borderline defenses (Lerner, Albert, & Walsh, 1987; Rosso et al., submitted).
Splitting and devaluation on both scales were most useful in distinguishing
BPD from schizophrenia and neurotic participants. Consistent with theory
and adding to the face validity of the borderline RDS defense scales, devaluation, splitting, and projection were significantly correlated with the experi-
mental self-report BPD measure and BPD diagnostic criteria (Berg, 1990;
Cooper et al., 1988; Rosso et al., submitted). Devaluation on the RDS was
significantly correlated with depression, anxiety, and social functioning difficulty (Cooper, Perry, & O'Connell, 1991). Projection was also correlated with
depressive symptoms. The presence of intellectualization predicted lower
amounts of anxiety and depression reinforcing the idea that certain "higher
level" defenses aid in mitigating against psychopathological states. Repression has been able to distinguish neurotic from borderline individuals (Rosso
et al., submitted). Ratings on the MCMI-III narcissism scales and diagnostic criteria by treating clinicians were positively correlated with both OMP
and PMI consistent with a conceptual understanding of narcissism and NPD
(Gritti, Marino, Lang, & Meyer, 2018; see also Berg, 1990; Gacono et al., 1992).

Nelson (2001) compared RDS borderline defenses with other psychological variables, including Exner's CS variables, Kwawer's Primitive Modes of Relating (PMR), and Gacono and Meloy's Extended Aggression scores. The study included a sample of mixed-gender outpatients from various sites, though no diagnostic data was provided. The majority of responses showed no RDS scores, with smaller proportions displaying one or two RDS scores. Correlations were observed between the RDS total score and the other systems. Notably, Devaluation significantly correlated with aggression, particularly AGM, AgPast, and AgC, while weak correlations were found for Projective Identification with AGM and AgC. Splitting was associated with MOR. The observed splitting in the sample may reflect difficulties in maintaining object constancy, the tendency to externalize bad objects while attempting to internalize good ones, or challenges in accessing good objects.

RDS scores did not significantly differentiate between psychopathic (PCL ≥ 30; N = 14) and non-psychopathic ASPD males (PCL < 30; N = 19; Gacono, 1988, 1990), though some trends aligned with theoretical expectations. Psychopathic males tended to exhibit higher levels of devaluation, splitting, and omnipotence, while those with moderate PCL scores showed greater idealization and projective identification. The frequent use of borderline defenses (devaluation, projective identification, and splitting) in ASPD participants supported Kernberg's (1975) view that individuals with ASPD are organized at a borderline level of personality functioning.

Moreover, psychopathic males displayed lower levels of primitive idealization and higher levels of denial (Gacono & Meloy, 1992). The absence of elevated idealization in these individuals also suggested the lack of pseudo-sublimatory channels, consistent with their failure to maintain a stable identity, which often manifests as an inability to sustain consistent employment or a career (Gacono, 1988, 1990). These findings highlight the severe pathology in psychopathic males, particularly in their reliance on splitting, high omnipotence, and inability to form attachments. Additionally, the use of projective identification and devaluation suggested borderline functioning (Gacono & Meloy, 1994).

Similar to their ASPD counterparts, perpetrators of sexual homicide (N = 20; 18 males, 2 females; Gacono & Meloy, 1994) exhibited high frequencies of devaluation (85%), projection (60%), and splitting (50%). In contrast to their non-sexually offending psychopathic ASPD counterparts, the presence of primitive idealization (55%) reflects an intrapsychic need that drives their compulsion to seek out others (victims). The occurrence of isolation (45%), projective identification (40%), and omnipotence (20%) are essential to their offending behavior (Gacono & Meloy, 1988). Projective identification (PJI) serves as the mechanism for the sexual acts and is described as "central to understanding sexual homicide ... the projection of malevolent traits onto the victim, a sustained identification with those traits, and a compulsion to omnipotently control them" (Gacono & Meloy, 1994, p. 290; also see Gacono, Meloy, & Bridges, 2000, 2008; Meloy et al., 1994). These individuals distort benign Rorschach images into aggressive representations through these "malevolent transformations" (e.g., "It's a flower. No, it's a flower with sharp thorns.")

In contrast to males (severe narcissism), psychopathic females (PCL-R $\geq$ 30; N = 115) exhibited more borderline defenses (M = 19.45) than neurotic (M = 15.43) or psychotic (M = 2.85) ones (Cunliffe & Gacono, 2008; Smith et al., 2021). These women produced high rates of all borderline defenses, suggesting a borderline personality organization. These psychopathic women were prone to attacking, devaluing, or splitting others as necessary to defend themselves against both external and internal threats. The production of denial responses (massive denial, hypomanic denial, and pollyannish denial) was common and, when combined with the production of other Rorschach variables, such as Hx, AB, and Mp without form quality, supported the presence of a malignant hysterical personality (Smith et al., 2021).

It is not surprising that the first five of the borderline defenses have been used in both the LDS and RDS and, therefore, have been the subject of adequate discussion and validation (also see Rosso et al., submitted). These scores also contain face validity with coding distinct from each other and other defenses. Their scoring can be easily linked to a conceptual understanding of the associated defense process. The utility, and perhaps the validity, of the other individual scores have ranged considerably (i.e., neurotic and psychotic defenses). At times many of the other scores appear over-inclusive, too broad, and, within their scoring criteria may contain some descriptor with only small nuances that separate them from other scores (i.e., POD and HYD). The literature does support the usefulness of these scales in differentiating among level of personality organization and revealing defensive constellations useful to identifying specific personality styles (Lerner, 1998; Meloy, Acklin, Gacono, & Murray, 1997; Schafer, 1954; Shapiro, 1965).

The LDS and RDS systems have strengths and weaknesses. Neither is particularly user friendly. They are time-consuming, challenging, and significant psychoanalytic training/clinical experience may be needed (Rosso et al., submitted). The LDS requires learning an additional system for coding form quality (Mayman, 1970) and relies for the most part on human representations which can, at times, reduce its usefulness in populations that produce few M or H variables. The RDS contains 132 individual criteria, far too many for scoring many of the individual defenses, some of which seem redundant or even unnecessary (i.e., ISO). Lerner et al. (1987) found that that the LDS were better at assessing more seriously disturbed inpatients while the RDS were better at assessing defenses in healthier outpatients. Lerner (1998) concluded that the RDS, despite their expansion to non-human content, showed "superior psychometric properties" (p. 294).

A Comprehensive Rorschach Defense System (CRDS)

The difficulties with the LDS and RDS led Gacono and Rosso to develop a hybrid system (see Chapter 9). Operating from the assumption that denial was present in most defenses, Gacono and Rosso used the RDS template and the LDS's level system for creating 13 defenses.

These included repression, intellectualization, isolation, rationalization, projection, projective identification, splitting, idealization (level 1 and 2), devaluation (level 1 and 2), denial (Lvl 1 and 2), pollyannish denial (Lvl 1 and 2), hypomanic denial, and omnipotence. Consistent with the LDS and CS level 2 special scores, level 2 defenses represented lower functioning mostly including indices of reality testing problems, primitive content, and cognitive slippage. Each defense was reformulated with definitions and examples to include CS referents when possible. For example: "Intellectualization uses logic, knowledge, and objectivity to create distance … may include Ay, Sc, Art …", while Higher levels of denial involved minimal distortion (adequate form F+, Fo) and lacked cognitive slippage (INC, FAB, CONTAM, ALOG). The goal was to make the defenses understandable to non-analytic practitioners and create coding more compatible with traditional CS coding.

Rosso and Gacono would modify the initial hybrid system. The defense mechanism of reaction formation has been included in the high-level denial defense mechanisms, pollyannish denial defense has been included in the first-level idealization defense; idealization and devaluation have both been differentiated into two distinct levels; projection and projective identification have been unified into the defense of projective identification, and the coding criteria have been significantly revised, also incorporating coding criteria from the LDS; the coding criteria for the splitting defense have been reformulated, incorporating those from the LDS; the hypomanic denial has been renamed omnipotent denial, and the coding criteria have been partially revised; and massive denial has been renamed psychotic denial, and the coding criteria have been significantly revised.

While this should be viewed as preliminary (Rosso et al., submitted), inter-rater reliability between two experienced psychologists was calculated on 20 randomly selected protocols (487 Rorschach responses and 423 coded defenses). Inter-rater reliability was almost perfect (Cohen's k =.84). Additionally, some preliminary validity results suggested those with borderline-level personality organization produced more Devaluation level 2, Splitting, PJI, and Psychotic denial responses compared to both non-clinical patients and neurotic level groups. Omnipotent Denial was a discriminating defense between the borderline and non-patient groups. The non-clinical patients yielded fewer defense scores compared to the other two groups, while the neurotic-level participants produced fewer defense scores than borderlines.

Conclusion

While the coding of individual defenses offers a rich yield adding to the interpretative value of the test, the broader Rorschach provides a wealth of information related to a patient's object relations and defensive functioning. Individual defense coding needs more systematic study. The newer systems introduced by Gacono and Rosso, as outlined in the following chapter, mark a new beginning for the coding of defenses.

As much as possible, the coding of defenses must be as easy to understand and rate as other CS variables. It is our hope that this chapter will renew interest in the formal assessment of defense operations on the Rorschach and inform new research that will continue to bring these scales into the 21st century and into future versions of the Comprehensive System.

When discussing Rorschach defenses, it is important to emphasize that most Rorschach data does not involve a projective process (Acklin, 1994; Exner, 2003; Rorschach, 1921/1942). As Exner (1989) stated,

> Unfortunately, the Rorschach has been erroneously mislabeled as a projective test for far too long, and that label has often encouraged interpreters to attempt to derive some meaning from the content of every answer. Many answers are simply the result of classifying the blot areas in ways that are compatible with the stimulus field. They are not projections. In fact, it is possible for a subject to give a reliable, valid protocol without including any projected material in the responses.
>
> (p. 527)

We concur with Exner's assertion and Acklin's (1994) findings regarding the nature of the Rorschach response process as a perceptual, representational, and symbolic task (Blatt, 1990; Rapaport, Gill, & Schafer, 1946; Schachtel, 1966; Weiner, 2003).

9 The Comprehensive Rorschach Defense System

A new coding system

Carl B. Gacono and Anna Maria Rosso

Introduction

The idea to develop a new Rorschach defense coding system sprang from our clinical and research use of the Lerner Defense Scales (LDS; Lerner & Lerner, 1980) and the Rorschach Defense Scales (RDS; Cooper & Arnow, 1986). We had noted their considerable utility as well as their limitations (also see Smith & Gacono, 2021), and, sought to design a new coding system that incorporated their strengths while overcoming their limitations.

This project evolved through four phases: (1) a study on the reliability and validity of the LDS (Rosso, Airaldi, & Camoirano, 2021); (2) a study on the reliability and validity of the RDS (Rosso, Gacono, Camoirano, & Smith, submitted); (3) the development of the new coding system, called the Comprehensive Rorschach Defense System (CRDS); and (4) the validation study of the CRDS. Our work, entitled "Beyond LDS and RDS toward the development of a valid and reliable measure of defenses," was supported by the 2022 Research Grant from the International Psychoanalytic Association (IPA).

In this chapter, we summarize the first two phases, focusing primarily on the findings that helped us identify the limitations of the LDS and RDS. We will also explain the rationale behind the construction of the CRDS and provide the complete coding system. The validation study of the CRDS will be presented in the following chapter (Rosso & Camoirano, Chapter 10 in this volume).

The study on the reliability and validity of the LDS

The LDS allows the coding of five defense mechanisms: splitting, devaluation, idealization, projective identification, and denial by evaluating responses that contain human figures, whether real or imaginary (for a more detailed description, see the previous chapter, Smith & Gacono, Chapter 8 in this volume).

Rosso et al. (2021) conducted a study focusing on: (a) inter-rater reliability; (b) common coding errors; and (c) the LDS's ability to differentiate

DOI: 10.4324/9781003536994-12

between neurotic and borderline personality levels, based on Psychodynamic Diagnostic Manual-2 (PDM-2) dimensional psychodynamic criteria, and a nonclinical group. The study included 80 clinical subjects (40 neurotic, 40 borderline) and 80 nonclinical subjects.

While supporting high levels of inter-rater agreement, some issues arose in the scoring of projective identification. Confusion between devaluation and projective identification was discovered for those responses where associative elaboration involved aggressive content. These errors largely stemmed from raters' incomplete understanding of the confabulatory nature of projective identification responses and their unfamiliarity with the Mayman coding system (1970) used by Lerner & Lerner. Unclear guidelines for responses like "astronaut," "two women dancing together," or "waiters," which some studies (e.g., Lerner, 2005; Lerner & Van-Der Keshet, 1995) associate with idealization or devaluation, created challenges in scoring higher levels of idealization and devaluation. These findings highlighted the need to clarify the coding criteria for projective identification, idealization, and devaluation in our system, aligning them more closely with the Exner Comprehensive System.

Consistent with previous studies (Lerner & Lerner, 1980, the Rosso et al. (2021) study demonstrated that the LDS successfully discriminated between neurotic and borderline personality organizations, with devaluation, projective identification, and denial distinguishing the two groups. Devaluation and projective identification correlated negatively with both the P and M Axes, supporting the LDS's validity in identifying personality organization levels.

The study found that individuals with neurotic personality organization used high-level denial more frequently than nonclinical subjects, while those with borderline personality organization used low-level denial more often than both neurotic and nonclinical groups. While supporting an underlying continuum for these defenses, it does raise concerns about including neurotic (higher level) forms of denial in scales designed for primitive defenses, as high-level denial may be misleading when weighted scores are used. The study showed that low-level denial correlated negatively with the P Axis, while no correlation emerged between high-level denial and projective identification (PI). Further analysis revealed that medium-level and low-level denial correlated with PI, suggesting more impaired mental functioning associated with severe reality distortion.

In terms of idealization, the findings supported previous research (Lerner & Van-Der Keshet, 1995) and aligned with Kernberg's (1980) view of idealization as a continuum from pathological to normal. The study found that the idealization subscale was more sensitive to the adaptive aspects of idealization, and the positive correlation between reflection responses and idealization supports the notion that reflection responses are indicative of adaptive narcissism. These results underscore the necessity of implementing two distinct codings for different levels of idealization: one reflecting a more mature form, and the other a more primitive one.

The study on the reliability and validity of the RDS

The RDS (Cooper & Arnow, 1986), in contrast with LDS, integrate both human and non-human content, along with aspects of the examinee-examiner relationship (see Schafer, 1954), to assess defensive mechanisms. The scales categorize 15 defenses according to levels of personality organization (for a more detailed description, see the previous chapter, Smith & Gacono, Chapter 8 in this volume).

Rosso et al. (submitted) aimed, using the same sample from the previous study (Rosso et al., 2021), to: (a) evaluate the concurrent validity of the RDS in distinguishing between individuals with neurotic and borderline levels of personality organization (assessed using PDM-2 criteria) and a nonclinical group; and (b) explore the correlations between the RDS and the LDS. Additionally, the study investigated how different levels of training and clinical experience influence the attainment of satisfactory reliability.

The study confirmed previous findings, showing that the borderline (BL) group exhibited the lowest frequency of neurotic defenses and the highest prevalence of borderline defenses, particularly devaluation, projection, and projective identification, all negatively correlated with the P and M Axes. Splitting distinguished the nonclinical group from the clinical groups but did not differentiate between the latter two, likely due to a sample artifact, as only 4 out of 40 subjects in the borderline group had low-level borderline functioning.

Primitive Idealization did not differentiate the groups, supporting its adaptive functions as noted in prior research, and confirming the need for a two-level coding system: Level 1 for more mature forms and Level 2 for primitive idealization. Both psychotic defenses, Hypomanic Denial and Massive Denial, were more prevalent in the borderline group and negatively correlated with the P and M Axes. The strongest correlation was observed between Massive Denial and both axes, indicating a significant impairment in reality testing and judgment, which points to more severe psychological dysfunction.

Projective identification (PJI) was higher in the nonclinical group than in the neurotic level group, which raised concerns about the measure's validity. Upon reviewing the nonclinical protocols, it was noted that many responses were coded using the PJI-B criteria (scoring PJI for animals causing harm by placing dangerous substances in objects), indicating that this discrepancy may be due to poorly defined criteria. Since projective identification is a dynamic process, it may be more appropriate to specify that harm must be explicitly stated in the response. This would prevent commonly used responses, such as "spiders" on Card X or "manta ray" on Card VI, from being mistakenly coded as PJI. The current study replicated previous findings on the concurrent validity of RDS and LDS, particularly regarding splitting and devaluation. It found a stronger correlation between the two idealization subscales and a slightly lower correlation between the two projective identification indexes. This result is consistent with the differences in the coding criteria of the two scales and highlighted the need to integrate these criteria into the new system.

Despite substantial inter-rater reliability between two highly experienced coders for this study (Cohen's k = .079), the subsequent study on the amount of training required to learn RDS coding revealed considerable difficulties and identified the most frequent errors made by inexperienced coders. Participants included graduate psychology students and licensed psychologists. By the end of the 50-hour course, only six graduate students achieved substantial agreement with the instructor (Cohen's k ranging from .53 to .71). In contrast, six licensed psychologists reached substantial agreement, and four achieved almost perfect agreement (Cohen's k ranging from .62 to .83). Of these psychologists, three had training in psychoanalytic psychotherapy, while one was trained in cognitive-behavioral therapy. The errors made by students were predominantly commission errors, indicating a lack of understanding of defense mechanisms. In contrast, experienced raters made omission errors, failing to code responses that should have been included. (For a detailed analysis of the errors, see Rosso et al., submitted.)

The RDS manual was found to be complex and lengthy, with, at times, unclear or redundant criteria that make it challenging to reliably code. We felt that the RDS coding system needed to be streamlined with, in some cases, clearer coding criteria. The descriptions of defenses in the manual are too concise and likely more understandable to those with psychoanalytic training, despite that even experienced psychoanalysts found some criteria difficult to learn. Additionally, some criteria are rarely used.

The Comprehensive Rorschach Defense System (CRDS)

We were interested in creating a coding system that would be accessible to all psychologists, regardless of whether they had psychoanalytic training. The system was designed to be simple, with concise and clear descriptions, incorporating only the essential criteria, and providing numerous examples for each criterion. We also included a section to highlighting potential coding errors. Additionally, we provided Revised Comprehensive System coding referents when possible. Finally, an appendix containing a comprehensive list of libidinal and aggressive content, which is useful for coding certain defense mechanisms (High-Level Denial, Isolation, and Splitting) is provided.

The final version of the coding system is the result of numerous revisions, shaped by our experience teaching the system in six graduate-level psychology courses. We are deeply grateful to the students who contributed to this process; their mistakes and requests for clarification were invaluable in helping us refine and perfect the system. Below, we outline how the CRDS differs from the LDS and the RDS.

How does the CRDS differ from the LDS?

Unlike the LDS, the CRDS does not focus exclusively on primitive defenses (such as splitting, projective identification, denial, devaluation, and idealization) or solely on human content responses. Instead, it considers all responses within the Rorschach protocol, incorporating defenses based on repression, including denial, reaction formation, isolation, intellectualization, and rationalization. In contrast to the 5-point continuum of the LDS, the defenses of idealization and devaluation are rated on two distinct levels. Within an object relations framework, the CRDS encompasses repression, cognitive defensive strategies for avoiding affect (such as isolation, intellectualization, and rationalization), primitive relational modes (including projective identification and splitting), defenses that enhance or diminish the perception of an individual (idealization, devaluation, omnipotent control), and various forms of denial (including high-level, omnipotent, and psychotic denial).

The two levels for both idealization and devaluation are regarded as conceptually separate, meaning their weighted sum is not calculated. The criteria for these levels have been refined and revised within the theoretical framework. Denial is no longer viewed as a single defense rated on three levels. The CRDS distinguishes between three distinct types of denial: high-level denial (HD), encompassing negation and reaction formation; omnipotent denial (OD); and psychotic denial (PD).

The coding criteria for splitting and projective identification have been preserved, with additional criteria identified through the RDS further supplementing them.

How does the CRDS differ from the RDS?

Some of the RDS were eliminated, and others were reformulated for greater clarity and to eliminate redundancy. This process resulted in a reduction of over half of the coding criteria, aiming to improve the system's validity, make it more user-friendly, and facilitate quicker learning, thereby enhancing inter-rater reliability.

In line with the conceptual framework, the following changes were implemented:

1 There is a significant difference regarding the criteria for coding repression. We have limited the coding of repression to responses that display an excessively dramatized emotional reaction or those that indicate extreme vagueness, as both serve to protect the individual from becoming aware of certain feelings. Some other criteria included in

the RDS may indicate a hysteriform style, which may not equate with repression. Hysterical mechanisms can appear in personality structures organized at varying levels, from mature to primitive. Unlike the RDS, we do not consider all responses without projective content as indicative of repression. "A butterfly" or "a lamp" may not necessarily indicate repression. Such responses can also result from emotional impoverishment, limited engagement with the test, or lower IQ. Therefore, we do not consider these responses as indicative of a specific defense mechanism. This issue will be addressed in detail in the validation study (see Chapter 10 in this volume);

2 The coding criteria for intellectualization, isolation, and rationalization were summarized, and those with questionable content validity were omitted;

3 The Pollyannish denial defense has been included in the first-level idealization defense because both refer to the need to maintain a positive view of life, possibly associated with the need to preserve a good internal object;

4 The defense mechanism of reaction formation has been included in the high-level denial defenses because, like other manifestations of high-level denial, it serves to avoid percepts or representations charged with libidinal or aggressive drive;

5 Projection and projective identification have been unified into the defense of projective identification, and the coding criteria have been significantly revised, also incorporating coding criteria from the LDS. According to Spillius (2012) and Sodré (2012), it is arguably not useful to distinguish between projection and projective identification, since "it is difficult to imagine a projection taking place in an external space or on something inanimate or abstract, without also thinking that what is projected, whatever it is, is not somehow personified" (Sodré, 2012, p. 132);

6 The coding criteria for the splitting defense have been summarized and more clearly reformulated, incorporating those from the LDS;

7 Omnipotence was renamed "Omnipotent Control" to emphasize that it reflects the need to exert control over others;

8 Idealization and devaluation, as previously mentioned, have both been differentiated into two distinct levels based on their intensity and potential degree of perceptual distortion;

9 The hypomanic denial has been renamed omnipotent denial, according to Kleinian theoretical framework, and the coding criteria have been partially revised;

10 Massive denial has been renamed psychotic denial, and the coding criteria have been significantly summarized.

The final version of the CRDS includes a total of 51 coding criteria.

The CRDS coding criteria

REPRESSION (REP)

Definition: A defense mechanism through which an individual excludes from consciousness painful or unacceptable thoughts, emotions, or memories, preventing them from being consciously perceived.

Coding criteria

A Dramatized overreactions.

   1 "Wow!"
   2 "My God!"
   3 "Gosh!"

B Extreme vagueness (lacking as sense of suspiciousness).

   1 "I'm sensing something here, but I just can't make it out."
   2 "I saw something but now I can't see anything."
   3 "There is something there, but I can't quite see it."
   4 "It just seems vague to me."
   5 "I don't see anything, I don't know … it doesn't mean anything to me."

HIGH-LEVEL DENIAL (HLD)

Definition: A defense mechanism by which an individual denies, minimizes, or reduces the intensity of painful feelings, ideas, or sources of conflict, without compromising reality testing.

Coding criteria

A Negation occurs in the free association or in the inquiry phase for percepts with definite form. If an afterthought or not related to the original percept (e.g., "It just feels like a female shape to me, not in any bodily sense") the negation is not coded. **Responses must have libidinal or aggressive contents/themes, good Form Quality (*o* or *u*), and absence of Critical Special Scores.**

   1 "It's not a lion."
   2 "Those people are not angry at each other."

B Minimization reduces or neutralizes threatening drive-laden material. Percepts are made less substantial, their impact less imminent. The absence or lessoning of dysphoric emotion may be stated. **Responses must have libidinal or aggressive contents/themes, good Form Quality (*o* or *u*), and absence of Critical Special Scores.**

   1 "It looks like the shadow of an evil monster." (AgC)
   2 "Here is a hint of the anger that this couple feels toward each other." (Mp, Hx, Fa)
   3 "It looks like a face. It isn't too happy looking." (Mp, Hx, Fa, MOR)
   4 "Two people looking at each other. They don't look very friendly toward each other." (Mp, Hx, Fa)
   5 "Looks like these two have just had a bit of a fight."
   6 "The face has a definite expression—almost a sad expression." (Mp, Hx, Fa, MOR)
   7 "Little bears." (AgC)
   8 "Little lions." (AgC)
   9 "Cute little children kissing."

C Repudiation/disavowal. **Responses must have libidinal or aggressive contents/themes, good Form Quality (*o* or *u*), and absence of Critical Special Scores.**

   1 "Two human beings fornicating." In Inquiry: "Did I say human beings? I didn't say that." those are two large apes. (Ma, H, Sx, DR)
   2 "A penis—no, don't write that down, it really looks like a snake instead." (Sx, DR)

D Humor or reference to cartoons is used to reduce or neutralize threatening drive-laden material. **Responses must have libidinal or aggressive contents/themes, good Form Quality (*o* or *u*), and absence of Critical Special Scores.**

   1 (Card I). "Two people face to face having an argument—their faces are so close together it is almost comical." (Ma, AG)
   2 (Card II). "Two elephants fighting it out, looking like Dumbo and a friend of his." (FMa, AG)
   3 (Card VI). "A squashed cat, it seems Sylvester cat when the tweety bird makes him dumb." (AgPast)

E The response includes figures or objects whose characteristics emphasize themes of obedience, altruism, cleanliness, politeness, sincerity, or kindness. Excessively courteous and polite modes can also be observed in the relationship with the psychologist. Also code when the responses includes strong anti-sentimental tones. In this way the individual negates the affect and transform it in its opposite (reaction formation is here considered as a type of negation).

1 "Two very clean and neat people."
2 "Two very kind women." (Mp, Hx)
3 "Two dogs sitting, looking very obedient." (FMp)
4 "One man helping the other lift a weight, must be a very good and helpful person." (Ma, COP)
5 "Excuse me, I don't want to be rude."
6 "Two dogs kissing. I can't stand that kind of slobbering." (Ma, DR)
7 "Two lovers, how melancholy they are!" (Mp, H, Hx, MOR)
8 "Two tender children, what a lie! Children are terrible." (DR)

Coding errors

High Level denial concerns only drive-laden material (both libidinal and aggressive). Do not code "maybe a butterfly," "it almost looks like a book," "it is not a chandelier, it looks more like a light bulb." Ensure the response contains drive-laden material. Consult Appendix as a guide for drive content.

INTELLECTUALIZATION (INT)

Definition: A defense mechanism through which an individual over-invests in cognitive and intellectual functioning to avoid contact with painful emotions and/or conflicts.

Coding criteria

A The response is presented in an overtly technical, scientific, intellectual manner, sometimes even using specialized language. Intellectualization occur with Art, and Ct. It is coded when the content is Ve, Arc, or Sc, and even An only if the language is particularly specialized.

1 "Two shakespearean characters." (Ct)
2 "This *ictu oculi* looks like a butterfly."
3 "An artifact from the Proterozoic era." (Ct)
4 "Reminiscent of what Thales of Miletus wrote."
5 "It seems like cerebrospinal fluid." (An)

B Emotionless comments expressing intellectual interest in the test.

1 "Could this be a painting, was the person who painted these cards an artist? What school of painting was it from?" (Art, DR)
2 "I think the person who made them wanted to elicit specific reactions, he will certainly have studied what colors elicit specific emotions." (DR)

C Expressions of doubt, rumination, long unproductive verbalizations.

   1 "I'm looking at the left and right, they would look the same at a first glance, but maybe they're not really, maybe this part here is slightly different, maybe it's subtly asymmetrical." (DR)

ISOLATION OF AFFECT (ISO)

Definition: A defense mechanism that allows the individual not to perceive the emotions connected to painful and/or conflictual thoughts.

Coding criteria

A Aggressive or sexual content is distanced in time or space, or is expressed in ways that mitigate the emotional impact of the percept.

   1 "An ancient rifle." (Wp, AgC)
   2 "An oriental sword." (Wp, Ct, AgC)
   3 "This object looks like a penis." (Sx)
   4 "This image could be described as a vagina." (Sx)
   5 "This drawing could indicate a fierce animal." (AgC)

B Affect is denied through devitalization.

   1 "A statue." (Art)
   2 "A painting with two people looking at each other." (H, Art)
   3 "Two people, like the drawings of primitive people in caves." (H, Art, Ct)
   4 "A robot." (Sc)

C Human or animal content is seen in very controlled, rigid or formal activities.

   1 "A ballet."
   2 "Two waiters in uniform." (H, Cg)
   3 "A circus dog, trained."
   4 "Two women bowing to each other." (Mp, H)
   5 "Two men in tight suits." (H, Cg)

D Geographic maps or landscapes seen as distant, isolated or inaccessible.

   1 "Mountains seen from an airplane." (Ge)
   2 "A view of Lake Michigan." (Ge)

RATIONALIZATION (RAT)

Definition: A defense mechanism through which an individual justifies unacceptable behaviors, thoughts, or emotions with logical or socially acceptable explanations, to avoid confronting the true motivations or emotions underlying them.

Coding criteria

A A very rational explanation is given to justify the response. Responses meeting the threshold for ALOG are not coded as Rationalization. Rationalization contains conventional reasoning.

1 "Two poodles glaring at each other. Dogs often do that." (Mp, INC, DR)
2 "Two putti. It must be because I just saw two of them." (DR, PER)
3 "Two lobsters. It must be because I'm hungry." (Fd, DR)
4 "Garden dwarfs. Maybe because there are several of them near my house." (PER)
5 "I always see x-rays. It must be because of my job." (PER)

Coding errors

Only drive-laden content distanced in time and/or space indicates Isolation. Responses such as "two pieces of antique furniture" or "two Chinese vases" should not be coded as Isolation. Code them as Intellectualization because of the Art or Ct Content. Code only geographic contents described as distant and physically inaccessible. Responses such as "a mountain full of snow on which two marmots are climbing" or "a restful lake, blue water, and big green trees around" do not indicate the defensive recourse to the avoidance of affect.

Not all personal references suggest rationalization. Thus, responses such as "a cat, it looks just like my sister's, "the Eiffel Tower, I liked seeing it when I was in Paris," should not be coded. Code only if the personal reference is evidently used to justify the response." Remember that responses meeting the threshold for ALOG are not coded as Rationalization. Rationalization contains conventional reasoning.

PROJECTIVE IDENTIFICATION (PROJ)

Definition: A defense mechanism by which an individual projects their unacceptable impulses, desires, emotions, and/or parts of themselves onto another, while simultaneously attempting to influence the other to adopt and live out these projections, thereby confirming their own rejected thoughts or feelings.

Coding criteria

A Confabulatory responses (i.e., elaborations in which inappropriate phases and circumstantial reasoning are present, coded as DRs in the Comprehensive System) involving humans, animals or even objects (only if affects or human features are attributed to them) in which verbalization indicate that the respondent identifies himself/herself with the projected feeling. When the identification is implicit, the confabulatory response makes the examiner feel that the respondent is really attuned with the projected feelings or state of mind. Include also all the human movement responses with *minus* form quality.

1 (Card I, D4). "A woman who is in great pain, giving birth, you can see her legs spread apart and she is screaming, she has her hands up in desperation." (Mao, DR2, Hx, AgV)

2 (Card II, D3). "A demonic figure looking at you." (Mp-, AgC, DR)

3 (Card II, D3). "A bloody butterfly, crawls on its blood, about to die, still tries to fly but can't make it, I don't know why it got this far, however it's obvious that it has to die, however it tried to get back up, you can see from all the blood it left behind." (DR2, MOR, AgPast)

4 (Card IV, W) "A bird that looks at you very badly." (DR, AgPot)

5 (Card IV, W). "An antbird trying to be a monster raised up on its paws, takes this awkward posture because it wants to feel strong and scare someone." (AgC, SM, Hx, DR2)

6 (Card IV, D1). "An inhuman face, eyes, is nested in this dying tree trunk, its expression is terribly bleak." (Mp, Fa, Hx, DR, MOR)

7 (V, Card VIII, W). "A character with a little long hair, the mustache, the hair, the eyes are a little bit hidden by the hair, they look a little bit like frog eyes, it's one of those faces that are a little bit closed, I don't know how to say, flattened on life, that also have a little bit of hidden aggression, one of those people who tend a little bit to hide." (Fa, Hx, DR2)

8 (Card VIII, W). "A clown, a creepy mask of a clown, it looks like one of those movies where the crazy killer wears a mask, these are the eyes and this is his sadistic grin, he enjoys terrorizing people." (Mp, Hx, DR2, PER, AgC, SM)

9 (Card IX, Dd99). "A frightened face, the expression of the eyes, they are downcast, the mouth open, it is a terrified woman, she is screaming." (Mp. Fa, Hx, DR, AgV)

10 (Card X, DdS22). "A kind of guardian, the mouth has a threatening smile, these are the eye orbits. One is frightened to look at him." (Hx, DR, SM, AgC)

11 (Card X, W). "Fireworks, here's a seagull (D3) in the middle, he's tremendously frightened, he's flying frantically to try to get away." (Mp, Hx, DR, AgV)

B Responses in which the location is Dd, and the content implies "eyes," especially if a particular expression is attributed to them. The determinant may be diffuse shading (Y; Comprehensive System).

1 (Card VI, Dd32). "Two eyes in this lighter part." (YF, Hd)

2 (Card VII, Dd99 in D3). "A ugly eye in this lighter part." (YF, Hd)

3 (Card IX, DdS22) "A hidden person who is afraid to come out." (Hx, AgV)

C Responses including aggressive and malevolent imagery, provided they explicitly or implicitly imply malevolent relationships in which victimization is evident (both in action or potential). *Do not score: "Two men fighting" or "An angry man" because they do not imply a victimization.*

1 (Card I). "A face full of hatred." (Mp, Fa, Hx)
2 (Card III, D9) "Two people with a sadistic grin." (Mp, Hx, SM)
3 (Card IV, W). "A malicious man." (Hx, AgC)
4 (Card VI, W). "This looks like an evil cat that's been run over." (Mp, INC, AgC, AgPast)
5 (Card VI, D1) "The skin of a bison, a crippled bison, poor creature! It's missing a piece of its leg." (AgPast, MOR)

D Responses or verbalizations that convey a sense of suspiciousness toward the testing situation, the Cards or the examiner.

1 "Is this a trap?"
2 "Is there some hidden meaning?"

E Responses in which a figure puts a substance or a feeling into another object for the purpose of controlling or destroying the recipient, or responses in which a human, an animal or an object is controlled by another figure or an external force.

1 (Card III, D2+D9) "These are the forces and energies that are controlling what these two people are doing. The force is going to make them have a bloody fight." (AgPot)
2 (Card III, D9+D2). "Two spirits controlling the two women." (AG)
3 (Card VI, W). "This man has electrodes in his neck."
4 (Card VI, W). "A manta ray, something dangerous both for its tail and for these sharp teeth." (AgC)
5 (Card VI, W). "A stingray, here its venomous stingers." (AgC)
6 (Card VI, Dd21). "Two pincers, two stingers, they are pointed, they have to sting someone." (AgC, AgPot)
7 (Card IX, D1+D3). "Two men immobilized by a witchcraft spell." (AgPast)
8 (Card X, D1+D12). "These tarantulas are injecting their poison into the grasshoppers." (AG, AgC)
9 (Card X, D14). "A probe in the sea, it is poisoning the sea."
10 (Card X, W). "Force keeps all these animals balanced suspended in the air."

F A vulnerable or valued object is protected from danger by placing it in another object.

1 (Card VII, W). "These statues are in a safe with thick walls." (AgV)
2 (Card VIII, D6). "An armor, a cuirass that protects the part of the chest, stomach and belly." (AgV)

3 (Card X, W). "These little innocent, weak-looking creatures seem to be trying to get inside these pink things. Maybe they are trying to find refuge from this world of vicious-looking crabs and insects." (AgV)

Coding errors

Psychologists who are unfamiliar with the Rorschach may find it difficult to understand when a response is extremely confabulatory. They tend to regard all movement responses as confabulatory, thus confusing projection as a psychological process that may be normal and desirable during test administration with a pathological tendency to permeate responses of their subjective experience beyond what can reasonably be seen in the Card. Confabulatory responses actually are those that exhibit extreme fantastic processing that strays beyond the limits of perceptual reality, so responses determined by human movement should not be coded as projective identification if they are of good form quality and do not exhibit EXTREME fantastic processing. In Comprehensive System-Revised they are coded DR. So, do not code projective identification if the response does not contain the Critical Special Score DR.

Following are some examples that should not be coded projective identification:

1 "Two women talking, could be two friends behind a piece of furniture." (Card VII)
2 "Two waiters who are carrying a tray, they are dressed in black and seem to be very careful not to drop the tray, they look a little stiff in their posture to me." (Card III)

Further coding errors occur when respondents interpret a Card or a portion of it as a person or animal and later describe it by also mentioning the eyes as one of its parts. Unless the eyes are placed in a Dd and a particular look is attributed beyond what perceptual reality can evoke, these responses do not indicate the use of projective identification.

Following are some examples that should not be coded projective identification:

1 "A Halloween mask, it's made like this, these are the holes for the eyes and mouth." (Card I)
2 "Two clowns at the circus dancing, these are their faces, eyes, mouth open, wide dress." (Card II)

Not all responses with aggressive content imply recourse to projective identification, but only those that implicitly or explicitly represent malicious intentions in an asymmetrical relationship in which victimization (past, ongoing, or potential) is thus evident.

Following are some examples that should not be coded projective identification,

1 "Two men wrestling, it's a hand-to-hand fight." (Card II) (Ma, AG)
2 "Two women arguing, each pulling this object in the middle, they are fighting over it." (Card III) (Ma, AG)

Responses in which an object or figure is protected because it is placed in another object, the theme of danger must be evident. For example, the response "Two little birds in the nest" should not be coded as projective identification because the respondent neither implicitly nor explicitly refers to a dangerous situation.

Do not code the responses "carpet" and "animal skin" unless there are additional embellishments in the response, such as "poor animal killed!"

SPLITTING (SPL)

Definition: A defense mechanism through which an individual polarizes experiences, themselves, and others into "extremely good" or "extremely bad," avoiding an integrated, articulated, and complex view, in order to prevent intolerable ambivalence.

Coding criteria

A Within object splitting: One part of a figure, object or phenomena of nature is seen as opposite to another part.

1 "A bird, it looks like a terrible bird of prey, its wings instead inspire lightness and benevolence." (Hx, AgC, AB)
2 "A huge being, its legs are looming and convey a sense of fear, its face, on the other hand, is small and sweet." (Mp, Hx)
3 "A landscape, the top part looks like a clear blue sky, the bottom part is threatening, like a tremendous hurricane that is coming to destroy everything." (mp, AgPot)
4 "A woman with two heads: one is benevolent and the other is malicious." (Mp, Hx, INC2, AgC).
5 "A diabolical woman disguised as a lovely butterfly." (Mp, Hx)
6 "An animal with the head of a harmless skunk and the tail of a dangerous reptile." (INC2)
7 "An eerie landscape: a restful lake in front of a looming, sinister mountain." (Mp, Hx, AgPot)

B Multiple object or concept splitting within a single response. Rapidly alternating objects or themes shift from very positive to very negative representations or from libidinal to aggressive (or vice versa) content. This occurs in an extraordinarily fluid fashion.

1 "A woman between two men with cloaks, one is evil and wants to attack her, the other is good and wants to save her." (Ma, AG, COP)
2 "An ugly insect … cute little lady bugs or butterflies." (DEV, ID)
3 "A Chinese mask … I saw an exhibition of Chinese art at the one in California, it was the most important exhibition in Los Angeles. I was fascinated with them. They looked so evil. Coloring is wrong. Chinese never use green and orange. Basic tools poorly defined as head, nose, and mouth." (ID, DEV).
4 "A large carnivore ready to strike. All I see is the eyes and a hostile mouth, what else is there to see. I wish I could see doves mating. Something soft and gentle." (DR, AgPot, ID)

C Rapidly alternating objects or themes shift from very positive to very negative representations or from libidinal to aggressive (or vice versa) content occur in sequential responses.

1 Sequence:
  a (Card II). "Two guys high-fiving each other." (Mao, COP)
  b (Card II). "Two men trying to kill each other, they are both wounded, you can see the blood." (Mao, AG, MOR, AgPast).

2 Sequence:
  a (Card III). "Looks like two shady guys." (DEV)
  b (Card III). "Two lovers looking into each other's eyes." (Mpo, COP)

3 Sequence:
  a (Card V). "A bat, an ugly, vicious bat." (DEV)
  b (Card V). "A beautiful butterfly in flight. It's harmless, just flying from flower to flower." (ID)

4 Sequence:
  a (Card VIII). "A noble coat of arms of an important lineage." (ID)
  b (Card VIII). "Two sewer rats." (DEV)

5 Sequence:
  a (Card IX). "A beautiful butterfly." (ID)
  b (Card IX). "A skull." (DEV)

6 Sequence:
  a (Card IX). "The dawning of a beautiful, peaceful day." (ID)
  b (Card IX). "The day after an explosion that destroyed everything, you can see the atomic fungus." (Ex, AgPast)

Coding errors

Opposing good/bad or idealized/devalued polarities must be marked and evident. No other polarities except good/bad and idealized/devalued are included. For example, the sequence "a small dog" and "an elephant" highlights the small-large polarity but does not indicate the use of splitting because it involves neither the good-bad nor the idealized-devalued polarity.

Following are some examples that should not be coded splitting.

1   "A butterfly" followed by "An insect."
2   "A little bird" followed by "A fly."
3   "A tulip" followed by "A nasty person."

IDEALIZATION

Definition: A defense mechanism through which an individual attributes extremely positive qualities to themselves and/or others, in order to avoid contact with painful emotional experiences of inadequacy and/or ambivalence.

Coding criteria

Idealization level 1 (ID1)

Idealization responses at level 1 evidence some mild embellishment and/or emphasis on pleasant and serene aspects of the life without any cognitive slippage. The responses must have good Form Quality (ordinary or unusual).

A   Mild positively enhancing qualities are added to figures, animals or objects. **Responses must have adequate form quality and absent Critical Special Scores.**

1   (Card II, D3). "A pretty coral."
2   (Card III, D2). "Some charming decorations for a party."
3   (Card III, D9). "Two nice people."
4   (Card VII, W). "Two friendly women."
5   (Card VII, D1). "Two smiling children."
6   (Card VIII, D2). "A beautiful colored butterfly."
7   (Card IX, W). "A pleasant landscape at sunset."

B References to well-known persons, character, and objects without implication of particular power or grandiosity **Responses must have adequate form quality and absent Critical Special Scores.**

   1 (Card VI, W). "Sylvester Cat."
   2 (Card X, D11). "Eiffel Tower."
   3 (Card X, D10). "Mustache, they look like those drawn by Salvator Dalì." [(Hd), Art]

C Objects related to strength, power, and worship. **Responses must have adequate form quality and absent Critical Special Scores.**

   1 "A noble crest"
   2 "A crown"
   3 "A totem"

D Figures engaged in positive and pleasant activities such as dancing, playing, or relaxing. **Responses must have adequate form quality and absent Critical Special Scores.**

   1 (Card IV). "There is a boy having a lot of fun sitting on a water plug. I mean a fire plug. His feet are in opposite directions. His head is back. I think he is laughing."
   2 (Card IX). "Two girls dancing with very full skirts. Their hair is blowing back from their heads. They seem to be enjoying themselves, carefree." (COP)

E Reference to positive qualities of the card or testing process.

   1 "Oh, isn't this one wonderful. It is very sweet."
   2 "How lovely and delicate, this one is."
   3 "This is really amazing. You must be very smart."

Idealization level 2 (ID2)

Idealization responses at level 2 evidence extreme embellishment and distortions and may include minus form and cognitive slippage. In case of Human Content, the real dimension is lost.

A Humans, animals, landscapes, or other objects are described in **blatant and excessively positive** terms.

   1 "A very rich woman full of jewelry, wearing a beautiful dress."
   2 "Two rampant lions in their regal majesty."
   3 "Queen Elizabeth's crown."

4 "Niagara Falls in their magnificence."
5 "A magic cup enveloped in divine fumes."
6 "Those mighty statues on the Notre Dame Cathedral, the Gargoyles."
7 "A majestic mountain."

B Objects of fame or enhancement of the human form. This would include officials, objects of fame or strength, athletic superstars.

1 "A bust of Napoleon."
2 "Looks like Jack Nicholson, the famous actor."
3 "Ever hear of an artist named Pablo Picasso? I think he did this one."
4 "An angel." (H)
5 "A fairy." (H)
6 "He looks like Pele, perhaps the best soccer player of all time."
7 "A character from a comic book drawn by a famous Japanese cartoonist." [(H), Art]

C The individual refers to himself, the examiner, testing procedure, or testing materials in blatantly positive terms. Also score when the examinee flatters the examiner.

1 "My creativity is very rich, I can really imagine a lot of things."
2 "You really seem like a person who understands others at first sight."
3 "Were these cards made by a famous painter? They could be exhibited in a museum of modern art."
4 "This desk of yours must be very old, it looks like an important antique, congratulations!"

Coding errors

Level 1, unlike level 2, does not involve references to marked aspect of celebrity, power, and grandiosity. To code Idealization level 2, percepts must be described in EXCESSIVELY positive terms. Responses such as "a nice dog," "a pleasant woman," "a distinguished man," "a beautiful vase" are coded as ID1. Code Idealization in case of good Form Quality (ordinary or unusual) and code Omnipotent Denial in case of *minus* Form Quality or in case of Critical Special Scores.

DEVALUATION

Definition: A defense mechanism through which an individual minimizes or denies the value of themselves, others, or an experience, in order to protect themselves from painful emotions such as loss, inadequacy, envy, failure, or frustration.

Coding criteria

Devaluation level 1 (DEV1)

_____

A Figures, animals, or insects which are commonly thought of as infa-
mous, repulsive, loathsome, or disgusting are identified without negative embellishments. This includes roaches, rats, vultures, leaches,
slugs, lice, maggots, ticks, fleas. Also included are mythological,
supernatural and fictional characters that have negatively tinged
connotations.

1 "This looks like Lucifer." (H)
2 "A witch on her broomstick." (H)
3 "A clown." (H)

B Figures in mildly negative activities or mildly negatively described figures placed in socially acceptable contexts.

1 "Two somewhat rude people talking loudly."
2 "Two old animals, not beautiful to look at."
3 "A woman dressed a little badly, her clothes a little frumpy."
4 "A guy with some dirt on his shirt."
5 "Two elderly men, they are a bit hunched over." (MOR)
6 "A slightly overweight woman."

Devaluation level 2 (DEV2)

_____

A Negative, critical, or pejorative terms (such as ugly, unattractive, disgusting, repulsive, gross, homely, ridiculous, stupid, weak, sick, diseased,
disfigured, deformed, distorted, defective, funny-looking, rotten, rot-
ting, decrepit, worn out, useless, worthless) are used to describe objects.

1 "A deformed man." (MOR)
2 "A tremendously fat woman."
3 "Two dwarf men." (MOR)
4 "A ragged carpet, to be thrown away." (MOR)
5 "A disgusting cat."

B Figures described in blatantly pejorative, negative, and/or socially
unacceptable terms, or whose activities, vocation, or social status
embodies a negatively tinged connotation, or socially unacceptable
behaviors. This excludes descriptions of intercourse or other sexual activities. Included are figures such as thieves, criminals, bums,

beggars, hobos, Ku Klux Klansmen, murderers, cannibals, savages, headhunters, slaves.

    1 "Two sorceresses."
    2 "A hooded robber."
    3 "A man who eats garbage."
    4 "Two gnomes." (H)

C Missing body parts. Only score when the missing body part is integrated with the final response.

    1 "A dog missing a paw." (MOR)
    2 "A woman without a head." (MOR)
    3 "A stumpy giant." (H)
    4 "A crippled bear." (MOR)

D Human figures or parts with physical characteristics of animals. Also responses involving humans, animals, human parts, or animal parts with incongruous combinations in the form of composite responses (INC1 and INC2).

    1 "Two women with bird beaks." (INC2)
    2 "A man with the head of a skunk." (INC2)
    3 "A dancer with the head of a rabbit." (INC2)
    4 "Two women with fish tails." (INC2)

E Examinee devalues an aspect of the Card, the testing experience, the examiner, themselves, or their own percepts.

    1 "It looks like a man who everybody thinks is great, but I think he stinks."
    2 "I hate this, it disgusts me."
    3 "These blots are aesthetically ugly."
    4 "I cannot believe this is the way you spend our time—how boring."
    5 "This looks like a bat; not this crap over here."
    6 "The outer part stuck me as an abortion. I saw it in a picture. It makes me feel like an idiot talking about Christmas."
    7 "Just image would be intimidating to me. I have a hang up about ugly things."

Coding errors

Popular responses without additional embellishment, "monster" on Card IV, and the responses "gnome," "elf," or similar on Card IX should not be coded.

OMNIPOTENT CONTROL (OMNI)

Definition: A defense mechanism that implies the perception of illusory power or control over oneself, others, or the environment, to protect oneself from emotions of inadequacy, frustration, or vulnerability.

Coding criteria

A The individual describes themselves with blatant and excessively positive terms making individual makes laudatory remarks to special abilities or testing process, or seeing themselves in the blot (i.e., percept
includes the self) or their possessions and this is elaborated with ag-
grandizing remarks.

   1 "Be prepared to write at length, my imagination is limitless. "
   2 "These are two racing bicycles about to cross the finish line, only I can
      see things like this in these two little dots, I have extraordinary visual
      acuity, I've always been told I have superior intelligence."
   3 "This looks like me when I went to my brother's wedding, no one was
      dressed more eccentrically and elegantly than me."

B In describing the percept the person uses the word "we" in referring to
themselves as the perceiver (the "editorial we")

C The respondent lectures, instruct, or display haughtiness toward the
examiner.

   1 "Also write this, "This test is shit" (the respondent imperiously dic-
      tates the sentence), did you write it? well, let's move on now."
   2 "Now I'm really bored, I feel like I've already explained myself well
      enough."
   3 "That's what I told them before and I've had this test 4–5 times from
      different people."
   4 "That pretty much says it."
   5 "Another bad one. I don't have any idea. A splotch of ink story—ac-
      cording to the doctor at the jail."
   6 "A young animal looking at reflection in a pool of water ... (?) I saw
      what I want to see."

Coding errors

During test administration, omnipotent control very often becomes evident
through the tone in which the examinee addresses the examiner. In these
cases, if the examiner has not highlighted in the protocol transcript the examinee's nonverbal behavior, including the tone of voice used, the coder
will not be able to capture this defense.

   Another frequent error is due to the fact that sometimes, especially in
the Italian language, it is common in colloquial usage to use "we," without implying the *plural maiestatis*. In these cases, the risk is to overestimate
the use of the editorial we. Therefore, even in these cases, it is necessary
for the psychologist to signal the use of "editorial we" in the protocol
transcript.

OMNIPOTENT DENIAL (OD)

Definition: A manic-type defense mechanism in which an individual denies painful emotions or realities, maintaining an euphoric or excessively positive attitude to avoid discomfort and confrontation with painful emotional experiences.

Coding criteria

A Embellished pollyannish objects that symbolize pretty and serene aspects of life such as flowers, dawns, sunsets, and toys. **These kind or responses must have minus form quality and/or Critical Special Scores.**

  1 (Card I, W). "A Christmas tree." (FQ minus)
  2 (Card II, W). "A flower." (FQ minus)
  3 (Card VI, D1). "A rose." (FQ minus)

B Figures described with pollyannish emphasis on fun, pleasure, pleasantness, happiness, and the like. Include figures engaged in activities such as dancing, playing, or relaxing. Euphoric emotion is emphasized. **These kind or responses must have minus form quality.**

  1 (Card III, D5). "A little bird chirping happily." (FQ minus)
  2 (Card VI, D1). "A man lying with outstretched arms relaxing." (FQ minus)
  3 (Card X, DdS22). "A smiling face." (FQ minus)

C Figures or animals described in ways that imply an incongruous combination (INC or FAB). This kind of response conveys a particular kind of denial in that it makes real what would be plausible in fairy tales or cartoons. Responses with INCOM2 or FABCOM2 must be coded Psychotic Denial, not Omnipotent Denial.

  1 "Two bears are cheerfully dancing the tango." (FAB)
  2 "Marine animals that are partying, crabs are circling, seahorses are jumping, fish are happily circling." (FAB)
  3 "Two elephants high-fiving each other." (FAB)

D Pollyannish concepts with or without reference to color.

  1 (Card III). "Love." (AB)
  2 (Card VII). "This one represents lightness and serenity." (AB)
  3 (Card VII). "Hope." (AB)
  4 (Card VIII). "Cheerfulness, joy. Orange conveys just these beautiful feelings to me!" (AB)
  5 (Card IX). "A new beginning." (AB)
  6 (Card IX). "The life, the color pink represents the beginning of life, the color green the lifeblood and the orange the warmth of friendship." (AB)
  7 (Card X). "Peace and cooperation between people and animals." (AB)

E Color is used in a personalized or idiosyncratic manner with positive qualities attributed to it. Avoidance or minimization of aggressive or dysphoric affect is the goal.

    1 (Card II). "A dark sky, maybe it is night, but soon it will be clear, the white in the middle indicates that a new beautiful day is coming." (AB)

    2 (Card II). "Two Santas, first I thought the red was blood … no! I said to myself! It's Santa's hat." (H)

F Arbitrary Form-Color Response. Form and color are incompatibly combined. This also includes all color projection responses (CP).

    1 (Card I, W). "A pretty colored flower." (CP)

    2 (Card II, D2). "Red lawn." (INC2)

    3 (Card VI, D3). "A totem pole with brightly colored feathers." (CP)

    4 (Card VII, W). "A rainbow. It is colorful." (CP)

    5 (Card VIII, D1). "Two pink cats." (INC2)

G Forced recourse to optimism ("happy end style") is evident in confabulatory responses or in deviant responses. If the response also meets the criteria for projective identification, code both.

    1 (Card I). "A bird losing bits of wings? No, how silly! is an airplane that is dropping confetti for a festive occasion." (MOR)

    2 (Card II). "Two men fighting, no, red is a color that gives joy, it's two dancers who are choreographing for a Christmas show, that's why they have red caps on and are dancing happily holding hands as they look at each other happily, they are thinking that they will celebrate Christmas with their families." (AG, COP).

    3 (Card III). "Two people who are very thin, but now they will soon recover and we can see them in great shape! soon they will go dancing and have a lot of fun." (MOR)

    4 (Card VI). "An animal that crashed into glass, but it is fine. Now we will see him recover and fly free and happy." (MOR)

    5 (Card IX). "A nice plate of salad and fish, there are also two fantastic lobsters! I really like lobsters, I always want to eat them, and I think I'll go to the restaurant tonight, I wanted to eat them and here I saw them!" (DR)

    6 (Card X). "A painter's palette, painting I've always liked, it makes me happy, that's why I saw it here." (DR)

H A **blatant** hypomanic mood is conveyed in action or figure or verbalization. Rather than emphasizing a superficial appraisal of fun or pleasantness, the focus is an elaboration of the level of energy (e.g., increased energy, gregariousness, overenthusiasm, restlessness, triumphant attitude, or stance).

    1 (Prior to Card I) "I'm so glad to take this test! I'm really in the mood today!"

2 (Card II). "Two people at a disco, they are wild, they will go on until dawn." (Ma)

3 (Card IV). "A happy man on his Harly Davidson, he's so happy and full of energy that he's going to drive all over California." (Mao, Hx)

4 (Card X). "This image really makes me happy, it's in tune with my mood today, I'm just thinking about the sun and the sea!"

Coding errors

A possibly frequent mistake concerns the confusion between Idealization Level 1—criteria C and D—and Omnipotent Denial criteria A and B. The psychologist must always remember to check the Form Quality of the response and code Idealization in case of good Form Quality (ordinary or unusual) and code Omnipotent Denial in case of *minus* Form Quality or Critical Special Scores.

PSYCHOTIC DENIAL (PD)

Definition: A defense mechanism through which an individual rejects, alters, and/or distorts significant aspects of reality, preventing confrontation with a painful or unsustainable truth.

Coding criteria

A Severe impairment of reality testing and judgment (the responses MUST contain CONTAM [Contamination] or INCOM2 [Bizarre Incongruous Combination] or FAB2 [Bizarre Fabulized Combination] or bizarre ALOG or MPD [Major Perception Distortion])

1 "An ice cream-soaked island." (CONTAM)

2 "It is a spiderbat." (CONTAM)

3 "Two bears climbing an ice cream cone." (FAB2)

4 "A group of miners burrowing deeply into the center of the earth." (Card I, W) (MPD)

5 "Two little old ladies who have the same roots and gossip (?) are resting on the same base, so they have the same roots." (ALOG)

6 "A dog with frog legs." (INCOM2)

A guide to identifying libidinal and aggressive content and themes

Libidinal content and themes[1]
(the following list is not exhaustive)

Oral images and themes

Sucking, nursing, breasts, nipples, famine, drought, starving, nausea, vomit, throat, teeth, gullet, stomach, belly, pig, hog, smoking, smoking materials, bird in nest, fat or thin human or animal, eating, drinking, cooking, preparation or serving of food, food (including all plants and animals that may be edible), drink, containers for food or drink, utensils for cooking or eating, hunger, appetite, persons with oral identity or social role (e.g., waiter, cook), places where food or drink is available, nurtures.

Mouth, lips, tongue (when seen in isolation, not just as one part pointed out in a face)

Anal images and themes

buttocks, feces, hemorrhoids, intestines, toilet, disgust, dirt, mud, bad smell,

Sexual images and themes

Sexual organs, ejaculation, intercourse, womb, menstruation, kissing, romance, lovers, bride, groom, boyfriend, nudity, exhibiting; undergarments, brassiere, corset, leering, peering, observing, prancing, transvestism, cross dressing (May include Sx and/or Cg)

Aggressive content and themes[2]
(the following list is not exhaustive)

Arrow, axe, barracuda, bat, battleship, bear, beast, blade, bomb, bullet, cage, claws, club, cobra, cockroach, copperhead, crocodile, demon, devil, dracula, dragon, explosion, fangs, fire, fist, Frankenstein, garrote, goblins, gun, hammer, hatchet, hurricane, jackal, jellyfish, killer whale, King Kong, knife, lion, missile, medusa, mummy, monster, needle, noose, panther, pick, pincers, rats, rifle, saw, scorpion, shark, sharp teeth, snake, spear, spider, spike, sticker bush, syringe, tarantula, tiger, tire-iron, tomahawk, tornado, torpedo, torch, vampire, venus fly trap, volcano, wasp, wolf, yellow jacket, or any object embellished with aggressive imagery (AgC) (e.g., "a butterfly with fangs," "a butterfly with claws").

Any response that implies that an aggressive act has occurred or is preparing to occur, or when the respondent identifies a perception as vulnerable to attack, exploitation, or indicates that the object has taken steps to protect itself from predation. (AgV, AgPast)

Notes

1 Holt, R. R. (1977). A method for assessing primary process and their control in Rorschach responses. In M. Rickers-Ovsiankina (Ed.), *Rorschach Psychology* (2nd ed.). New York: Krieger.
2 Gacono C. B., & Meloy, J. R. (1994). *The Rorschach assessment of aggressive and psychopathic personality*. Hillsdale, NJ: Lawrence Erlbaum Associates, Publishers.

10 The validation of the Comprehensive Rorschach Defense System

Anna Maria Rosso and Andrea Camoirano

Introduction

The Comprehensive Rorschach Defense System (CRDS; Gacono & Rosso, this volume, Chapter 9) was developed to establish a psychometrically sound system for assessing defense mechanisms through the Rorschach test.

A review of the literature (see Smith & Gacono, 2022) and recent empirical studies (Rosso, Airaldi, & Camoirano, 2021; Rosso, Gacono, Camoirano, & Smith, submitted) have highlighted the strengths and limitations of two existing measures: the Lerner Defense Scale (LDS; Lerner & Lerner, 1980) and the Rorschach Defense Scales (RDS; Cooper & Arnow, 1986). While both instruments have demonstrated utility in clinical and research contexts, they also exhibit notable constraints. The LDS is restricted to the analysis of human-content responses on the Rorschach and focuses exclusively on primitive defenses, such as splitting, idealization, devaluation, projective identification, and denial. The RDS, although broader in scope, has encountered difficulties in achieving inter-rater reliability, primarily due to the extensive training required, the need for a strong psychoanalytic theoretical foundation, and substantial clinical experience.

The development of the CRDS sought to retain the advantages of both the LDS and the RDS while addressing their respective limitations. The previous chapter outlines the methodological process that led to the final version of the CRDS, emphasizing the steps taken to enhance its theoretical coherence and practical applicability.

This chapter presents the validation of the CRDS, which was conducted through four interrelated studies. The first study investigated the training duration necessary to achieve reliable coding; the second and third studies examined its concurrent and convergent validity, respectively; and the fourth study assessed its divergent validity. Together, these studies provide a comprehensive evaluation of the system's psychometric properties and its potential for broader application in both clinical and research settings.

DOI: 10.4324/9781003536994-13

Study 1: How much training and what type is required to become a reliable coder?

This study employed a within-subjects design to examine the impact of training on proficiency in coding the CRDS. Specifically, it aimed to investigate: (a) the types of errors associated with different levels of training, and (b) the level of expertise required to achieve sufficiently accurate CRDS coding.

Method

Participants and procedures

To address these questions, a training course on CRDS coding was conducted as part of an academic teaching program led by one of the authors (A.M.R.). The course was attended by 10 graduate psychology students with no prior clinical experience and no in-depth knowledge of psychodynamic psychology. Their academic background included only one course in dynamic psychology and one in psychodynamically oriented clinical psychology. The program in which they were enrolled primarily focused on cognitive psychology, with a strong emphasis on cognitive development.

Students received academic credit for completing the course, which included a final assessment to certify their eligibility for credit. The course consisted of five sessions, each lasting four hours. Beginning with the second session, the final hour of each class was devoted to an individual exercise. During the subsequent session, these exercises were reviewed, questions and concerns were addressed by the instructor, and the class collectively coded a new Rorschach protocol according to the CRDS. A new individual exercise was then assigned.

This structured approach provided a framework for systematically evaluating the progression of coding skills and the role of training in achieving inter-rater reliability.

Over the course of the training, students completed a total of four exercises. The first exercise (T1) was conducted after seven hours of instruction, during which they received a brief overview of the Rorschach and a detailed explanation of the CRDS coding system. The second exercise (T2) was administered after an additional four hours of practice, the third (T3) after another four hours, and the final exercise (T4) following a total of 19 hours of training. This training included seven hours of lectures, three hours of individual exercises, six hours of group exercises, and three hours dedicated to reviewing and correcting individual exercises.

The final exercise also served as the course's concluding assessment, which students were required to pass in order to earn academic credit. All four exercises were designed to be of equal complexity. Each involved coding 45 Rorschach responses, which included three responses representing each type of defense and three responses that did not reflect the use of any defense mechanism.

Results

Errors made in the first (T1) and final (T4) exercises were analyzed qualitatively and categorized into three types: confusion errors, where the student coded the wrong defense; commission errors, where the student erroneously assigned one or more defenses to a response that did not involve any defense; and omission errors, where the student failed to identify one or more defenses evident in the response. Confusion errors decreased from 43 in the first exercise to 10 in the final exercise, commission errors dropped from 13 to 5, and omission errors fell from 31 to 3.

An analysis of errors in the final exercise showed that most were associated with Omnipotent Denial (OD). Specifically, OD was confused with mature denial (HLD) in five cases and with Level 2 Idealization (ID2) in three cases.

The percentage of correct responses showed progressive improvement across the training sessions. At T1, the mean accuracy was 80.3% (range: 76%–91%); at T2, it was 79.4% (range: 67%–91%). At T3, accuracy increased to 84% (range: 71%–94%), and by T4, it reached 95% (range: 87%–100%). These results highlight a steady improvement in coding proficiency, culminating in near-perfect performance by the final exercise.

Since the T1 variable did not follow a normal distribution, nonparametric methods were used for the analyses. A nonparametric Friedman test was conducted to examine differences among repeated measures. When the Friedman test revealed significant results, post hoc analyses were performed using the Wilcoxon signed-rank test. Effect sizes (r) were calculated by dividing the test statistic (Z) by the square root of the number of cases, following Rosenthal's (1994) method, and interpreted according to Cohen's (1988) guidelines: small ($0.1 \leq r < 0.3$), medium ($0.3 \leq r < 0.5$), and large ($r > 0.5$).

No significant difference was found in the percentage of correct responses between T1 and T2. However, a large effect size was observed for the improvement from T2 to T3 ($r = .58$) and from T3 to T4 ($r = .85$).

Additionally, the level of agreement between each participant and the course instructor was calculated for each of the four assessments using Cohen's kappa (κ). Agreement ranged from .81 to .91 at T1, .74 to .95 at T2, . 86 to .98 at T3, and .88 to 1.00 at T4, indicating progressively higher levels of inter-rater reliability as training progressed.

Discussion

The results indicate that a relatively small amount of training is sufficient to achieve a satisfactory level of reliability in coding the system. Notably, even after only seven hours of training, all students reached a substantial level of agreement with the instructor during the first exercise. This agreement improved further, reaching near-perfect levels by the final assessment after 19 hours of training.

While no precise data are available regarding the amount of time each student spent independently studying the coding system, it is plausible that the significant improvement between the penultimate and final exercises may also be attributed to increased motivation. Given that the final exercise served as the evaluation required for academic credit, students were likely particularly driven to perform well and may have dedicated additional time to individual study.

Nevertheless, the fact that all students achieved reliable coding after the first exercise is a highly encouraging outcome. This finding suggests that the system is accessible even to psychologists without prior training in psychodynamic theory or clinical experience. It provides strong evidence for the system's usability and its potential for broader application across diverse professional contexts.

However, it remains uncertain whether these somewhat surprising results may, at least in part, be attributable to the fact that the instructor was one of the authors of the CRDS and therefore particularly adept at conveying the coding system. Further studies are necessary to examine the replicability of these findings under different teaching conditions.

The analysis of errors made in the final exercise, although limited in number, highlights the importance of dedicating particular attention during both teaching and learning to clearly distinguishing among mature denial, omnipotent denial, and idealization.

In this regard, it may be helpful to closely examine the specific responses that were erroneously coded. These included: "Minnie and Mickey Mouse kissing," "Chip and Dale from the cartoons arguing and chasing each other," "What a nice conclusion! The red part that seemed like blood is actually a streamer!" and "It looks like the Rockefeller Center Christmas tree—I think it's the most beautiful Christmas tree in the world!"

The first two responses indicate the use of mature denial, defined as "a defense mechanism by which an individual denies, minimizes, or reduces the intensity of painful feelings, ideas, or sources of conflict, without compromising reality testing." These responses meet Criterion D: "Humor or reference to cartoons is used to reduce or neutralize threatening drive-laden material. Responses must have libidinal or aggressive content/themes, good Form Quality (o or u), and an absence of Critical Special Scores."

It is crucial not to confuse these with omnipotent denial, defined as "a manic-type defense mechanism in which an individual denies painful emotions or realities, maintaining a euphoric or excessively positive attitude to avoid discomfort and confrontation with painful emotional experiences." Omnipotent denial is coded according to Criterion C: "Figures or animals described in ways that imply an incongruous combination (INC or FAB). This kind of response conveys a particular kind of denial in that it makes real what would be plausible in fairy tales or cartoons."

The third response reflects the use of omnipotent denial, as defined by Criterion F: "Forced recourse to optimism ('happy end style') is evident in confabulatory responses or in deviant responses."

The fourth response, on the other hand, indicates the use of idealization, defined as "a defense mechanism through which an individual attributes extremely positive qualities to themselves and/or others in order to avoid contact with painful emotional experiences of inadequacy and/or ambivalence."

From a Kleinian theoretical perspective (Klein, 1946), both idealization and omnipotent denial are considered manic defenses, which may lead to confusion between the two. However, a careful reading of the CRDS coding manual should help prevent such misclassifications, as the distinctions between these mechanisms are clearly outlined.

This study highlights the need to further investigate how specific challenges in distinguishing among related defense mechanisms may reflect broader complexities in the theoretical constructs underlying the coding system. These findings raise important questions about the interpretive demands placed on coders and the extent to which such challenges might influence the reliability and utility of the system in both research and clinical practice.

Study 2: Concurrent validity

The evolution of diagnostic frameworks in mental health has long been a topic of critical discussion among clinicians and researchers. Over time, significant strides have been made in standardizing diagnostic criteria, with tools such as the *Diagnostic and Statistical Manual of Mental Disorders* (DSM) playing a pivotal role in shaping clinical practice and research. However, despite its utility, the DSM has faced persistent criticism for its inability to fully capture the complexity of psychological functioning.

Although the DSM-IV included a Defensive Functioning Scale (DFS) within its multiaxial framework—a noteworthy attempt to incorporate psychodynamic principles—it offered only limited integration of psychoanalytic concepts. The DFS categorized defense mechanisms into a hierarchy ranging from mature to immature, providing a means to assess how individuals navigate internal conflicts and external stressors. However, its application was hindered by a lack of empirical validation and the subjective nature of assessing defenses, limiting its clinical utility. When the DSM-5 was published in 2013, it eliminated the multiaxial system, including the DFS, as part of an effort to streamline the diagnostic framework and enhance its empirical foundation.

In response to the DSM's limitations, psychoanalysts and psychodynamic researchers sought to create a diagnostic framework that would better address the complexities of human psychological functioning. This effort culminated in the publication of the *Psychodynamic Diagnostic Manual* (PDM) in 2006. Unlike the symptom-focused, categorical approach of the DSM, the PDM introduced a dimensional, person-centered framework that captured the richness of personality organization, mental functioning, and subjective experience.

Developed collaboratively by leading psychoanalytic organizations, including the International Psychoanalytical Association and the American Psychoanalytic Association, the PDM aimed to provide a psychodynamically informed understanding of mental health. Drawing particularly on Otto Kernberg's structural model of personality organization (Kernberg, 1975, 1984), it sought to bridge psychodynamic theory and clinical practice while offering a triaxial structured framework that includes personality patterns (Axis P), profiles of mental functioning (Axis M), and symptomatic expressions and subjective experience (Axis S).

Defense mechanisms are pivotal to understanding psychological functioning within both the P and M Axes, as they provide crucial insights into personality structure and mental capacities. In the P Axis, defenses are evaluated as integral components of personality organization, with an emphasis on identifying the predominant mechanisms employed by the individual and assessing their level of maturity. This evaluation considers how these defenses shape self-perception and influence interpersonal relationships, highlighting their role in maintaining or disrupting adaptive functioning.

In the M Axis, defensive functioning is examined in the context of specific mental capacities, such as emotional regulation and impulse control, offering a more nuanced perspective on how defenses facilitate or hinder psychological resilience. By linking defenses to both personality structure and core mental processes, the PDM allows for a dynamic and comprehensive understanding of their impact on overall psychological functioning.

The second edition of the PDM (*PDM-2*; Lingiardi & McWilliams, 2017) addressed feedback from the first edition, incorporated advances in research and clinical practice, and made the system more empirically grounded, while retaining the core principles of the original manual.

To operationalize the diagnostic framework outlined in the PDM-2, the *Psychodiagnostic Chart-2* (PDC-2; Gordon & Bornstein, 2015, 2018) was developed and included as an appendix in the manual. The PDC-2 is a clinician-rated tool designed to assess key domains of psychological functioning identified by the PDM-2, including personality organization, mental capacities, and symptom patterns. By providing a structured and accessible method for applying psychodynamic criteria, the PDC-2 bridges the gap between the manual's theoretical constructs and their practical application in clinical assessment, enhancing its utility in both research and practice.

This study aims to assess the concurrent validity of the CRDS by examining its correlation with the PDC-2. Specifically, it seeks to determine the extent to which the CRDS, as a psychodynamic tool for evaluating defense mechanisms, aligns with the PDC-2's dimensional framework for assessing personality organization and mental functioning.

Method

Participants

Eighty clinical subjects participated in this study. They were self-referred outpatients who underwent psychological assessment prior to initiating psychotherapy at a private clinical psychology service in northern Italy between 2017 and 2019. The sample included 37 females and 43 males, with ages ranging from 18 to 65 years (M = 39.43, SD = 9.06). Educational backgrounds varied from 8 to 23 years (M = 13.90, SD = 4.05).

Each participant was diagnosed according to the *Psychodynamic Diagnostic Manual-2* (PDM-2). Specifically, 40 subjects were classified as having a neurotic level of personality organization (NL), while the remaining 40 were diagnosed with borderline personality organization (BL). Following intake interviews and psychological assessments, all participants were evaluated using the PDC-2 (Gordon & Bornstein, 2015, 2018) on both the P Axis and M Axis.

Participants in the Neurotic Level group received P Axis scores ranging from 6 to 8 (M = 6.48, SD = 0.64) and M Axis scores ranging from 46 to 54 (M = 49.05, SD = 2.56). Those in the Borderline Level group had P Axis scores ranging from 3 to 5 (M = 4.23, SD = 0.66) and M Axis scores ranging from 31 to 46 (M = 38.25, SD = 4.59).

Measures

RORSCHACH TEST

The Rorschach test was administered following the guidelines of the Comprehensive System (Exner, 2003). The collected protocols were subsequently coded according to the CRDS. Scores for each defense were then converted into percentages, using the total number of protocol responses as the denominator.

PSYCHODIAGNOSTIC CHART-2

The study specifically utilized Sections I and III of the PDC-2, which correspond to the assessment of personality organization (P Axis) and mental functioning (M Axis), respectively.

Section I evaluates the subject's level of personality organization on a 10-point scale, contributing to the global P Axis score. This score reflects critical dimensions such as identity (the ability to perceive and understand oneself accurately and deeply), object relations (the capacity to form and sustain stable and satisfying relationships), defensive style (ranging from primitive to mature defenses), and reality testing. Scores are categorized as follows: 1–2 (Psychotic), 3–5 (Borderline), 6–8 (Neurotic), and 9–10 (Healthy).

Section III focuses on 12 domains of mental functioning, assessed through a series of 5-point ratings, culminating in a global M Axis score ranging from 5 to 60. These scores classify mental functioning into levels of impairment or health: healthy/optimal (54–60), good/adequate (47–53), mild impairment (40–46), moderate impairment (33–39), and significant/severe limitations (12–18). The domains assessed include cognitive and affective regulation, identity integration, relational capacity, defensive mechanisms, and self-directedness, offering a comprehensive assessment of the subject's psychological strengths and vulnerabilities.

Recent research (Gordon & Bornstein, 2018; Hinrichs et al., 2019) has supported the psychometric validity of the PDC-2, highlighting its strong internal consistency, inter-rater reliability, retest reliability, and convergent validity. Specifically, inter-rater agreement was reported as .76 for Section I and .85 for Section III (Gordon & Bornstein, 2018), underscoring the robustness of the PDC-2 as a tool for psychodynamic assessment.

Procedure

Rorschach protocols, derived from archival datasets and administered by licensed psychologists trained in Rorschach methodology, were analyzed for this study. All protocols were independently examined by both authors, with one author blinded to the participants' clinical group assignments. The PDC-2 was completed during the consultation process by the psychotherapists, each of whom had conducted at least four sessions with the respective patient.

Each participant had provided written informed consent for their anonymized protocols to be used in future research. The study received approval from the Institutional Review Board of the Italian Psychoanalytical Society (IRB approval 01/22/2023) and was conducted in accordance with the Ethical Principles of Psychologists and Code of Conduct of the American Psychological Association, as well as the principles outlined in the Declaration of Helsinki.

Results

Preliminary analyses

No significant differences were found between the two clinical groups regarding gender ($\chi^2 = .50$, $p = .50$), age ($t = .386$, $p = .714$), and the number of Rorschach responses (R) ($t = -1.045$, $p = .299$). However, individuals organized at a borderline level exhibited lower levels of education ($t = 4.341$, $p < .0001$). Consistently, education showed a significant positive correlation with both Axis P ($r = .509$, $p < .0001$) and Axis M ($r = .531$, $p < .0001$).

CRDS variables were not normally distributed, as skewness and kurtosis values fell outside the accepted range of ±2 (George & Mallery, 2010), rendering them unsuitable for parametric procedures. The Mann–Whitney U test revealed significant gender-related effects for Intellectualization ($z = -2.010$, $p = .044$), Omnipotent Control ($z = -2.127$, $p = .033$), and Omnipotent Denial ($z = -1.990$, $p = .047$), with males exhibiting higher levels on all three variables.

Spearman correlation analyses between age, education, and CRDS scores revealed that Intellectualization and Omnipotent Control correlated positively with age ($r = .220$, $p = .049$; and $r = .318$, $p = .004$, respectively). Additionally, Intellectualization and Psychotic Denial were significantly correlated with education, the former positively and the latter negatively ($r = .409$, $p < .0001$; and $r = -.338$, $p = .002$, respectively). This finding is not unexpected, considering that educational attainment is associated with higher levels of psychological functioning. Given that the majority of participants had earned a university degree, it is reasonable to assume that their higher cognitive functioning contributed to their ability to pursue advanced levels of education.

Inter-rater reliability

Regarding the CRDS, inter-rater reliability was found to be almost perfect (Cohen's $\kappa = .88$).

Comparison between clinical groups

The Mann–Whitney U test comparing the two clinical groups revealed that the Neurotic Level group scored higher than the Borderline Level group on Rationalization, Idealization Level 1, and the total number of mature defenses (small effect sizes). In contrast, the Borderline Level group exhibited higher scores on High-Level Denial, Idealization Level 2, and Omnipotent Control (small effect sizes); Omnipotent Denial and the total number of defenses (medium effect sizes); Devaluation Level 2 (large effect size); and Projective Identification and Psychotic Denial (very large effect sizes). Table 10.1 presents the descriptive statistics and a summary of these results.

Correlations between CRDS scores and PDC-2 scores

Spearman correlation analyses between CRDS scores and PDC-2 scores revealed weak but significant correlations between the P Axis score and

Table 10.1 Descriptive statistics and comparisons between neurotic and borderline groups

| Variable | NL = 40 | | BL = 40 | | Z | p | d |
	M	SD	M	SD			
HLD	0.35	0.70	0.53	0.64	−1.627	.104	−0.27
INT	1.65	2.34	1.28	1.48	−.761	.447	0.19
ISO	1.42	1.63	1.35	1.29	−.158	.874	0.05
RAT	0.45	0.74	0.23	0.57	−1.754	.079	0.34
REP	0.48	0.85	0.40	0.74	−.235	.814	0.10
ID1	3.25	2.38	2.20	1.90	−2.500	.012	0.49
Mature D	9.03	5.14	6.73	4.13	−.1953	.051	0.50
ID2	0.57	0.90	0.97	1.47	−.550	.583	−0.34
DEV1	1.23	1.12	1.53	1.58	−.015	.888	−0.22
DEV2	0.80	1.96	2.93	2.30	−5.352	<.0001	−1.03
OMNI	0.05	0.22	0.28	1.20	−.505	.614	−0.32
SPL	0.58	1.72	1.30	1.41	−3.539	<.0001	−0.26
PROJ	0.60	1.03	3.27	3.24	−4.817	<.0001	−1.30
OD	0.85	1.07	1.70	2.00	−1.616	.100	−0.55
PD	0.25	0.94	1.85	1.93	−4.833	<.0001	−1.27
Defenses T	13.95	7.09	20.55	9.72	−3.248	.001	−0.79

Notes: NL = Neurotic Level Personality Organization group; BL = Borderline Level Personality Organization group; M = mean; SD = standard deviation; Z = z-statistic; p = p-value; d = Cohen's measure of effect size ($|d|$ < 0.20: negligible; $0.20 ≤ |d|$ < 0.50: small; $0.50 ≤ |d|$ < 0.80: moderate; $|d| ≥ 0.80$: large); HLD = High-Level Denial; INT = Intellectualization; ISO = Isolation; RAT = Rationalization; REP = Repression; ID1 = Idealization Level 1; Mature D = total number of HLD, INT, ISO, RAT, REP, and ID1; ID2 = Idealization Level 2; DEV1 = Devaluation Level 1; DEV2 = Devaluation Level 2; OMNI = Omnipotent Control; SPL = Splitting; PROJ = Projective Identification; OD = Omnipotent Denial; PD = Psychotic Denial; Defense T = total number of scored responses for defenses.

both Idealization Level 1 (positive) and the total number of scored defenses (negative). Moderate negative correlations were observed between the P Axis score and Devaluation Level 2, Splitting, Projective Identification, and Psychotic Denial.

The M Axis score showed weak, positive, and significant correlations with Rationalization and Idealization, and weak, negative, and significant correlations with the total number of scored defenses. Additionally, it demonstrated moderate negative correlations with Splitting, Projective Identification, and Psychotic Denial, as well as a strong negative correlation with Devaluation Level 2. The results are summarized in Table 10.2.

Discussion

The results support the concurrent validity of the CRDS, particularly its ability to distinguish between individuals with neurotic-level personality organization and those with borderline-level personality organization. The total number of mature defenses—rather than individual mature

Table 10.2 Correlations between PDC-2 and CRDS scores

	P Axis	M Axis
HLD	−.158	−.173
INT	.070	.128
ISO	−.007	−.014
RAT	.181	.221*
REP	.068	.070
ID1	.266*	.240*
Mature D	.213	.180
ID2	−.104	−.054
DEV1	.021	−.018
DEV2	−.597***	−.600***
OMNI	−.050	.001
SPL	−.423***	−.440***
PROJ	−.520***	−.450***
OD	−.149	−.188
PD	−.561***	−.576***
Defense T	−.347**	−.331**

Notes: P Axis = Level of Personality Organization score on the Psychodiagnostic Chart-2; M Axis = Mental Functioning score on the Psychodiagnostic Chart-2; HLD = High-Level Denial; INT = Intellectualization; ISO = Isolation; RAT = Rationalization; REP = Repression; ID1 = Idealization Level 1; Mature D = total number of HLD, INT, ISO, RAT, REP, and ID1; ID2 = Idealization Level 2; DEV1 = Devaluation Level 1; DEV2 = Devaluation Level 2; OMNI = Omnipotent Control; SPL = Splitting; PROJ = Projective Identification; OD = Omnipotent Denial; PD = Psychotic Denial; Defense T = total number of scored responses for defenses.

$*: p < .05;$
$**: p < .01;$
$***: p < .001.$

defenses—was found to effectively discriminate between the two groups. In contrast, all primitive defenses demonstrated discriminatory power, even when considered individually. Notably, Level 2 Devaluation, Projective Identification, and Psychotic Denial emerged as the most significant contributors to this differentiation, showing the largest effect sizes.

It should also be noted that the BL group resorted more frequently to the use of defenses in their responses to the Rorschach. This finding, which will be discussed further, suggests that the emotional stimulation induced by the Rorschach cards generates greater distress in these individuals, leading to more frequent activation of defensive processes.

When comparing the results of this study with two previous studies (Rosso et al., 2021; Rosso et al., submitted) that examined the concurrent validity of the LDS and the RDS on the same clinical samples, it becomes evident that the CRDS is significantly more effective than the other two systems in discriminating between the neurotic and borderline groups.

Regarding the LDS, only Devaluation and Projective Identification defenses were found to be higher in the borderline group, with small and moderate effect sizes, respectively, whereas Idealization, Denial, and Splitting were unable to discriminate between the two clinical groups (Rosso et al., 2021). Similarly, the RDS showed no concurrent validity for Idealization defenses (Rosso et al., submitted). The hypothesis that this limitation was due to the need to distinguish between mature and primitive forms of Idealization is thus supported by the present findings: Level 1 Idealization was significantly higher in the neurotic personality organization group, whereas primitive Idealization was more frequently employed by individuals with borderline personality organization.

Projective Identification, Hypomanic Denial, and Massive Denial, as coded by the RDS, were able to discriminate between the two groups, but with effect sizes smaller than those found in the present study ($d = 0.92$ vs. 1.30; 0.34 vs. 0.55; and 0.92 vs. 1.27, respectively).

Important differences between the two studies also emerge regarding the discriminant power of Repression. When Repression was coded according to RDS criteria, a significant difference was found between the two clinical groups (Rosso et al., submitted). However, when coded according to CRDS criteria, no significant difference emerged.

As highlighted in the previous chapter, the CRDS differs considerably from the RDS in terms of the coding criteria for Repression. According to the CRDS, only responses that display overly dramatized emotional reactions or extreme vagueness are coded as indicative of Repression. In our view, this type of response may reflect an attempt to defend against contact with distressing internal representations.

Consequently, many responses that would have been coded as Repression under the RDS criteria—such as simple responses like "a butterfly" or "a woman"—were excluded in our system. Although such responses may occasionally signal Repression, they may also reflect the absence of defensive activity, limited engagement with the test, or an ideational-affective impoverishment of a different nature, as observed in conditions such as severe alexithymia or depressive psychopathological states. As a result, many responses that would have been categorized as Repression using the RDS criteria were not coded as such in the CRDS.

For these reasons, the CRDS includes an additional variable indicating the percentage of responses coded as defenses, calculated using the total number of Rorschach responses as the denominator. As shown in Table 10.1, subjects with a neurotic personality organization exhibited a higher frequency of uncoded responses, with a large effect size.

It is possible, and perhaps even probable, that this finding reflects a more frequent use of Repression; however, only a careful qualitative assessment of each protocol can confirm this interpretation. Protocols with a low number of coded defenses should be evaluated with particular attention. In such cases, we recommend the combined use of the CRDS and the Reality–Fantasy Scale Version 2 (RFS-2; Tibon-Czopp, 2022), which assesses an individual's capacity to enrich thought with imaginative activity while maintaining adherence to reality.

Following Winnicott's (1971) theoretical perspective, the RFS-2 evaluates the ability to access the transitional space of experience. As Chabert (1987) noted, the Rorschach can be understood as a test of mental functioning, requiring the subject to achieve a compromise between the imaginary and reality.

The Rorschach administration instruction—"I'm going to show you a series of inkblots and ask you what they might be"—asks the individual to draw upon their inner world to produce an interpretation that still respects the perceptual reality of the blot. Those who succeed in this compromise demonstrate the capacity to use imagination in a balanced way while maintaining a realistic perception of external reality. In these cases, contact with one's inner world enriches psychological functioning, leading to imaginative activity that remains anchored to reality.

In contrast, some records are poor, characterized by dry, rigid thinking anchored to what is immediately obvious. This type of thinking corresponds to what Marty & de M'Uzan (2010) described as *pensée opératoire* ("operational thinking"), revealing a failure of preconscious processes and the rigidity of mental activity focused solely on facts.

The RFS-2 thus serves to assess the capacity to maintain a transitional space and allows clinicians to distinguish between protocols characterized by a low number of coded defenses due to impoverished psychological functioning (e.g., alexithymic conditions) and those that reflect mature psychological functioning characterized by an adaptive use of Repression.

Study 3: Convergent validity

The *Defense Mechanism Rating Scales* (DMRS; Perry, 1990) and its subsequent Q-sort version (*DMRS-Q*; Di Giuseppe, Perry, Petraglia, et al., 2014) are currently considered the gold standard for the empirical measurement of defense mechanisms (Lingiardi & McWilliams, 2017). In Chapter 7, we described these two instruments in detail and reviewed the empirical research on defense mechanisms conducted since their development.

In the present study, we investigated the convergent validity of the CRDS by asking the therapists of 20 patients included in the clinical groups considered in Study 2—10 with neurotic-level personality organization and 10 with borderline-level personality organization—to complete the DMRS-Q in order to calculate the correlations between the scores obtained from the two instruments.

Method

Participants

The twenty patients were randomly selected, with 10 drawn from the neurotic personality organization group and 10 from the borderline personality organization group. The sample included 11 males and 9 females, ranging in age from 17 to 58 years (M = 36.85, SD = 11.74), with educational backgrounds ranging from 8 to 23 years (M = 14.45, SD = 4.20).

Participants in the neurotic-level group received P Axis scores ranging from 6 to 8 (M = 6.50, SD = 0.71) and M Axis scores ranging from 47 to 54 (M = 49.20, SD = 2.62). Those in the borderline-level group had P Axis scores ranging from 3 to 5 (M = 4.50, SD = 0.70) and M Axis scores ranging from 33 to 46 (M = 40.60, SD = 3.78).

Measures

The *DMRS-Q* is the Q-sort version of the DMRS. It consists of 150 items, with five items corresponding to each of the 30 defenses identified according to the Hierarchical Theory of Defense Mechanisms. This theory organizes defenses into seven levels, which are further grouped into three broad categories: immature, neurotic, and mature defenses.

The immature defense category includes acting out, help-rejecting complaining, passive aggression, splitting of the self-image, splitting of the image of others, denial, rationalization, autistic fantasy, omnipotence, and idealization of the self-image and the image of others.

The neurotic defense category includes affect isolation, intellectualization, undoing, repression, dissociation, reaction formation, and repression.

The mature defense category encompasses positive coping strategies such as affiliation, altruism, anticipation, humor, assertiveness, self-observation, sublimation, and repression.

For a more detailed description of the DMRS-Q and its theoretical foundations, see Chapter 7.

Procedure

The therapists of the 20 patients, who were unaware of the CRDS coding results, were asked to complete the DMRS-Q using the coding procedure available through the online platform at https://webapp.dmrs-q.com, which calculates three core scores: individual defense mechanism scores, scores for each hierarchical defense level, and the overall defensive functioning (ODF) score.

Following the instructions provided in the manual (Di Giuseppe & Perry, 2021), scores were calculated for immature, neurotic, and mature defense levels. These three scores were used in the data analyses alongside the ODF score.

Defenses coded according to CRDS criteria were simultaneously categorized into two groups: neurotic defenses and primitive defenses. In accordance with the psychoanalytic theory that informed the development of the CRDS, the first group included Repression, Intellectualization, Isolation, High-Level Denial, Rationalization, and Level 1 Idealization, whereas the second group included Level 2 Idealization, Level 1 Devaluation, Level 2

Devaluation, Omnipotent Control, Splitting, Projective Identification, Omnipotent Denial, and Psychotic Denial.

As in the previous study, the variable relating to the number of protocol responses that did not receive a defense coding was also included. For each CRDS variable, the percentage of coded responses was calculated based on the total number of responses provided across the entire Rorschach protocol.

Results

Because both CRDS and DMRS-Q variables were normally distributed, with skewness and kurtosis values within the accepted range of ±2 (George & Mallery, 2010), they were suitable for parametric procedures; therefore, Pearson's correlation analyses were conducted.

No significant differences were found between females and males on the variables of interest (*ps* ranged from .126 to .981), and no significant correlations were found between DMRS-Q and CRDS scores and either age or education (*ps* ranged from .137 to .944 for age and from .081 to .944 for education).

ODF scores and mature defenses coded on the DMRS-Q correlated strongly and positively with the number of responses that received no defense code on the CRDS, and strongly and negatively with primitive defenses coded on the CRDS. Neurotic defenses coded on the DMRS-Q correlated significantly with neurotic defenses coded on the CRDS. Immature defenses coded on the DMRS-Q correlated strongly and positively with primitive defenses coded on the CRDS, while a significant negative correlation was found with the number of responses that did not receive a defense code on the CRDS.

The results are summarized in Table 10.3.

Table 10.3 Correlations between DMRS-Q and CRDS scores

	1	2	3	4	5	6	7
1. Mature Defenses DMRS-Q	–						
2. Neurotic Defenses DMRS-Q	.050	–					
3. Immature Defenses DMRS-Q	−.964***	−.295	–				
4. ODF	.972***	.242	−.988***	–			
5. Neurotic Defenses CRDS	−.014	.503*	−.129	.115	–		
6. Primitive Defenses CRDS	−.685**	−.101	.705**	−.686**	−.279	–	
7. No Coded Defenses CRDS	.606**	−.121	−.567**	.569**	−.234	−.805***	–

* : $p < .05$;
** : $p < .01$;
*** : $p < .001$.

Discussion

The results strongly support the convergent validity of the CRDS. Although the DMRS-Q and the CRDS were developed from different theoretical frameworks and include different sets of defenses, the levels of correlation observed are more than satisfactory. In particular, the strong correlation ($r = .705$) between the scores for immature/primitive defenses assessed by the two instruments is noteworthy. The correlation between the scores for neurotic defenses measured by the two instruments was also moderate and significant.

The slightly lower correlation for neurotic defenses, although still significant, is likely due to definitional differences between the systems: the DMRS-Q classifies Rationalization and Denial among immature defenses, whereas the CRDS, in accordance with psychoanalytic theory, categorizes both Rationalization and High-Level Denial among neurotic defenses.

It should also be noted that, as in Study 2, the number of Rorschach responses that did not receive a defense coding correlated positively and significantly with both the category of mature defenses on the DMRS-Q and the ODF scores. This finding seems to support previously formulated hypotheses suggesting that individuals with more mature psychological functioning experience less distress in response to the emotional stimuli elicited by the Rorschach, and therefore use fewer defenses and/or that the absence of coded defensive responses may reflect the adaptive use of Repression.

Although the results of the present study are particularly promising, the small sample size warrants caution in interpretation and highlights the need for further research on the convergent validity of the CRDS.

Study 4: Divergent validity

The relationship between defense mechanisms and intelligence has been investigated in only a few studies, which have yielded mixed results (Pievsky et al., 2016). One study (Haan, 1963) reported that the use of defenses such as displacement, isolation, denial, and repression was associated with a decrease in IQ, whereas Vaillant (1993) found no relationship between intelligence and the maturity level of defenses. As Pievsky and colleagues noted, Cramer has conducted the most extensive research on this topic, using the Defense Mechanism Manual (DMM; Cramer, 1991) to assess the defense mechanisms of denial, projection, and identification. Cramer found that intelligence did not affect defense mechanisms during childhood, adolescence, or emerging adulthood (Cramer, 1999, 2008, 2009), whereas among adults, denial and projection were positively associated with intelligence, and the Vocabulary subtest of the WAIS-R was positively related to identification (Cramer, 2003, 2004).

One of the most recent studies was conducted by Pievsky and colleagues (2016), who examined the relationship between defense mechanisms and intelligence using the Wechsler Adult Intelligence Scale (WAIS) and the Defense Style Questionnaire (DSQ-40; Andrews, Singh, & Bond, 1993). They found a positive association between Full-Scale IQ and the use of mature defenses, while no significant relationship emerged between FSIQ and the use of immature or neurotic defenses.

In contrast, a few years later, Stenius et al. (2021), using the same measures for both defenses and intelligence, did not find any significant relationships.

Given these findings from the literature review, we investigated the divergent validity of the CRDS by examining its correlations with a measure of intelligence.

Method

Participants

Data were collected from 60 volunteer participants drawn from a nonclinical community sample. Participants ranged in age from 18 to 62 years (M = 29.55, SD = 11.09); 25 were male (41.7%). The mean number of years of education was 14.83 (SD = 2.29; range = 8–21).

Measures

RORSCHACH TEST

The Rorschach test was administered in accordance with the guidelines of the Comprehensive System (Exner, 2003). The collected protocols were subsequently coded using the CRDS. Scores for each defense were then converted into percentages, using the total number of responses in the protocol as the denominator.

STANDARD PROGRESSIVE MATRICES

The Raven's Standard Progressive Matrices (SPM; Raven, 1938), generally considered a measure of general cognitive ability, is designed to assess an individual's capacity to identify perceptual patterns and solve problems through analogical reasoning, without relying on language skills or formal education. It consists of five series, each containing 12 items that progressively increase in complexity, requiring increasingly higher levels of cognitive processing to interpret and solve visual information. The SPM's psychometric properties are well documented, demonstrating high reliability and validity as a measure of nonverbal and fluid intelligence (Raven, Raven, & Court, 1998). The

Italian version of the Raven's SPM (Busdraghi, Mandolesi, Sutera, & Vezzani, 2024) was administered. Raw scores were obtained and subsequently converted into percentiles using age-based normative tables. The resulting percentile values were then used in the data analyses.

Procedure

All participants were recruited by graduate students from among their acquaintances using a solicitation letter (available upon request) written by the first author. The letter, which also served as an informed consent form, made it clear that no feedback regarding individual results would be provided and identified the project as a study investigating the psychometric properties of a new psychological scale. In accordance with the procedures described in the letter, participants who signed the informed consent form were subsequently contacted by other graduate students—previously extensively trained in Rorschach administration—who were not personally acquainted with them, in order to schedule an appointment. Data were collected anonymously; each participant was assigned an identification number, and no compensation was provided.

Both authors independently coded the Rorschach protocols according to the CRDS, and inter-rater reliability was subsequently calculated. In cases of disagreement, a consensus was reached.

Results

Preliminary Analyses

CRDS variables were not normally distributed, as skewness and kurtosis values fell outside the accepted range of ±2 (George & Mallery, 2010), rendering them unsuitable for parametric procedures.

No significant differences were found between females and males on the variables of interest (ps ranging from .107 to .994). Neither age nor education was significantly correlated with CRDS scores or SPM percentile values (rs ranging from −.204 to .228, and from −.171 to .228, respectively).

Inter-Rater Reliability

Regarding the CRDS, inter-rater reliability was found to be almost perfect (Cohen's κ = .86).

Correlations between SPM and CRDS scores

No significant correlations were found between SPM and CRDS scores (ρs ranging from −.160 to .172).

Discussion

The findings provide substantial support for the discriminant validity of the CRDS. No significant correlations emerged between any of the defense mechanisms assessed by the CRDS and the scores on the Raven's SPM.

This lack of association suggests that the CRDS measures constructs that are distinct from general cognitive ability, as assessed through nonverbal, fluid intelligence tasks. This outcome aligns with the theoretical expectation that defense mechanisms represent unconscious psychological processes, which are not directly influenced by levels of cognitive functioning. These results are relevant given previous mixed findings in the literature regarding the relationship between intelligence and defense mechanisms.

Nonetheless, an important limitation should be acknowledged. The use of a nonclinical, community-based sample may limit the generalizability of the findings to clinical populations, where defensive functioning may manifest differently.

11 Exploring psychic functioning through the Comprehensive Rorschach Defense System

A case study

Anna Maria Rosso

Introduction

This chapter presents a Rorschach protocol with the aim of illustrating how the Comprehensive Rorschach Defense System (CRDS; Gacono & Rosso, this volume, Chapter 9), used in conjunction with the Rorschach Comprehensive System, can offer a nuanced understanding of psychic functioning. The integration of these tools makes it possible to move beyond diagnostic classification as defined by DSM-5-TR criteria (APA, 2022) and to deepen psychodynamic diagnostic formulation in accordance with the Psychodynamic Diagnostic Manual-2 (PDM-2; Lingiardi & McWilliams, 2017).

The PDM-2 represents the most recent and comprehensive effort to conceptualize and classify psychopathology within a psychodynamic framework. It adopts a multidimensional diagnostic approach structured around three axes: the P Axis, which assesses the level of personality organization and identifies personality syndromes; the M Axis, which provides a detailed evaluation of mental functioning; and the S Axis, which addresses symptom patterns with particular attention to the patient's subjective experience.

The P Axis, which largely echoes Kernberg's (1975) conceptualization, includes (a) the assessment of the level of personality organization—neurotic, borderline, or psychotic—based on the ability to see oneself in a complex, stable, and accurate manner (identity), the ability to maintain intimate, stable, and satisfying relationships (object relations), the level of defensive functioning, and the capacity to understand conventional notions of reality (reality testing); and (b) the identification of personality syndromes, defined by constitutional–maturational patterns that may contribute to the disorder, central preoccupations and affects, pathogenic beliefs about self and others, and predominant defensive mechanisms.

The M Axis refers to 12 mental functions that include affective and cognitive processes (e.g., emotion regulation, attention and learning, capacity to experience, communicate, and understand affect, mentalization, and reflective functioning); identity and relationships (e.g., differentiation and integration, capacity for intimacy, regulation of self-esteem, and internal

DOI: 10.4324/9781003536994-14

experience); defense and coping (e.g., impulse control, defensive function-ing, adaptive capacity, resilience, and psychological resources); and self-awareness and self-direction (e.g., psychological mindedness, capacity to construct and adhere to standards and ideals, and a sense of meaning and purpose).

The PDM-2 was developed by psychoanalysts who recognized not only the value but also the pressing necessity, of empirical research to ensure the survival and continued development of psychoanalysis. This move-ment toward empirical validation has required a significant investment in efforts to operationalize psychoanalytic constructs and to develop assess-ment tools.

The Rorschach test, when interpreted according to the guidelines of the Comprehensive System, can significantly contribute to supporting diag-nostic hypotheses formulated within the framework of the PDM-2. How-ever, it does not offer sufficiently specific information regarding defensive functioning—an area of crucial importance for understanding the nature of a patient's anxieties, as well as their capacity to tolerate emotional ex-perience and to maintain contact with their internal world. The CRDS was developed precisely to address this gap.

Anthony: when riding a Harley can't even be imagined

A clinical vignette on narcissistic fragility, defensive passivity, and the denial of aggression

Anthony, a 35-year-old man, was assessed in the context of a court-man-dated child custody evaluation. Eight years before the evaluation, he had a son, Thomas, with Angela. Both described their relationship as intense and troubled. Although the pregnancy had not been planned, Angela wel-comed it with enthusiasm, and Anthony accepted it positively, feeling very close to her despite their having dated for only a few months.

The relationship quickly deteriorated, and when Thomas was one year old, Angela left Anthony and moved to another city. Anthony, in turn, moved back in with his mother. Angela described him as emotionally and physically unavailable, immature, lacking initiative, prone to outbursts of anger, and generally irresponsible as a parent. Anthony explained that his physical distance from his son and a delicate spinal surgery that required long rehabilitation prevented him from relocating and establishing a re-lationship with Thomas. Angela, who later remarried, regularly brought Thomas to visit his father, though only for a few hours. After recovering, Anthony visited Thomas every 10 to 15 days, usually during holidays at Angela's home.

After the breakup, Anthony returned to live with his widowed mother, who had raised him alone since his father died when Anthony was nine. He describes a routine life: working in a factory, spending time with friends at a neighborhood bar, and avoiding serious relationships until he met Christine, his current partner.

He reports no significant life events aside from his father's death. He never wanted to study, completed compulsory education at 14, and has worked in the same factory since age 17. He dislikes change, never moved out of his mother's home, and prefers familiar places and people who accept him. He reports low self-confidence in relationships, noting that Angela had shown the first interest in him. After that relationship ended, he remained single until Christine, who pursued him openly. Although he does not feel particularly attracted to her, he appreciates feeling loved and emotionally supported.

At Christine's urging, Anthony hired a lawyer to contest his current visitation rights. He stated:

> When Thomas was little, I was fine with seeing him together with his mother. I didn't know what to do alone with him. He seemed bored with me. I didn't know what to say or suggest. But now, with Christine, things are different. She's full of ideas and knows how to engage Thomas. We can take him to the mountains, to the beach, or the playground. Christine says I give up too easily, and that I shouldn't. She says they don't respect me and think I'm not capable of being a father.

Anthony has difficulty expressing emotional involvement; during the interviews, he appears mild and calm. Christine, by contrast, is emotionally intense and combative—she presents herself as deeply angry and appears to be waging a personal battle, immersing herself in Anthony's situation with passionate engagement.

Convinced that Anthony's rights as a father were being violated, Christine persuaded him to hire a lawyer known for his aggressive stance. The lawyer demanded that Thomas begin spending several days a week, alternating weekends, and part of the school holidays with his father—even in the mother's absence. Christine, an impulsive woman with limited awareness of Thomas's fears and needs, approached the matter as she did her political activism and labor struggles: as a fight. The defense of Anthony's paternal rights had become her personal cause, and Anthony, for his part, adhered to it rather passively.

Angela, meanwhile, remained openly resentful toward Anthony. Since the judge ordered a court-appointed evaluation, the conflict increasingly took the shape of a battle between the two women. Each, in different ways, expressed and acted out her bitterness. Anthony appeared to understand that his relationship with Thomas could not be rebuilt overnight, yet he did not shy away from supporting Christine's assertive efforts. Not surprisingly, the more Anthony and Christine insisted that Thomas see them, the more the child resisted—suffering visibly—and the more tensions escalated between all parties involved.

Diagnostic Hypotheses According to DSM-5-TR and PDM-2 Criteria

According to the DSM-5-TR descriptive diagnostic criteria (APA, 2022), a diagnostic hypothesis of Avoidant Personality Disorder (AvPD) can be formulated. Anthony avoids work activities that involve significant inter-personal contact due to fears of criticism, disapproval, or rejection; he is reluctant to engage in relationships unless certain of being liked; he is inhibited in new interpersonal situations and experiences pervasive feelings of inadequacy. He perceives himself as unattractive and inferior to others and is notably unwilling to take personal risks or engage in new activities.

From the perspective of the PDM-2 psychodynamic diagnostic framework, Anthony presents with a poorly defined sense of self and a limited capacity to establish and maintain intimate, stable, and fulfilling relationships, while reality testing appears to be relatively intact. He shows deficits in affect regulation and learning, in experiencing, expressing, and understanding emotions, and in mentalization. Self-directedness—defined as the ability to pursue personal goals—is severely impaired.

These features raise a differential diagnostic consideration between depressive personality pattern and the depressed/empty type of narcissistic personality pattern, presumably organized at a high borderline level. While diminished self-esteem, fear of rejection, and self-devaluation may suggest a depressive personality, the presence of humiliation, the absence of guilt and of genuine concern for relationships or loss more convincingly point toward a narcissistic personality pattern of the depressed/empty type.

The contribution of the Rorschach test—Comprehensive System

The Rorschach protocol, coded and interpreted according to the guidelines of the Comprehensive System (Exner, 2003), provides valuable insights into the psychodynamic structure of Anthony's psychological functioning. The results indicate that Anthony is markedly self-focused (EgoI = 0.61) and highly preoccupied with his own needs and sense of personal worth (Fr + rF = 1)—narcissistic features that contribute to a tendency to avoid responsibility, suffer intensely from failure or frustration, and avoid relationships unless they serve to affirm his self-image.

These narcissistic needs for validation appear largely unmet, as Anthony shows signs of painful, ruminative introspection focused on the unsatisfactory aspects of himself (FV = 1; FD = 1). It is likely that recent difficulties within the family have further intensified his feelings of inadequacy. He also exhibits a limited capacity for a realistic sense of self and shows signs of identity diffusion, which may impair both his decision-making and the quality of his interpersonal relationships (H: (H) + Hd + (Hd) = 3:4).

Presumably due to deep narcissistic vulnerability, he appears cautious and guarded in interpersonal contexts, seemingly fearful of being hurt or exposed emotionally (positive HVI). He likely comes across as reserved and hesitant, revealing little of his inner life to others, and tends to avoid intimate relationships in favor of more superficial ones that allow him to maintain distance (SumT = 0). At the same time, he seems to long for harmonious, idealized relationships, possibly because he struggles to tolerate the conflictual dimensions intrinsic to real interpersonal engagement (COP = 5; AG = 0).

Although Anthony appears capable of managing life's difficulties without becoming overtly distressed (AdjD = +1), this composure likely reflects not true resilience but rather a defensive avoidance of emotional pain (eb = 4:2; m = 1; SumSh = 2; FV = 1; FT = 0; FC' = 0; FY = 1). His calm demeanor, even under stressful conditions—such as those surrounding the assessment—may mask a lack of emotional reactivity (D = +1; m = 1; Y = 1). While he appears able to control his behavior and avoid emotional outbursts, it is unlikely that he has access to or insight into his internal emotional struggles, or that he would spontaneously seek psychotherapeutic help.

Anthony shows a pervasive introversive style (EB = 8:2.5; EBPer = 3.2), he rigidly relies on reasoning in his approach to life and decision-making, leaving no room for feelings and intuition. That may expose him to encounter serious difficulties in emotionally engaging situations in which he may go into disorganization, showing major lapses in the judgment and reality testing. In some circumstances, in fact, he gives evidence of a serious impairment in his ability to think logically and coherently (Sum6 = 7; WSum6 = 26; Level 2 = 1; FAB = 4) and this happens only in responses to the colored Cards, confirming how destabilizing the affects are for him. When not prompted by intense emotions, he is able to think logically and coherently and has adequate ideational flexibility, showing that he is able to modify his ideas according to evidence (a:p = 7:5). In accordance with his hypervigilant style, he is very attentive to the environment, ready to grasp and analyze every aspect of it, without letting the complexity of situations and the relationships between their different aspects slip by (Zf = 16; Zd = −1.0; DQ+ = 12; DQo = 6; DQv = 0; W:D:Dd = 9:7:2). His ability to process information presumably denotes good intellectual abilities that he does not, however, seem to be able to fully utilize, probably due to his propensity to set himself limited goals relative to his potential (W:M = 9:8). Although he is usually able to perceive events and evaluate situations realistically, his reality testing shows lapses more often than normally expected (XA% = .72; WDA% = .81; X-% = .28; P = 7; X+% = .50; Xu% = .22). Examination of *minus* responses reveals that they appear only at the colored Cards, confirming Anthony's considerable difficulty in coming to terms with affect.

The contribution of the Comprehensive Rorschach Defense System

While the structural interpretation based on the Comprehensive System provided substantial evidence to support the diagnostic hypothesis formulated according to PDM-2 criteria, it did not offer an in-depth understanding of the dynamics underlying Anthony's mental functioning. In contrast, analysis of the Rorschach protocol using the CRDS is expected to shed light on the nature of Anthony's defensive operations, their motivational underpinnings (i.e., the anxieties that elicit them), and the quality of his object relations.

After coding Anthony's protocol in accordance with CRDS guidelines, we could proceed either by analyzing the quantitative indicators that emerged (see Appendix D) or by examining the sequence of responses and the corresponding defenses. We favor this second approach and recommend it generally, as it allows the clinician to build a more nuanced understanding of the patient in stages—without relying too early on quantitative data that, while informative, risk reducing the clinical picture to a classificatory scheme. In Anthony's case, the quantitative analysis would support the PDM-2-based diagnostic hypothesis of a narcissistic personality syndrome organized at a high borderline level. However, it would not move beyond an objectifying understanding, which—though preferable to the descriptive diagnosis of AvPD under DSM-5-TR—remains largely limited to a classificatory perspective.

By analyzing the sequence of Anthony's responses, we propose instead to use the CRDS as a tool to explore the anxieties that activate his defensive patterns. In clinical work, it is crucial to consider anxiety and defense in relation to one another rather than in isolation (Spillius, 1988). Identifying the specific responses in which defenses appear not only clarifies which defenses are being used but—an even more clinically relevant question—reveals the anxieties against which Anthony is defending himself.

From the outset, Anthony conveys that he is animated—and simultaneously frightened—by an aggressive oral drive. His first response to Card I, *"A wolf, a fox mask, carnival type,"* suggests that the anxiety aroused by oral aggression first mobilizes a high-level defense of denial (the wolf becomes a wolf mask, then further softened into a fox mask), followed by a level 1 defense of idealization (the image is transformed into something associated with a festive, harmless setting—carnival). This progression indicates a shift from danger to playfulness, effectively neutralizing the threatening dimension.

Given this opening, we pay close attention to Anthony's response to Card II, where the presence of red may stimulate both libidinal and aggressive drives. He produces two responses: *"Two garden dwarfs hugging each other from behind"* and *"Two puppy dogs turned toward each other, as if kissing."* Here, the libidinal drive is privileged, but is then managed through affect isolation and devaluation (human figures are depersonalized as statues and diminished by being cast as dwarfs), followed by denial of the sexual content, expressed through a regressive and tender imagery.

This same internal conflict continues on the next card, which also features red. He sees two girls—first holding a large soup pot, then handing something over, pulling something, playing, folding sheets. Aggression is again neutralized through idealization (*"they're playing"*). Up to this point, Anthony has been able to contain his anxiety through relatively mature defenses. However, as the libidinal tension increases, it surpasses his capacity for regulation. The anxiety becomes more intense and disorganizing, leading to the activation of a more primitive defense—psychotic denial—signaling a breakdown in thought organization. This is evident in a Space-fusion response characterized by major perceptual distortion: *"A woman's underwear suit, a babydoll, a bra, a bow as decoration on the navel, and briefs."*

At the following card, freed from the emotional pressure elicited by red, Anthony regains his capacity for reality testing and allows himself to identify with an idealized masculine figure: *"A motorcyclist, a giant motorboat, a proud motorcyclist"* (he imitates the posture), *"the big boots ... the steering wheel with the things hanging down ... as if they were ornaments on the motorcycle or vest, things that embellish—or that they think embellish—those things that are actually tacky."* This response marks a return to a more organized mental state, with the reemergence of cohesive imagery and symbolic control.

The anxiety elicited by this card is initially managed through idealization. However, in the final part of the response—*"or according to them they embellished ... those things that are actually tacky"*—the defense falters, revealing Anthony's deeper fear of identifying with an assertive, masculine self capable of enjoying his own vitality. A similar conflict appears on Card V, where the butterfly, initially described as swooping freely, is then diminished into a passive figure being carried away. The same dynamic is seen in Card VI, where a stingray—typically perceived as a venomous animal—is repeatedly described as harmless: *"leaning in, precise in positioning, well spread out, well placed, well ordered."*

Here, Anthony appears to have temporarily regained control over his anxiety related to aggressive impulses, primarily through high-level denial.

Yet his narcissistic fragility makes it difficult to sustain this organization. The subsequent cards, particularly those involving soft gray (Card VII) and pastel tones (the last three chromatic cards), tend to elicit regressive responses in individuals with narcissistic vulnerability.

On Card VII, Anthony first resorts to devaluation, followed by idealization—signaling the use of splitting as a means of preserving a positive internal object. On Card VIII, libidinal and aggressive drives converge, producing a response marked by intense anxiety and corresponding psychotic denial: *"two animals, two lions, two pumas climbing more than clinging, then the bust of a woman ... and these lions clinging to the shoulders."*

In the following response, he attempts to use the more mature defense of isolation by devitalizing the female figure and turning her into a mannequin. However, the poor form quality suggests the defense is ineffective. On Card IX, he begins with idealization to safeguard the internal object, but the emergence of oral-aggressive content (*"two griffins"*) triggers the activation of omnipotent denial—a more primitive defense that recurs in subsequent responses.

It appears that, in order to cope with the distress generated by aggressive drive impulses, Anthony must rely on a primitive form of denial. This defense gives rise to relational representations that are forcibly benevolent, increasingly infused with emotions of joy and euphoria, and embedded in a regressive context.

Discussion

The clinical illustration demonstrated how the CRDS, used in conjunction with the Comprehensive System (CS; Exner, 2003), enables an in-depth understanding of psychic functioning and can enhance the psychodynamic diagnostic process. The CRDS allowed us to move beyond the structural diagnosis of Anthony's personality to explore the dynamics of his mental functioning, particularly the quality of his anxieties and object relations.

The DSM-5-TR proved useful from a descriptive standpoint, highlighting Anthony's pronounced tendency to avoid involvement and responsibility, accompanied by a fear of being unappreciated and persistent feelings of inadequacy. The psychodynamic classification, based on PDM-2 criteria, supported the structural diagnostic hypothesis of a narcissistic personality syndrome of the depressed/empty type, organized at a high borderline level.

This hypothesis was substantially confirmed by the Rorschach interpretation according to the CS, which added important insights into Anthony's psychological functioning, allowing us to go beyond classification and understand him more fully as a person.

What emerged was a portrait of a man deeply preoccupied with his self-worth, insecure in his sense of identity, prone to self-torment over perceived flaws, guarded and fearful in interpersonal relationships, and largely unable to recognize or manage conflict. Likely as a result of defensive efforts to deny aggression, he tends to depict interpersonal relationships as overly positive and harmonious. The CS also revealed his difficulty in tolerating emotional pain and a defensive tendency to avoid contact with affect, along with a rigid investment in thinking processes at the expense of emotional sensitivity. At times, affective activation disorganizes his thought processes. The CS further indicated good intellectual potential, which Anthony does not seem to fully access—possibly due to his inclination to set goals that fall short of his capacities.

While the CS contributed significantly to our understanding of Anthony, the CRDS added a deeper layer of insight.

Anthony is terrified by his oral-aggressive impulses (e.g., wolf, large soup pot, race, lions, griffins), which he attempts to manage primarily through idealization. When this defense proves insufficient due to the intensity of the anxiety, he resorts to omnipotent denial. In certain instances, these defenses fail to contain his internal disorganization, which then manifests in the form of psychotic denial.

He appears able to access libidinal drive only within a regressive, idealized, childlike framework. Outside of this dimension, libidinal excitation threatens to disorganize his thought processes. Sexual themes, in particular, evoke psychotic denial—likely because male sexual identification is, in his internal world, inseparable from intolerable aggression. Activity, too, is perceived as dangerous and must be inhibited; passivity offers a sense of calm, shielding him from the feared emergence of aggressive impulses.

Anthony seems compelled to live in passivity, defensively denying his aggression in order to avoid engaging in object relations marked by conflict. These would expose him to the dual threat of a hostile, frustrating object and his own retaliatory rage.

Throughout his life, he has fallen in love only once—an intense and destabilizing experience with Angela, which likely triggered drive states he was unable to process. Since then, he has largely avoided emotional entanglements and now experiences a moderate, emotionally contained relationship with Christine, a woman who appears to fight on his behalf and may, via projective identification, embody his disowned aggression. His passivity, driven by anxiety around aggressive drives, likely also interferes with his capacity to make full use of his intellectual resources and to set appropriate goals for himself.

The CRDS, through the analysis of defenses emerging across the sequence of Rorschach responses, offered valuable insight into the unconscious motivational dynamics underlying Anthony's AvPD. It contributed a genuinely dynamic understanding of his psychological functioning.

One might object that interpretations based on response content lack validity, being highly subjective and dependent on the psychoanalytic orientation of the examiner. While this concern is not unfounded—since psychoanalytic interpretation often relies on a chain of inferential reasoning—the risk of arbitrary or ungrounded interpretations can be minimized by adhering to established methodological guidelines. As Schafer (1954) emphasized, interpretive claims must be supported by sufficient evidence; and as Lerner (1998) later argued, inferences should privilege the experiential level and avoid excessive reliance on abstract or overly theoretical constructs.

APPENDICES

Appendix A

Anthony's Rorschach protocol

TAV. I	
(1) a wolf, a wolf mask, fox mask, a Carnival mask, can I also turn it over? [as you like], a wolf mask, fox mask, carnivalesque type, no, I can't see anything else in it (continues to observe the card, turns it over, poses it) [may you take your time] yes, yes (continues to observe the card, turning it in the different positions) no, the only verse I can find something in it is this, I can see the ears, nostrils, eyes, face, elongated nose like wolf, fox, something like that	Examiner repeats response (ERR) S: (WS) the snout, ears, eyes, nostrils
TAV. II	
(2) this one would look like two garden dwarfs hugging from behind, the red cap, the body, the feet	ERR S: (W) they look like they are hugging, but seen from behind E: what makes them look like seen from behind? S: I don't know, it gives me that impression there, I can't see any face, like they are hugging with their arm raised E: you were telling me with the cap, what makes it look like a cap to you? S: the classic garden dwarf one, it must be that living in the suburbs I see a lot of them in the houses around me
(3) in a different way I see you two puppies back to back turning with their heads toward each other, yes, the muzzle, the ears, two puppy dogs, two little doggies (he keeps looking at the card turning it to the different positions) turned like this toward each other as if they were kissing	ERR S: (D1) one here, here the other, paws, ears, muzzle, turn like this

TAV. III

(prolonged latency)

(4) there I see two girls holding something, like it's a pot, the big soup pot ones, actually like they're tending something because they both look like they're turned around, I don't know--two girls like they're playing a game of pulling something, I don't know

ERR
S: (D1) the back, the legs, kind of like pulling, like folding sheets
E: what makes them look like sheets?
S: I don't see the sheets, I see the girls bowing, like folding a sheet more than pulling

(5) Then I can see there a woman's underwear outfit, a babydoll, something like that, a bra, a center bow

ERR
S: (DdS99: DdS24+D3+D7) here part of the bra, the bow as a decoration on the navel and the slip

TAV. IV

(6) here I see a motorcyclist, one of those giant motorcycles, the big boots, the motorcycle wheel, a proud biker, posing (imitates posture), I don't know how to describe it, the big boots nice and big (turns and turns the card over and over while continuing to observe it), nothing else, I was reminded of the motorcyclist!

ERR
S: (W) the motorcycle wheel, the motorcycle, the boots, proud (imitates posture), the steering wheel with things dangling
E: what dangling things?
S: as if they were an adornment to the motorcycle or the jacket, as if they were embellishing or according to them embellishing, like bangs, something like that, those things that are actually tacky

TAV. V

(7) a butterfly, its wings, body, tail, head

ERR
S: (W) In free swooping let's say, not in free swooping, getting carried, the body, the wings

TAV. VI

(8) A stingray, what is it called? A stingray, lying down, camouflaged under the sand ... it will be the impact though ... a stingray ... it comes from looking at it like this (puts the card flat) as when it is resting on the seabed (turns the board over and over while continuing to look at it) I can't see anything else

ERR
S: (W) I imagined it this way, looking at it from above.
E: what do you mean?
S: because it's very precise in positioning, it seems to me well spread out, well open, I've seen them at the aquarium, well placed, I don't know, well ordered

TAV. VII

(9) looks like an ethnic necklace, tacky I think of them, South American types

ERR
S: (W) here it looks like the hooking behind the nape of the neck
E: what makes it look ethnic to you?
S: I don't know, multiple parts connected by a thread

(10) then I see two little girls there, one in front of the other, however I see the tail up as if they are jumping, playing on a trampoline, on a rope	ERR S: (W) two little girls, like on a trampoline, here is the base, the face, the tail up
TAV. VIII (11) two animals ... lions, cougars, clinging, climbing more than clinging, then the bust of a woman, the shoulders with the beginning of a dress, the flounced ones, wide, and these two lions clinging to the shoulders (he turns the card)	ERR here the shoulders, the bra, the beginning of one of those flouncy tango dancer type skirts E: what makes it look like that to you? S: because it widens, it's more fluffy, more puffy, maybe these orange shades make it look puffy
(12) upside down looks like a mannequin on display in a store, a shirt and skirt	ERR S: (D6) the short blouse, like shoulder covers, then the shirt underneath and then a denim type skirt E: what makes it look like jeans to you? S: the blue color looks like denim, then the shades, like lighter and darker jeans, also the blouse is shaded, the colors are very shaded, they look like those blouses that you see around that look ruined and instead they are just made like that, kind of faded, lighter and darker
TAV. IX (he sighs) (13) looks like another carnival mask to me.	ERR S: (D2) its shape
(14) if not, I can see us like two griffins	ERR S: (D3) It looks like the ridge, I don't know what it's called.
(15) or two seahorses	ERR S: (D3) the shape, one facing the other, saying nicely hello
(16) or a shrimp looking in the mirror, reflection, it's behind something	ERR S: (D3) as if looking in a mirror, here he is resting on a seabed, put like this (imitates posture) E: what makes it look like a seabed to him? E: I don't know, like he's behind something because part of the butt can't be seen, I said shrimp also because of the orange color, reflected in the mirror because they are the same exact here

(17) the muzzle of a horse with some kind of adornment	ERR S: (Dd22+D12) the shape, a horse's head, then this like a lapel, like those horse decorations
TAV. X (18) it looks like a coral reef underwater landscape, tropical, I see two seahorses, two shrimps, it almost looks like they are playing, they are going to tickle the seahorses' noses, playful, these look like cuttlefish, squid, two fish with claws, it almost looks like all these are playfully teasing the seahorses, these pinching their noses, these jumping on them being much smaller, a playful atmosphere, it's colorful, two tickling each other in the sides	ERR S: (W) seahorses (D9), here the crabs (D1), as if they're pulling their noses out of spite, here I'm reminded of the hermit crab (D7), as if they're tickling his sides, these two (D8) jumping on his head because they're smaller, like a cartoon, all colorful, I like it, here two more little fish (D12), yes, they are all playing, these green ones going to poke the others as if to tickle them, these ones below giving each other the momentum, yes, a playful atmosphere let's say, they are all having fun, even the seahorses, as if they are the adults and all the others are the pups.

Appendix B

Sequence of scores

Card	Resp. No	Location and DQ	Loc. No.	Determinant(s) and Form Quality	(2)	Content(s)	Pop	Z Score	Special Scores
I	1	WSo	1	Fo		(Ad), Art		3.5	
II	2	W+	1	Mp.FCo	2	(H), Cg		4.5	PER, COP, GHR
	3	D+	1	Mao	2	A	P	3.0	COP, FAB, GHR
III	4	D+	1	Mao	2	H, Hh	P	3.0	COP, GHR
	5	DdS+	99	F-		Cg, Art, Sx		4.5	
IV	6	W+	1	Ma.mpo		H, Cg, Sc, Art	P	4.0	GHR
V	7	Wo	1	FMpo		A	P	1.0	DV
VI	8	Wo	1	FMpu		A		2.5	PER
VII	9	Wo	1	Fu		Ay, Cg		2.5	
	10	W+	1	Mao	2	H, Sc	P	2.5	COP, GHR
VIII	11	W+	1	FMa.FV-	2	A, Cg, Hd, Sx	P	4.5	FAB2, PHR
	12	D+	6	FC.FY-		Cg,(H)		3.0	PHR
IX	13	Do	2	Fo		(Hd), Art			GHR
	14	Do	3	Fu	2	(A)			
	15	D+	3	Mau	2	A		2.5	FAB, PHR
	16	D+	3	FD.Fr.Mp.FC-		A, Ls, Hh		2.5	FAB, PHR
	17	Dd+	22	F-		Ad, Art		2.5	
X	18	W+	1	Ma.CFo	2	Ls, Hx, Art, A	P	5.5	COP, FAB, INC, GHR

Appendix C

Rorschach structural summary

Location	
Zf	= 16
ZSum	= 51.5
ZEst	= 52.5
W	= 9
(Wv	= 0)
D	= 7
W+D	= 16
Dd	= 2
S	= 2

Determinants

Blend	Single	
M.FC	M	= 4
M.m	FM	= 2
FM.FY	m	= 0
FC.FY	FC	= 0
FD.Fr.M.CF	CF	= 0
M.FC	C	= 0
	Cn	= 0
	FC'	= 0
	C'F	= 0
	C'	= 0
	FT	= 0
	TF	= 0
	T	= 0
	FV	= 0
	VF	= 0
	V	= 0
	FY	= 0
	YF	= 0
	Y	= 0
	Fr	= 0
	rF	= 0
	FD	= 0
	F	= 6
	(2)	= 8

Contents	
H	= 3
(H)	= 2
Hd	= 1
(Hd)	= 1
Hx	= 1
A	= 1
(A)	= 1
Ad	= 1
(Ad)	= 1
An	= 0
Art	= 6
Ay	= 1
Bl	= 0
Bt	= 0
Cg	= 6
Cl	= 0
Ex	= 0
Fd	= 0
Fi	= 0
Ge	= 0
Hh	= 2
Ls	= 2
Na	= 0
Sc	= 2
Sx	= 2
Xy	= 0
Idio	= 0

S-Con		
☐	FV+VF+V+FD > 2	
■	Col-Shd Blends > 0	
■	Ego < .31 or > .44	
☐	MOR > 3	
☐	Zd > ±3.5	
☐	es > EA	
☐	CF + C > FC	
■	X+% < .70	
☐	S > 3	
☐	P < 3 or > 8	
☐	Pure H < 2	
☐	R < 17	
3	Total	

DQ		
		(FQ-)
+	= 12	(5)
o	= 6	(0)
v/+	= 0	(0)
v	= 0	(0)

FQ			
	FQx	MQual	W+D
+	= 0	0	0
o	= 9	6	9
u	= 4	1	4
-	= 5	1	3
none	= 0	0	0

Special Scores		
	Lvl-1	Lvl-2
DV	= 1x1	0x2
INC	= 1x2	0x4
DR	= 0x3	0x6
FAB	= 4x4	1x7
ALOG	= 0x5	
CON	= 0x7	
	Raw Sum6 = 7	
	Wgtd Sum6 = 26	
AB	= 0	GHR = 7
AG	= 0	PHR = 4
COP	= 5	MOR = 0
CP	= 0	PER = 2
		PSV = 0

RATIOS, PERCENTAGES, AND DERIVATIONS

R = 18		L = 0.50			
EB	= 8 : 2.5	EA	= 10.5	EBPer	= 3.2
eb	= 4 : 2	es	= 6	D	= +1
		Adj es	= 6	Adj D	= +1
FM = 3		SumC'	= 0	SumT	= 0
m = 1		SumV	= 1	SumY	= 1

AFFECT

FC:CF+C	=	3 : 1
Pure C	=	0
SumC' : WSumC	=	0 : 2.5
Afr	=	0.80
S	=	2
Blends:R	=	6 : 18
CP	=	0

INTERPERSONAL

COP = 5	AG = 0	
GHR:PHR	=	7 : 4
a:p	=	7 : 5
Food	=	0
SumT	=	0
Human Content	=	7
Pure H	=	3
PER	=	2
Isolation Index	=	0.11

IDEATION

a:p	= 7 : 5	Sum6	= 7
Ma:Mp	= 6 : 2	Lvl-2	= 1
2AB+(Art+Ay)	= 7	WSum6	= 26
MOR	= 0	M-	= 1
		M none	= 0

MEDIATION

XA%	= 0.72
WDA%	= 0.81
X-%	= 0.28
S-	= 1
P	= 7
X+%	= 0.50
Xu%	= 0.22

PROCESSING

Zf	= 16
W:D:Dd	= 9 : 7 : 2
W : M	= 9 : 8
Zd	= -1.0
PSV	= 0
DQ+	= 12
DQv	= 0

SELF-PERCEPTION

3r+(2)/R	= 0.61
Fr+rF	= 1
SumV	= 1
FD	= 1
An+Xy	= 0
MOR	= 0
H:(H)+Hd+(Hd)	= 3 : 4

PTI = 1	☐ DEPI = 3	☐ CDI = 0	☐ S-CON = 3	☐ HVI = Yes	☐ OBS = No

Appendix D

Comprehensive Rorschach Defense System

Defense	Response(s)	Frequency
Repression		
Higher Level Denial	1, 7, 8,	3
Intellectualization		
Isolation	2, 12	2
Rationalization	2	1
Projective Identification		
Splitting	4,10	2
Idealization Level 1	1, 4, 10, 13	4
Idealization Level 2	6,	1
Devaluation Level 1	2, 6, 9	3
Devaluation Level 2		
Omnipotent Control		
Omnipotent Denial	15, 16, 18	3
Psychotic Denial	5, 11	2
Total Scored	21	

References

Acklin, M. W. (1994). Some contributions of cognitive science to the Rorschach Test. *Rorschachiana*, 19(1), 129–145. https://doi.org/10.1027/1192-5604.19.1.129

Acklin, M. W. (1997). Psychodiagnosis of personality structure: Psychotic personality organization. In J. R. Meloy, M. W. Acklin, C. B. Gacono, & J. F. Murray (Eds.), *Contemporary Rorschach interpretation* (pp. 11–20). Mahwah, NJ: Lawrence Erlbaum Associates Publishers.

Akhtar, S. (2020). Repression: A critical assessment and update of Freud's 1915 paper. *The American Journal of Psychoanalysis*, 80(3), 241–258. https://doi.org/10.1057/s11231-020-09261-z

Akkerman, K., Lewin, T. J., & Carr, V. J. (1999). Long-term changes in defense style among patients recovering from major depression. *Journal of Nervous and Mental Disease*, 187(2), 80–87. https://doi.org/10.1097/00005053-199902000-00003

Alliance of Psychoanalytic Organizations. (2006). *Psychodynamic diagnostic manual (PDM)*. Silver Spring, MD: Author.

American Psychiatric Association (APA). (2022). *Diagnostic and statistical manual of mental disorders* (5th ed., text rev.; DSM-5-TR). Washington, DC: American Psychiatric Publishing, Inc. https://doi.org/10.1176/appi.books.9780890425787

American Psychological Association (APA). (2013). *Diagnostic and statistical manual of mental disorders: DSM-5™*, (5th ed.). Washington, DC: American Psychiatric Publishing, Inc. https://doi.org/10.1176/appi.books.9780890425596

Andrews, G., Pollock, C., & Stewart, G. (1989). The determination of defense style by questionnaire. *Archives of General Psychiatry*, 46(5), 455–460. https://doi.org/10.1001/archpsyc.1989.01810050069011

Andrews, G., Singh, M., & Bond, M. (1993). The Defense Style Questionnaire. *Journal of Nervous and Mental Disease*, 181, 246–256. http://dx.doi.org/10.1097/00005053-199304000-00006

Bachrach, H. M., Weber, J. J., & Solomon, M. (1985). Factors associated with the outcome of psychoanalysis (clinical and methodological considerations): Report of the Columbia Psychoanalytic Center Research Project: IV. *International Review of Psycho-Analysis*, 12(4), 379–389.

Balint, M. (1955). Friendly expanses—Horrid empty spaces. *International Journal of Psychoanalysis*, 36, 225–241.

Balint, M. (1956). Pleasure, object and libido. Some reflexions on Fairbairn's modifications of psychoanalytic theory. *British Journal of Medical Psychology*, 29, 162–167. https://doi.org/10.1111/j.2044-8341.1956.tb00912.x

Balint, M. (1959). *Thrills and regressions*. New York, NY: International Universities Press.

Balint, M. (1968). *The basic fault*. London, UK: Tavistock.

Baranger, M., Baranger, W., Rogers, S., & Churcher, J. (2008). The analytic situation as a dynamic field. *The International Journal of Psychoanalysis, 89*(4), 795–826. https://doi.org/10.1111/j.1745-8315.2008.00074.x

Bayle, G. (1996). Présentation du rapport: Les clivages. *Revue Française de Psychanalyse, 60* (Spec Issue), 1303–1547. https://doi.org/10.3917/rfp.g1996.60n5.1303

Békés, V., Prout, T. A., Di Giuseppe, M., Wildes Ammar, L., Kui, T., & Arsena, G., et al. (2021). Initial validation of the defense mechanisms rating scales Q-sort: A comparison of trained and untrained raters. *Mediterranean Journal of Clinical Psychology, 9*. https://doi.org/10.13129/2282-1619/mjcp-3107

Berg, J. L. (1990). Differentiating ego functions of borderline and narcissistic personalities. *Journal of Personality Assessment, 55*(3–4), 537–548. https://doi.org/10.1080/00223891.1990.9674089

Bhatia, M., Petraglia, J., de Roten, Y., Banon, E., Despland, J.-N., & Drapeau, M. (2016). What defense mechanisms do therapists interpret in-session? *Psychodynamic Psychiatry, 44*(4), 567–586. https://doi.org/10.1521/pdps.2016.44.4.567

Bion, W. R. (1957). Differentiation of the psychotic from non-psychotic personalities. *The International Journal of Psychoanalysis, 38*, 266–275.

Bion, W. R. (1959). Attacks on linking. *The International Journal of Psychoanalysis, 40*, 308–315.

Bion, W. R. (1962a). The psycho-analytic study of thinking. *The International Journal of Psychoanalysis, 43*, 306–310.

Bion, W. R. (1962b). *Learning from experience*. London, UK: Heinemann.

Bion, W. R. (1963). *Elements of psychoanalysis*. London, UK: Heinemann.

Bion, W. R. (1965). *Transformations: Change from learning to growth*. London, UK: Heinemann.

Blass, R. B. (2015). Conceptualizing splitting: On the different meanings of splitting and their implications for the understanding of the person and the analytic process. *The International Journal of Psychoanalysis, 96*(1), 123–139. https://doi.org/10.1111/1745-8315.12326

Blatt, S. J. (1990). The Rorschach: A test of perception or an evaluation of representation. *Journal of Personality Assessment, 55*(3–4), 394–416. https://doi.org/10.1080/00223891.1990.9674079

Blatt, S. J., Brenneis, C. B., Schimek, J. G., & Glick, M. (1976). Normal development and psychopathological impairment of the concept of the object on the Rorschach. *Journal of Abnormal Psychology, 85*(4), 364–373. https://doi.org/10.1037/0021-843X.85.4.364

Blatt, S. J., & Lerner, H. D. (1983). The psychological assessment of object representation. *Journal of Personality Assessment, 47*(1), 7–28. https://doi.org/10.1207/s15327752jpa4701_2

Blechner, M. J. (2009). Research, curriculum, and diversity. *Contemporary Psychoanalysis, 45*(3), 306–310. https://doi.org/10.1080/00107530.2009.10746004

Bond, M., Gardner, S. T., Christian, J., & Sigal, J. J. (1983). Empirical study of self-rated defense styles. *Archives of General Psychiatry, 40*(3), 333–338. https://doi.org/10.1001/archpsyc.1983.01790030103013

Bornstein, R. F. (2007). Nomothetic psychoanalysis. *Psychoanalytic Psychology, 24*(4), 590–602. https://doi.org/10.1037/0736-9735.24.4.590

Breuer, J., & Freud, S. (1893). On the psychical mechanism of hysterical phenomena: Preliminary communication from studies on hysteria. In *The standard edition of the complete psychological works of Sigmund Freud* (Vol. 2, pp. 1–17). London, UK: Hogarth Press.

Britton, R. (2000). *Belief and imagination: Explorations in psychoanalysis*. London, UK: Routledge.

Brook, J. A. (1992). Freud and splitting. *International Review of Psycho-Analysis, 19*(3), 335–350.

Busch, F. N., & Milrod, B. L. (2010). The ongoing struggle for psychoanalytic research: Some steps forward. *Psychoanalytic Psychotherapy, 24*(4), 306–314. https://doi.org/10.1080/02668734.2010.519234

Busdraghi, C., Mandolesi, L., Sutera, F., & Vezzani, C. (2024). *Raven's 2 – Matrici Progressive di Raven: Edizione Italiana [Raven's 2- Raven's Progressive Matrices]*. Firenze: Giunti Psychometrics.

Chabert, C. (1987). *La psychopatologie a l'epreuve du Rorschach* [The psychopathology the test of Rorschach]. Paris: Dunod.

Chiesa, M. (2010). Research and psychoanalysis: Still time to bridge the great divide? *Psychoanalytic Psychology, 27*(2), 99–114. https://doi.org/10.1037/a0019413

Cohen, J. (1988). *Statistical power analysis for the behavioral sciences* (2nd ed.). Hillsdale, NJ: Lawrence Erlbaum Associates.

Cohen, J., & Kinston, W. (1984). Repression theory: A new look at the cornerstone. *The International Journal of Psychoanalysis, 65*(4), 411–422.

Collins, R. (1983). *Rorschach correlates of borderline personality*. Unpublished doctoral dissertation, University of Toronto.

Constantinides, P., & Beck, S. M. (2010). Toward developing a scale to empirically measure psychotic defense mechanisms. *Journal of the American Psychoanalytic Association, 58*(6), 1159–1188. https://doi.org/10.1177/0003065110396875

Cooper, S. H., & Arnow, D. (1984). Prestage versus defensive splitting and the borderline personality: A Rorschach analysis. *Psychoanalytic Psychology, 1*(3), 235–248. https://doi.org/10.1037/h0085105

Cooper, S. H., & Arnow, D. (1986). *Rorschach Defense Scales*. Unpublished manuscript.

Cooper, S. H., & Bond, M. (1992). *The Psychodynamic Intervention Ratings Scales (PIRS)*, 2002 revision. Montreal: Authors (1992 and revised in 1996, 1998, 2002).

Cooper, S. H., Perry, J. C., & Arnow, D. (1988). An empirical approach to the study of defense mechanisms: I. Reliability and preliminary validity of the Rorschach defense scales. *Journal of Personality Assessment, 52*(2), 187–203. https://doi.org/10.1207/s15327752jpa5202_1

Cooper, S. H., Perry, J. C., & O'Connell, M. (1991). The Rorschach Defense Scales: II. Longitudinal perspectives. *Journal of Personality Assessment, 56*(2), 191–201. https://doi.org/10.1207/s15327752jpa5602_1

Coriat, I. H. (1917). Some statistical results of the psychoanalytic treatment of the psychoneuroses. *Psychoanalytic Review, 4*, 208–216.

Cramer, P. (1991). *The development of defense mechanisms: Theory, research, and assessment*. New York, NY: Springer-Verlag.

Cramer, P. (1999). Ego functions and ego development: Defense mechanisms and intelligence as predictors of ego level. *Journal of Personality, 67*(5), 735–760. https://doi.org/10.1111/1467-6494.00071

Cramer, P. (2003). Personality change in later adulthood is predicted by defense mechanism use in early adulthood. *Journal of Research in Personality, 37*(1), 76–104. https://doi.org/10.1016/S0092-6566(02)00528-7

Cramer, P. (2004). Identity change in adulthood: The contribution of defense mechanisms and life experiences. *Journal of Research in Personality, 38*(3), 280–316. https://doi.org/10.1016/S0092-6566(03)00070-9

Cramer, P. (2008). Identification and the development of competence: A 44-year longitudinal study from late adolescence to late middle age. *Psychology and Aging, 23*(2), 410–421. https://doi.org/10.1037/0882-7974.23.2.410

Cramer, P. (2009). The development of defense mechanisms from pre-adolescence to early adulthood: Do IQ and social class matter? A longitudinal study. *Journal of Research in Personality, 43*(3), 464–471. https://doi.org/10.1016/j.jrp.2009.01.021

Cunliffe, T. B., & Gacono, C. B. (2008). A Rorschach understanding of antisocial and psychopathic women. In C. B. Gacono, F. B. Evans, N. Kaser-Boyd, & L. A. Gacono (Eds.), *The handbook of forensic Rorschach assessment* (pp. 361–378). New York, NY: Routledge.

de Roten, Y., Djillali, S., von Roten, F. C., Despland, J.-N., & Ambresin, G. (2021). Defense mechanisms and treatment response in depressed inpatients. *Frontiers in Psychology, 12.* https://doi.org/10.3389/fpsyg.2021.633939

Despland, J.-N., de Roten, Y., Despars, J., Stigler, M., & Perry, J. C. (2001). Contribution of patient defense mechanims and therapist interventions to the development of early therapeutic alliance in a brief psychodynamic investigation. *Journal of Psychotherapy Practice & Research, 10*(3), 155–164.

DeWitt, K. N., Milbrath, C., & Simon, N. M. (2018). Wallerstein's Scales of Psychological Capacities: A clinically useful measure of character change. *Psychoanalytic Psychology, 35*(1), 115–126. https://doi.org/10.1037/pap0000139

Di Giuseppe, M., & Perry, J. C. (2021). The hierarchy of Defense Mechanisms: Assessing defensive functioning with the Defense Mechanisms Rating Scales Q-sort. *Frontiers in Psychology, 12.* https://doi.org/10.3389/fpsyg.2021.718440

Di Giuseppe, M., Perry, J. C., Petraglia, J., Janzen, J., & Lingiardi, V. (2014). Development of a Q-Sort Version of the Defense Mechanism Rating Scales (DMRS-Q) for clinical use. *Journal of Clinical Psychology, 70*(5), 452–465. https://doi.org/10.1002/jclp.22089

Drapeau, M., De Roten, Y., Perry, J. C., & Despland, J.-N. (2003). A study of stability and change in defense mechanisms during a brief psychodynamic investigation. *Journal of Nervous and Mental Disease, 191*(8), 496–502. https://doi.org/10.1097/01.nmd.0000082210.76762.ec

Drapeau, M., Stelmaszczyk, K., Baucom, D., Henry, M., & Hébert, C. (2018). A process study of long-term treatment: Comparing a successful and a less successful outcome. *Psychoanalytic Psychotherapy, 32*(4), 368–384. https://doi.org/10.1080/02668734.2018.1558414

Eagle, M. (2000a). Repression, part I of II. *Psychoanalytic Review, 87*(1), 1–38.

Eagle, M. (2000b). Repression: Part II of II. *Psychoanalytic Review, 87*(2), 161–187.

Erle, J. B., & Goldberg, D. A. (1979). Problems in the assessment of analyzability. *The Psychoanalytic Quarterly, 48*(1), 48–84.

Erle, J. B., & Goldberg, D. A. (1984). Observations on assessment of analyzability by experienced analysts. *Journal of the American Psychoanalytic Association, 32*(4), 715–737. https://doi.org/10.1177/000306518403200401

Exner, J. E. (1989). Searching for projection in the Rorschach. *Journal of Personality Assessment, 53*(3), 520–536. https://doi.org/10.1207/s15327752jpa5303_9

Exner, J. E. (2003). *The Rorschach: A comprehensive system. Vol. I. Basic foundations and principles of interpretation.* New York, NY: Wiley.

Exner, J. E., Fontan, P., & Andronikof, A. (2022). *The Rorschach: A comprehensive system-revised. Interpretation and technical manual.* Fort Mill, SC: Rorschach Workshop International Rorschach Institute.

Fairbairn, W. R. D. (1940). Schizoid factors in the personality. In W. R. D. Fairbairn (Ed.) (1952), *Psychoanalytic studies of the personality* (pp. 3–27). London, UK: Routledge.

Fairbairn, W. R. D. (1941). A revised psychopathology of the psychoses and psychoneuroses. In W. R. D. Fairbairn (Ed.) (1952), *Psychoanalytic studies of the personality* (pp. 28–58). London, UK: Routledge.

Fairbairn, W. R. D. (1943). Repression and the return of bad objects (with special reference to the "war neuroses"). In W. R. D. Fairbairn (Ed.) (1952), *Psychoanalytic studies of the personality* (pp. 59–81). London, UK: Routledge.

Fairbairn, W. R. D. (1944). Endopsychic structure considered in terms of object-relationships. In W. R. D. Fairbairn (Ed.) (1952), *Psychoanalytic studies of the personality* (pp. 82–131). London, UK: Routledge.

Fairbairn, W. R. D. (1951). Addendum. In W. R. D. Fairbairn (Ed.) (1952), *Psychoanalytic studies of the personality* (pp. 132–136). London, UK: Routledge.

Fairbairn, W. R. D. (1963). Synopsis of an object-relations theory of the personality. *International Journal of Psychoanalysis, 44,* 224–225.

Feldman, F. (1968). Results of psychoanalysis in clinic case assignments. *Journal of the American Psychoanalytic Association, 16*(2), 274–300. https://doi.org/10.1177/000306516801600209

Feldman, M. (2009). Chapter 2: Splitting and projective identification. In *Doubt, conviction and the analytic process: Selected papers of Michael Feldman* (Vol. 65, pp. 21–33). London: Routledge.

Ferenczi, S. (1932). *The clinical diary of Sandor Ferenczi* [J. Dupont (Ed.), M. Balint & N.Z. Jackson (Trans.)]. Cambridge, MA and London, UK: Harvard University Press.

Ferenczi, S. (1933). Confusion of tongues between adults and the child. In M. Balint (Ed.), *Final contribution to the problems and methods of psychoanalysis*, E. Mosbacher (Trans.) London, UK: Karnac Books, 1980, pp. 156–167.

Ferro, A., & Civitarese, G. (2015). *The analytic field and its transformations.* Routledge.

Fonagy, P., & Target, M. (1994). The efficacy of psychoanalysis for children with disruptive disorders. *Journal of the American Academy of Child & Adolescent Psychiatry, 33*(1), 45–55. https://doi.org/10.1097/00004583-199401000-00007.

Fonagy, P., & Target, M. (1996). Predictors of outcome in child psychoanalysis: A retrospective study of 763 cases at the Anna Freud Centre. *Journal of the American Psychoanalytic Association, 44*(1), 27–77. https://doi.org/10.1177/000306519604400104

Frank, A. (1969). The unrememberable and the unforgettable: Passive primal repression. *The Psychoanalytic Study of the Child, 24,* 48–77. https://doi.org/10.1080/00797308.1969.11822686

Frank, A., & Muslin, H. (1967). The development of Freud's concept of primal repression. *Psychoanalytic Study of the Child, 22,* 55–76.

Freud, A. (1936). *The ego and the mechanisms of defense.* New York, NY: International Universities Press.

Freud, S. (1893a). Frau Emmy von N, case histories from studies on hysteria. In *The standard edition of the complete psychological works of Sigmund Freud* (Vol. 2, pp. 48–105). London, UK: Hogarth Press.

Freud, S. (1893b). Miss Lucy R, case histories from studies on hysteria. In *The standard edition of the complete psychological works of Sigmund Freud* (Vol. 2, pp. 106–124). London, UK: Hogarth Press.

Freud, S. (1893c). Katharina, case histories from studies on hysteria. In *The standard edition of the complete psychological works of Sigmund Freud* (Vol. 2, pp. 125–134). London, UK: Hogarth Press.

Freud, S. (1893d). Fräulein Elisabeth von R, case histories from studies on hysteria. In *The standard edition of the complete psychological works of Sigmund Freud* (Vol. 2, pp. 135–181). London, UK: Hogarth Press.

Freud, S. (1893e). The psychotherapy of hysteria from studies on hysteria. In *The standard edition of the complete psychological works of Sigmund Freud* (Vol. 2, pp. 253–305). London, UK: Hogarth Press.

Freud, S. (1894a). Draft H. Paranoia. In *The complete letters of Sigmund Freud to Wilhelm Fliess, 1887–1904* (Vol. 42, pp. 107–112). Cambridge, MA: Belknap Press of Harvard University Press.

Freud, S. (1894b). The neuro-psychoses of defense. In *The standard edition of the complete psychological works of Sigmund Freud* (Vol. 3, pp. 41–61). London, UK: Hogarth Press.

Freud, S. (1895). Draft K. The neuroses of defense (A Christmas Fairy Tale), January 1, 1896: [enclosed with letter]. In *The complete letters of Sigmund Freud to Wilhelm Fliess, 1887–1904* (Vol. 42, pp. 162–169). Cambridge, MA: Belknap Press of Harvard University Press.

Freud, S. (1896). Further remarks on the neuro-psychoses of defense. In *The standard edition of the complete psychological works of Sigmund Freud* (Vol. 3, pp. 157–185). London, UK: Hogarth Press.

Freud, S. (1897). Letter from Freud to Fliess, September 21, 1897. In *The complete letters of Sigmund Freud to Wilhelm Fliess, 1887–1904* (Vol. 42, pp. 264–267). Cambridge, MA: Belknap Press of Harvard University Press.

Freud, S. (1898). The psychical mechanism of forgetfulness. In *The standard edition of the complete psychological works of Sigmund Freud* (Vol. 3, pp. 287–297). London, UK: Hogarth Press.

Freud, S. (1900). The interpretation of dreams. In *The standard edition of the complete psychological works of Sigmund Freud* (Vol. 4, pp. ix–627). London, UK: Hogarth Press.

Freud, S. (1901). The psychopathology of everyday life: Forgetting, slips of the tongue, bungled actions, superstitions and errors (1901). In *The standard edition of the complete psychological works of Sigmund Freud* (Vol. 6, pp. vii–296). London, UK: Hogarth Press.

Freud, S. (1905). Three essays on the theory of sexuality (1905). In *The standard edition of the complete psychological works of Sigmund Freud* (Vol. 7, pp. 123–246). London, UK: Hogarth Press.

Freud, S. (1909a). Analysis of a phobia in a five-year-old boy. In *The standard edition of the complete psychological works of Sigmund Freud* (Vol. 10, pp. 1–150). London, UK: Hogarth Press.

Freud, S. (1909b). Notes upon a case of obsessional neurosis. In *The standard edition of the complete psychological works of Sigmund Freud* (Vol. 10, pp. 151–318). London, UK: Hogarth Press.

Freud, S. (1910). Leonardo da Vinci and a memory of his childhood. In *The standard edition of the complete psychological works of Sigmund Freud* (Vol. 11, pp. 57–138). London, UK: Hogarth Press.

Freud, S. (1911a). Formulations on the two principles of mental functioning. In *The standard edition of the complete psychological works of Sigmund Freud* (Vol. 12, pp. 213–226). London, UK: Hogarth Press.

Freud, S. (1911b). Psycho-analytic notes on an autobiographical account of a case of paranoia (Dementia Paranoides). In *The standard edition of the complete psychological works of Sigmund Freud* (Vol. 12, pp. 1–82). London, UK: Hogarth Press.

Freud, S. (1913). Totem and Taboo: Some points of agreement between the mental lives of savages and neurotics (1913 [1912–13]). In *The standard edition of the complete psychological works of Sigmund Freud* (Vol. 13, pp. vii–162). London, UK: Hogarth Press.

Freud, S. (1914) On narcissism: An introduction. In *The standard edition of the complete psychological works of Sigmund Freud* (Vol. 14, pp. 67–102). London, UK: Hogarth Press.

Freud, S. (1915a). Instincts and their vicissitudes. In *The standard edition of the complete psychological works of Sigmund Freud* (Vol. 14, pp. 109–140). London, UK: Hogarth Press.

Freud, S. (1915b). Repression. In *The standard edition of the complete psychological works of Sigmund Freud* (Vol. 14, pp. 141–158). London, UK: Hogarth Press.

Freud, S. (1915c). The unconscious. In *The standard edition of the complete psychological works of Sigmund Freud* (Vol. 14, pp. 159–215). London, UK: Hogarth Press.

Freud, S. (1916). Some character types met in psychoanalytic work. In *The standard edition of the complete psychological works of Sigmund Freud* (Vol. 16, pp. 309–333). London, UK: Hogarth Press.

Freud, S. (1917). Mourning and melancholia. In *The standard edition of the complete psychological works of Sigmund Freud* (Vol. 14, pp. 237–258). London, UK: Hogarth Press.

Freud, S. (1920). Beyond the pleasure principle. In *The standard edition of the complete psychological works of Sigmund Freud* (Vol. 18, pp. 1–64). London, UK: Hogarth Press.

Freud, S. (1922). Some neurotic mechanisms in jealousy, paranoia and homosexuality. In *The standard edition of the complete psychological works of Sigmund Freud* (Vol. 18, pp. 221–232). London, UK: Hogarth Press.

Freud, S. (1923). The ego and the id. In *The standard edition of the complete psychological works of Sigmund Freud* (Vol. 19, pp. 1–66). London, UK: Hogarth Press.

Freud, S. (1924a). Neurosis and psychosis. In *The standard edition of the complete psychological works of Sigmund Freud* (Vol. 19, pp. 147–154). London, UK: Hogarth Press.

Freud, S. (1924b). The loss of reality in neurosis and psychosis. In *The standard edition of the complete psychological works of Sigmund Freud* (Vol. 19, pp. 181–188). London, UK: Hogarth Press.

Freud, S. (1925). Negation. In *The standard edition of the complete psychological works of Sigmund Freud* (Vol. 19, pp. 233–240). London, UK: Hogarth Press.

Freud, S. (1926). Inhibitions, symptoms and anxiety. In *The standard edition of the complete psychological works of Sigmund Freud* (Vol. 20, pp. 75–176). London, UK: Hogarth Press.

Freud, S. (1927). Fetishism. In *The standard edition of the complete psychological works of Sigmund Freud* (Vol. 21, pp. 147–158). London, UK: Hogarth Press.

Freud, S. (1938a). Splitting of the ego in the process of defense. In *The standard edition of the complete psychological works of Sigmund Freud* (Vol. 23, pp. 271–278). London, UK: Hogarth Press.

Freud, S. (1938b). An outline of psycho-analysis. In *The standard edition of the complete psychological works of Sigmund Freud* (Vol. 23, pp. 139–208). London, UK: Hogarth Press.

Freud, S. (1950). Project for a scientific psychology (1950 [1895]). In *The standard edition of the complete psychological works of Sigmund Freud* (Vol. 1, pp. 281–391). London, UK: Hogarth Press.

Gacono, C. B. (1988). *A Rorschach analysis of object relations and defensive structure and their relationship to narcissism and psychopathy in a group of antisocial offenders* (Doctoral dissertation, United States International University).

Gacono, C. B. (1990). An empirical study of object relations and defensive operations in antisocial personality disorder. *Journal of Personality Assessment, 54*(3/4), 589. https://doi.org/10.1080/00223891.1990.9674022

Gacono, C. B., & Meloy, J. R. (1988). The relationship between cognitive style and defensive process in the psychopath. *Criminal Justice and Behavior, 15*(4), 472–483. https://doi.org/10.1177/0093854888015004004

Gacono, C. B., & Meloy, J. R. (1992). The Rorschach and the DSM-III—R antisocial personality: A tribute to Robert Lindner. *Journal of Clinical Psychology, 48*(3), 393–406. https://doi.org/10.1002/1097-4679(199205)48:3<393::AID-JCLP2270480319>3.0.CO;2-Z

Gacono, C. B., & Meloy, J. R. (1994). *The Rorschach assessment of aggressive and psychopathic personalities.* Mahwah, NJ: Lawrence Erlbaum Publishers Associates.

Gacono, C. B., Meloy, J. R., & Berg, J. L. (1992). Object relations, defensive operations, and affective states in narcissistic, borderline, and antisocial personality disorder. *Journal of Personality Assessment, 59*(1), 32–49. https://doi.org/10.1207/s15327752jpa5901_4

Gacono, C. B., Meloy, J. R., & Bridges, M. R. (2000). A Rorschach comparison of psychopaths, sexual homicide perpetrators, and nonviolent pedophiles: Where angels fear to tread. *Journal of Clinical Psychology, 56*(6), 757–777. https://doi.org/10.1002/(SICI)1097-4679(200006)56:6<757::AID-JCLP6>3.0.CO;2-I

Gacono, C. B., Meloy, J. R., & Bridges, M. R. (2008). A Rorschach understanding of psychopaths, sexual homicide perpetrators, and nonviolent pedophiles. In C. Gacono, B. Evans, N. Kaser- Boyd, & L. Gacono (Eds.), *The handbook of forensic Rorschach assessment* (pp. 379–402). Mahwah, NJ: Lawrence Erlbaum.

George, D., & Mallery, M. (2010). *SPSS for Windows step by step: A simple guide and reference, 17.0 update* (10th ed.). Boston, MA: Pearson.

Gillieron, E. (1989). Short psychotherapeutic interventions (four sessions). *Psychotherapy and Psychosomatics, 51*(1), 32–37. https://doi.org/10.1159/000288131

Gleser, G. C., & Ihilevich, D. (1969). An objective instrument for measuring defense mechanisms. *Journal of Consulting and Clinical Psychology, 33*(1), 51–60. https://doi.org/10.1037/h0027381

Gordon, R. M., & Bornstein, R. F. (2015). The Psychodiagnostic Chart-2 v.8.1 (PDC-2). https://doi.org/10.13140/RG.2.1.3905.4169. https://www.researchgate.net/publication/292592861_Digital_Pychodiagnostic_Chart-2_PDC-2_v81

Gordon, R. M., & Bornstein, R. F. (2018). Construct validity of the Psychodiagnostic Chart: A transdiagnostic measure of personality organization, personality syndromes, mental functioning, and symptomatology. *Psychoanalytic Psychology, 35*(2), 280–288. https://doi.org/10.1037/pap0000142.

Greenson, R. R. (1967). *The technique and practice of psycho-analysis.* New York, NY: International Universities Press.

Grinberg, L. (1979). Countertransference and projective counteridentification. *Contemporary Psychoanalysis, 15*(2), 226–247. https://doi.org/10.1080/00107530.1979.10745579

Gritti, E. S., Marino, D. P., Lang, M., & Meyer, G. J. (2018). Assessing narcissism using Rorschach-based imagery and behavior validated by clinician reports: Studies with adult patients and nonpatients. *Assessment, 25*(7), 898–916. https://doi.org/10.1177/1073191117715728

Grotstein, J. S. (1981). *Splitting and projective identification.* Northvale, NJ: Jason Aronson.

Grotstein, J. S. (2000). *Who is the dreamer who dreams the dream? A study of psychic presences.* New York: Routledge.

Grotstein, J. S. (2007). *A beam of intense darkness: Wilfred Bion's legacy to psychoanalysis.* London: Karnac Books.

Grotstein, J. S. (2009). *But at the same time and on another level: Psychoanalytic theory and technique in the Kleinian/Bionian mode.* London: Routledge

Haan, N. (1963). Proposed model of ego functioning: Coping and defense mechanisms in relationship to IQ change (Monograph No. 571). *Psychological Monographs: General and Applied, 77*(8), 1–23. https://doi.org/10.1037/h0093848

Hamburg, D. A., Bibring, G. L., Fisher, C., Stanton, A. H., Wallerstein, R. S., Weinstock, H. I., & Haggard, E. (1967). Report of ad hoc committee on central fact-gathering data of the American Psychoanalytic Association. *Journal of the American Psychoanalytic Association, 15*(4), 841–861. https://doi.org/10.1177/000306516701500407.

Hartmann, H. (1939). *Ego psychology and the problem of adaptation.* New York, NY: International Universities Press.

Hartmann, H. (1950). Psychoanalysis and developmental psychology. In *Essays on ego psychology.* New York, NY: International Universities Press.

Hartmann, H. (1951). Technical implications of ego psychology. In *Essays on ego psychology.* New York, NY: International Universities Press.

Hartmann, H. (1955). Notes on theory of sublimation. In *Essays on ego psychology.* New York, NY: International Universities Press.

Hartmann, H., & Kris, E. (1946). The genetic approach in psychoanalysis. *Yearbook of Psychoanalysis, 2,* 1–22.

Hartmann, H., Kris, E., & Loewenstein, R. M. (1946). Comments on the formation of psychic structure. *The Psychoanalytic Study of the Child, 2,* 11–38. https://doi.org/10.1080/00797308.1946.11823535

Hartmann, H., Kris, E., & Loewenstein, R. M. (1949). Notes on the theory of aggression. In A. Freud, H. Hartmann, & E. Kris (Eds.), *The psychoanalytic study of the child* (Vol. 3/4, pp. 9–36). Madison, CT: International Universities Press.

Hartmann, H., Kris, E., & Loewenstein, R. M. (1951). Some psychoanalytic comments on "culture and personality." In *Psychoanalysis and culture; essays in honor of Géza Róheim* (pp. 3–31). Madison, CT: International Universities Press.

Hersoug, A. G., Bøgwald, K.-P., & Høglend, P. (2005). Changes of defensive functioning. Does interpretation contribute to change? *Clinical Psychology & Psychotherapy, 12*(4), 288–296. https://doi.org/10.1002/cpp.444

Hersoug, A. G., Sexton, H. C., & Høglend, P. (2002). Contribution of defensive functioning to the quality of working alliance and psychotherapy outcome. *American Journal of Psychotherapy, 56*(4), 539–554.

Hinrichs, J., Dauphin, V. B., Munday, C. C., Porcerelli, J. H., Kamoo, R., & Christian-Kliger, P. (2019). Assessing level of personality organization with the psychodiagnostic chart: A validity study. *Journal of Personality Assessment, 101*(2), 181–190. https://doi.org/10.1080/00223891.2018.1436062

Hinshelwood, R. D. (1989). *A dictionary of Kleinian thought*. London, UK: Free Association Books.

Hinshelwood, R. D. (2006). Melanie Klein and repression: An examination of some unpublished notes of 1934. *Psychoanalysis and History, 8*(1), 5–42. https://doi.org/10.3366/pah.2006.8.1.5

Hinshelwood, R. D. (2008). Repression and splitting: Towards a method of conceptual comparison. *The International Journal of Psychoanalysis, 89*(3), 503–521. https://doi.org/10.1111/j.1745-8315.2008.00055.x

Høglend, P., & Perry, J. C. (1998). Defensive functioning predicts improvement in major depressive episodes. *Journal of Nervous and Mental Disease, 186*(4), 238–243. https://doi.org/10.1097/00005053-199804000-00006

Holt, R. R. (1977). A method for assessing primary process manifestations and their control in Rorschach responses. In M. A. Rickers-Ovsiankina (Ed.), *Rorschach psychology* (2nd ed., pp. 375–420). Huntington, NY: Krieger.

Joseph, B. (1985). Transference: The total situation. *The International Journal of Psychoanalysis, 66*(4), 447–454.

Joseph, B. (1987). Projective identification: Clinical aspects. In J. Sandler (Ed.), *Projection, identification, projective identification* (pp. 65–76). London: Routledge.

Joseph, B. (1988). Projective identification: Some clinical aspects. In *Melanie Klein today: Developments in theory and practice, Vol. 1: Mainly theory* (pp. 138–150). London: Routledge

Joseph, B. (2012). Projective identification: Some clinical aspects. In E. B. Spillius, & O' Shaughnessy (Eds.) *Projective identification: The fate of a concept* (pp. 98–111). London: Routledge

Kantrowitz, J. L., Katz, A. L., Paolitto, F., Sashin, J., & Solomon, L. (1987). Changes in the level and quality of object relations in psychoanalysis: Follow up of a longitudinal, prospective study. *Journal of the American Psychoanalytic Association, 35*(1), 23–46. https://doi.org/10.1177/000306518703500102

Kernberg, O. (1967). Borderline personality organization. *Journal of the American Psychoanalytic Association, 15*, 641–685.

Kernberg, O. F. (1970). A psychoanalytic classification of character pathology. *Journal of the American Psychoanalytic Association, 18*(4), 800–822. https://doi.org/10.1177/000306517001800403

Kernberg, O. F. (1975). *Borderline conditions and pathological narcissism*. New York, NY: Jason Aronson.

Kernberg, O. F. (1976). *Object relations theory and clinical psychoanalysis*. New York, NY: Jason Aronson.

Kernberg, O. F. (1980). *Internal world and external reality*. New York, NY: Aronson.

Kernberg, O. F. (1982). Self, ego, affects and drives. *Journal of the American Psychoanalytic Association, 30*, 893–917.

Kernberg, O. F. (1984). *Severe personality disorders: Psychotherapeutic strategies.* New Haven, CT: Yale University.

Kernberg, O. F. (1986). *Severe personality disorders: Psychotherapeutic strategies.* New Haven, CT: Yale University Press.

Kernberg, O. F. (2001). Object relations, affects, and drives: Toward a new synthesis. *Psychoanalytic Inquiry, 21*(5), 604. https://doi.org/10.1080/07351692109348963.

Kernberg, O. F. (2004). *Aggressivity, narcissism, and self-destructiveness in the psychotherapeutic relationship: New developments in the psychopathology and psychotherapy of severe personality disorders.* New Haven, CT: Yale University Press.

Kernberg, O. F. (2018). *Treatment of severe personality disorders: Resolution of aggression and recovery of eroticism.* Washington, DC: American Psychiatric Association Publishing.

Kinston, W., & Cohen, J. (1986). Primal repression: Clinical and theoretical aspects. *The International Journal of Psychoanalysis, 67*(3), 337–355.

Kinston, W., & Cohen, J. (1988). Primal repression and other states of mind. *The Scandinavian Psychoanalytic Review, 11*(2), 81–105. https://doi.org/10.1080/01062301.1988.10592521

Klein, M. (1924). The role of the school in the libidinal development of the child. *International Journal of Psychoanalysis, 5*, 312–331.

Klein, M. (1927). Symposium on child-analysis. *International Journal of Psychoanalysis, 8*, 339–370.

Klein, M. (1928). Early stages of the Oedipus conflict. *International Journal of Psychoanalysis, 9*, 167–180.

Klein, M. (1930). The importance of symbol-formation in the development of the ego. *International Journal of Psychoanalysis, 11*, 24–39.

Klein, M. (1931). A contribution to the theory of intellectual inhibition. *International Journal of Psychoanalysis, 12*, 206–218.

Klein, M. (1932). *The Psychoanalysis of Children.* (The International Psycho-analytical Library, No 22). London, UK: Hogarth Press.

Klein, M. (1935). A contribution to the psychogenesis of manic-depressive States. *International Journal of Psychoanalysis, 16*, 145–174.

Klein, M. (1937). Love, guilt and reparation. In *Writings of Melanie Klein* (Vol. I). London, UK: Hogarth.

Klein, M. (1940). Mourning and its relation to manic-depressive States. *International Journal of Psychoanalysis, 21*, 125–153.

Klein, M. (1945). The Oedipus complex in the light of early anxieties. *International Journal of Psychoanalysis, 26*, 11–33.

Klein, M. (1946). Notes on some schizoid mechanisms. *International Journal of Psychoanalysis, 27*, 99–110.

Klein, M. (1952). Some theoretical conclusions regarding the emotional life of the infant. In Klein, M. (1975), *Envy and gratitude and other works, 1946–1963.* New York, NY: Delacorte Press.

Klein, M. (1957). *Envy and gratitude; a study of unconscious sources.* New York: Basic Books.

Knapp, P. H., Levin, S., McCarter, R. H., Wermer, H., & Zetzel, E. (1960). Suitability for psychoanalysis: A review of one hundred supervised analytic cases. *The Psychoanalytic Quarterly, 29*, 459–477.

Knight, R. P. (1941). Evaluation of the results of psychoanalytic therapy. *The American Journal of Psychiatry, 98*, 434–446. https://doi.org/10.1176/ajp.98.3.434

Kohut, H. (1971). *The analysis of the self.* New York, NY: International Universities Press.

Kohut, H. (1977). *The restoration of the self.* Chicago, IL: University of Chicago Press.

Kohut, H. (1984). *How does analysis cure?* Chicago, IL: University of Chicago Press.

Kohut, H., & Wolf, E. S. (1978). The disorders of the self and their treatment: An outline. *The International Journal of Psychoanalysis, 59*, 413–425.

Kramer, U., Despland, J., Michel, L., Drapeau, M., & de Roten, Y. (2010). Change in defense mechanisms and coping over the course of short-term dynamic psychotherapy for adjustment disorder. *Journal of Clinical Psychology, 66*(12), 1232–1241. https://doi.org/10.1002/jclp.20719

Laplanche, J., & Pontalis, J. B. (1973). *The language of psychoanalysis*. London, UK: Hogarth Press.

Lerner, H., Albert, C., & Walsh, M. (1987). The Rorschach assessment of borderline defenses: A concurrent validity study. *Journal of Personality Assessment, 51*(3), 334–348. https://doi.org/10.1207/s15327752jpa5103_1

Lerner, H. D., Sugarman, A., & Gaughran, J. (1981). Borderline and schizophrenic patients. A comparative study of defensive structure. *Journal of Nervous & Mental Disease, 169*(11), 705–711. https://doi.org/10.1097/00005053-198111000-00004

Lerner, P. M. (1998). *Psychoanalytic perspectives on the Rorschach*. Hillsdale, NJ: Analytic Press.

Lerner, P. M. (2005). Defense and its assessment: The Lerner defense scale. In R. F. Bornstein & J. M. Masling (Eds.), *Scoring the Rorschach: Seven validated systems* (pp. 237–269). New York, NY: Lawrence Erlbaum Associates Publishers.

Lerner, P. M., & Lerner, H. (1980). Rorschach assessment of primitive defense in borderline personality structure. In J. Kwawer, P. M. Lerner, & A. Sugarman (Eds.), *Borderline phenomena and the Rorschach test* (pp. 257–274). New York, NY: International Universities Press.

Lerner, P. M., & Van-Der Keshet, Y. (1995). A note on the assessment of idealization. *Journal of Personality Assessment, 65*, 77–90. https://doi.org/10.1207/s15327752jpa6501_6

Leuzinger-Bohleber, M., Stuhr, U., Ruger, B., & Beutel, M. (2003). How to study the 'quality of psychoanalytic treatments' and their long-term effects on patients' well-being: A representative, multi–perspective follow-up study. *International Journal of Psychoanalysis, 84*, 263–290.

Levine, M., & Spivack, G. (1964). *The Rorschach index of repressive style*. Springfield, IL: Charles C Thomas.

Lindfors, O., Knekt, P., Lehtonen, J., Virtala, E., Maljanen, T., & Härkänen, T. (2019). Effectiveness of psychoanalysis and long-term psychodynamic psychotherapy on personality and social functioning 10 years after start of treatment. *Psychiatry Research, 272*, 774–783. https://doi.org/10.1016/j.psychres.2018.12.082

Lingiardi, V. (2023). *I meccanismi di difesa* [The defense mechanisms]. Milano: Raffaello Cortina.

Lingiardi, V., Gazzillo, F., & Waldron, S. Jr. (2010). An empirically supported psychoanalysis: The case of Giovanna. *Psychoanalytic Psychology, 27*(2), 190–218. https://doi.org/10.1037/a0019418

Lingiardi, V., & McWilliams, N. (Eds.). (2017). *Psychodynamic Diagnostic Manual: Second Edition (PDM-2)*. New York, NY: Guilford Press.

Mahler, M. S. (1971). A study of the separation-individuation process: And its possible application to borderline phenomena in the psychoanalytic situation. *The Psychoanalytic Study of the Child, 26*, 403–424. https://doi.org/10.1080/00797308.1971.11822279

Mahler, M. S., Pine, F., & Bergman, A. (1975). *The psychological birth of the human infant. Symbiosis and individuation*. New York, NY: Basic Books.

Marty, P., & de M'Uzan, M. (2010). Operational thinking (1963). In Birksted-Breen, D., Flanders, S., Gibeault, A., Alcorn, D., Leighton, S., & Weller, A. (2010). *Reading French psychoanalysis* (pp. 449–458). London and New York: Routledge.

Mayman, M. (1970). Reality contact, defense effectiveness, and psychopathology in Rorschach form-level scores. In B. Klopfer, M. Meyer, & F. Brawer (Eds.), *Developments in Rorschach technique: Aspects of personality structure* (Vol. III, pp. 11–46). New Jork, NY: Harcourt, Brace & Jovanovich.

Meloy, J. R., Acklin, M. W., Gacono, C. B., & Murray, J. F. (1997). *Contemporary Rorschach interpretation*. Mahwah, NJ: Lawrence Erlbaum Associates Publishers.

Meloy, J. R., Gacono, C. B., & Kenney, L. (1994). A Rorschach investigation of sexual homicide. *Journal of Personality Assessment, 62*(1), 58–67. https://doi.org/10.1207/s15327752jpa6201_6

Mihura, J. L., Meyer, G. J., Dumitrascu, N., & Bombel, G. (2013). The validity of individual Rorschach variables: Systematic reviews and meta-analyses of the comprehensive system. *Psychological Bulletin, 139*(3), 548–605. https://doi.org/10.1037/a0029406.

Nelson, A. R. G. (2001). *An exploratory study of the construct validity of empirical and content approaches to the Rorschach Inkblot Test.* (Doctoral dissertation, Argosy University/Twin Cities).

Ogden, T. H. (1979). On projective identification. *The International Journal of Psychoanalysis, 60*(3), 357–373.

Ogden, T. H. (1992). *Projective identification and psychotherapeutic technique.* Northvale, NJ: Jason Aronson.

Ogden, T. H. (1994). The analytic third: Working with intersubjective clinical facts. *The International Journal of Psychoanalysis, 75*(1), 3–19.

Ogden, T. H. (1997). Reverie and interpretation. *The Psychoanalytic Quarterly, 66*(4), 567–595.

Ogden, T. H. (2016). *Reclaiming unlived life: Experiences in psychoanalysis.* New York, NY: Routledge.

Ogden, T. H. (2019). Ontological psychoanalysis or "what do you want to be when you grow up?" *The Psychoanalytic Quarterly, 88*(4), 661–684. https://doi.org/10.1080/00332828.2019.1656928

Ogden, T. H. (2024). Ontological psychoanalysis in clinical practice. *The Psychoanalytic Quarterly, 93*(1), 13–31. https://doi.org/10.1080/00332828.2024.2314776.

Perry, J. C. (1990). *Defense Mechanism Rating Scales* (5th ed.). Boston, MA: The Cambridge Hospital.

Perry, J. C. (2001). A pilot study of defenses in adults with personality disorders entering psychotherapy. *Journal of Nervous and Mental Disease, 189*(10), 651–660. https://doi.org/10.1097/00005053-200110000-00001

Perry, J. C., Beck, S. M., Constantinides, P., & Foley, J. E. (2009). Studying change in defensive functioning in psychotherapy using the defense mechanism rating scales: Four hypotheses, four cases. In R. A. Levy & J. S. Ablon (Eds.), *Handbook of evidence-based psychodynamic psychotherapy: Bridging the gap between science and practice.* (pp. 121–153). Totowa, NJ: Humana Press/Springer Nature. https://doi.org/10.1007/978-1-59745-444-5_6.

Perry, J. C., & Bond, M. (2012). Change in defense mechanisms during long-term dynamic psychotherapy and five-year outcome. *The American Journal of Psychiatry, 169*(9), 916–925. https://doi.org/10.1176/appi.ajp.2012.11091403

Perry, J. C., & Bond, M. (2017). Addressing defenses in psychotherapy to improve adaptation. *Psychoanalytic Inquiry, 37*(3), 153–166. https://doi.org/10.1080/0735 1690.2017.1285185

Perry, J. C., & Henry, M. (2004). Studying defense mechanisms in psychotherapy using the Defense Mechanism Rating Scales. In U. Hentschel, G. Smith, J. G. Draguns, & W. Ehlers (Eds.), *Defense mechanisms: Theoretical, research and clinical perspectives* (pp. 165–192). Amsterdam, The Netherlands: Elsevier.

Perry, J. C., & Høglend, P. (1998). Convergent and discriminant validity of overall defensive functioning. *Journal of Nervous and Mental Disease, 186*(9), 529–535. https://doi.org/10.1097/00005053-199809000-00003

Perry, J. C., & Ianni, F. F. (1998). Observer-rated measures of defense mechanisms. *Journal of Personality, 66*(6), 993–1024. https://doi.org/10.1111/1467-6494.00040

Perry, J. C., Petraglia, J., Olson, T. R., Presniak, M. D., & Metzger, J. A. (2012). Accuracy of defense interpretation in three character types. In R. A. Levy, J. S. Ablon, & H. Kächele (Eds.), *Psychodynamic psychotherapy research: Evidence-based practice and practice-based evidence* (pp. 417–447). Totowa, NJ: Humana Press - Springer. https://doi.org/10.1007/978-1-60761-792-1_25

Perry, J. C., Presniak, M. D., & Olson, T. R. (2013). Defense mechanisms in schizotypal, borderline, antisocial, and narcissistic personality disorders. *Psychiatry: Interpersonal & Biological Processes, 76*(1), 32–52. https://doi.org/10.1521/psyc.2013.76.1.32

Pfeffer, A. Z. (1959). A procedure for evaluating the results of psychoanalysis. *Journal of the American Psychoanalytic Association, 7*, 418–444. https://doi.org/10.1177/000306515900700302

Pfeffer, A. Z. (1961). Follow-up study of a satisfactory analysis. *Journal of the American Psychoanalytic Association, 9*, 698–718. https://doi.org/10.1177/000306516100900407

Pfeffer, A. Z. (1963). The meaning of the analyst after analysis: A contribution to the theory of therapeutic results. *Journal of the American Psychoanalytic Association, 11*(2), 229–244. https://doi.org/10.1177/000306516301100202

Pievsky, M. A., Persaud, U. D., Tiersky, L. A., Freer, B. D., Abuelhiga, L. S., Mazzola, K. S., & Eyzerovich, E. (2016). The relationship between defense style and intelligence. *Journal of the American Psychoanalytic Association, 64*(5), 1013–1020. https://doi.org/10.1177/0003065116676096

Presniak, M. D., Olson, T. R., Porcerelli, J. H., & Dauphin, V. B. (2010). Changes in defensive functioning in a case of avoidant personality disorder. *Psychotherapy: Theory, Research, Practice, Training, 47*(1), 134–139. https://doi.org/10.1037/a0018838

Rapaport, D., Gill, M., & Schafer, R. (1946). *Diagnostic psychological testing: The theory, statistical evaluation, and diagnostic application of a battery of tests: Volume II*. The Year Book Publishers. https://doi.org/10.1037/10582-000

Raven, J. (1938). *Progressive matrices: A perceptual test of intelligence*. London, UK: H.K. Lewis.

Raven, J. C., Raven, J. E., & Court, J. H. (1998). *Manual for Raven's Progressive Matrices and Vocabulary Scales*. San Antonio, TX: Harcourt Assessment.

Rayner, E. (1991). *The independent mind in British psychoanalysis*. London, UK: Free Association Books.

Reich, W. (1933). *Character analysis*. New York, NY: Noonday Press, 1949.

Rorschach, H. (1942). *Psychodiagnostics*. New York, NY: Grune and Stratton (Original work published 1921).

Rosenfeld, H. (1964). On the psychopathology of narcissism: A clinical approach. *International Journal of Psycho-Analysis, 45*, 332–337.

Rosenfeld, H. (1971). A clinical approach to the psychoanalytic theory of the life and death instincts: An investigation into the aggressive aspects of narcissism. *The International Journal of Psychoanalysis, 52*(2), 169–178.

Rosenthal, R. (1994). Parametric measures of effect size. In Cooper, H., & Hedges, L. V. (Eds). *The handbook of research synthesis* (pp. 231–244). New York, NY: Russell Sage Foundation.

Rosso, A. M., Airaldi, C., & Camoirano, A. (2021). Inter-rater reliability and construct validity of the Lerner defense scale in clinical and non-clinical groups. *Frontiers in Psychology, 12*, 708886. https://doi.org/10.3389/fpsyg.2021.708886

Rosso, A. M., Gacono, C. B., Camoirano, A., & Smith, J. M. (submitted). Is the Rorschach Defense Scale a reliable and valid tool for evaluating psychotherapy processes and outcomes?

Roy, C. A., Perry, J. C., Luborsky, L., & Banon, E. (2009). Changes in defensive functioning in completed psychoanalyses: The Penn Psychoanalytic Treatment Collection. *Journal of the American Psychoanalytic Association, 57*(2), 399–415. https://doi.org/10.1177/0003065109333357

Sandler, J. (1985). *The analysis of defense.* New York, NY: International University Press.

Sandler, J. (1990). On internal object relations. *Journal of the American Psychoanalytic Association, 38*(4), 859–880. https://doi.org/10.1177/000306519003800401

Sandler, J., & Freud, A. (1981a). Discussions in the Hampstead Index on 'The Ego and the Mechanisms of Defense': IV. The mechanisms of defense, Part 1. *Bulletin of the Anna Freud Centre, 4,* 151–199.

Sandler, J., & Freud, A. (1981b). Discussions in the Hampstead Index on 'The Ego and the Mechanisms of Defense': V. The mechanisms of defense, Part 2. *Bulletin of the Anna Freud Centre, 4,* 231–277.

Sandler, J., Holder, A., Dare, C., & Dreher, A. U. (1997). *Freud's models of the mind: An introduction.* Madison, CT: International Universities Press, Inc.

Sandler, J., & Sandler, A. M. (1978). On the development of object relationships and affects. *The International Journal of Psychoanalysis, 59*(2–3), 285–296.

Sashin, J. I., Eldred, S. H., & Van Amerongen, S. T. (1975). A search for predictive factors in institute supervised cases: A retrospective study of 183 cases from 1959–1966 at the Boston Psychoanalytic Society and Institute. *The International Journal of Psychoanalysis, 56*(3), 343–359.

Savvopoulos, S., Manolopoulos, S., & Beratis, S. (2011). Repression and splitting in the psychoanalytic process. *The International Journal of Psychoanalysis, 92*(1), 75–96. https://doi.org/10.1111/j.1745-8315.2010.00363.x

Schachtel, E. G. (1966). *Experiential foundations of Rorschach's test.* New York, NY: Basic Books.

Schafer, R. (1954). *Psychoanalytic interpretation in Rorschach testing: Theory and application.* New York, NY: Grune & Stratton.

Sechaud, E. (2015). The double nature of splitting. *The International Journal of Psychoanalysis, 96*(1), 141–143. https://doi.org/10.1111/1745-8315.12325

Segal, H. (1964). *Introduction to the work of Melanie Klein.* London: Hogarth Press.

Shapiro, D. (1965). *Neurotic styles.* New York, NY: Basic Books.

Smith, J. M., & Gacono, C. B. (2022). Revisiting the coding of defenses: Cooper, Perry, & Arnow (1988) Rorschach Defense Scales. In J. M. Smith, Y. Weinberger-Katzav, & P. Fontan (Eds.), *The Rorschach: A comprehensive system – revised®, supplementary scales handbook.* Fort Mill SC: Rorschach Workshops, International Rorschach Institute.

Smith, J. M., Gacono, C. B., & Cunliffe, T. B. (2021). *Understanding female offenders: Psychopathy, criminal behavior, assessment, and Treatment.* Cambridge, MA: Academic Press.

Smith, J. M., Weinberger-Katzav, Y., & Fontan, P. (Eds.) (2022). *The Rorschach: A comprehensive system – revised®, supplementary scales handbook.* Fort Mill SC: Rorschach Workshops, International Rorschach Institute.

Sodré, I. (2012). *Who's who? Notes on pathological identifications.* In E. Spillius & E. O'Shaughnessy (Eds.), *Projective identification: The fate of a concept* (pp. 132–146). London: Routledge.

Spillius, E. (2012). Developments by British Kleinian analysts. In E. Spillius & E. O'Shaughnessy (Eds.), *Projective identification: The fate of a concept* (pp. 49–60). London: Routledge.

Spillius, E., & O'Shaughnessy, E. (2012). *Projective identification: The fate of a concept.* London: Routledge.

Spillius, E. B. (1988). *Melanie Klein today.* London/New York, NY: Routledge.

Stenius, J., Knekt, P., Heinonen, E., Holma, J., Antikainen, R., & Lindfors, O. (2021). Predicting the working alliance over the course of long-term psychodynamic psychotherapy with the Rorschach Ego Impairment Index, self-reported defense style, and performance-based intelligence: An evaluation of three methodological approaches. *Psychoanalytic Psychology, 38*(1), 58–67. https://doi.org/10.1037/pap0000318

Tanzilli, A., Di Giuseppe, M., Giovanardi, G., Boldrini, T., Caviglia, G., Conversano, C., & Lingiardi, V. (2021). Mentalization, attachment, and defense mechanisms: A Psychodynamic Diagnostic Manual-2-oriented empirical investigation. *Research in Psychotherapy: Psychopathology, Process and Outcome, 24*(1), 31–41. https://doi.org/10.4081/ripppo.2021.531

Tibon-Czopp, S. (2022). The Reality-Fantasy Scale. In J. M. Smith, Y. Weinberger-Katzav, & P. Fontan (Eds.), *The Rorschach: A comprehensive system – revised®, supplementary scales handbook*. Fort Mill SC: Rorschach Workshops, International Rorschach Institute.

Vaillant, G. E. (1976). *Adaption to life*. Boston, MA: Little, Brown.

Vaillant, G. E. (1993). *Wisdom of the ego*. Cambridge: Harvard University Press.

Vaillant, G. E., Bond, M., & Vaillant, C. O. (1986). An empirically validated hierarchy of defense mechanisms. *Archives of General Psychiatry, 43*(8), 786–794. https://doi.org/10.1001/archpsyc.1986.01800080072010

Van der Keshet, Y. (1988). *Anorexic patients and ballet students: A Rorschach analysis*. Unpublished doctoral dissertation, University of Toronto.

Wallerstein, R. S. (1986). *Forty-two lives in treatment: A study of psychoanalysis and psychotherapy*. New York, NY: Guilford.

Wallerstein, R. S. (2005). Outcome research. In E. S. Person, A. M. Cooper, & G. O. Gabbard (Eds.), *The American psychiatric publishing textbook of psychoanalysis*. (pp. 301–315). Washington, DC: American Psychiatric Publishing.

Weber, J. J., Solomon, M., & Bachrach, H. M. (1985). Characteristics of psychoanalytic clinic patients: Report of the Columbia Psychoanalytic Center Research Project: I. *International Review of Psycho-Analysis, 12*(1), 13–26.

Wechsler, D. (1981). *Manual for the Wechsler Adult Intelligence Scale—Revised*. New York, NY: Psychological Corporation.

Weiner, I. B. (2003). *Principles of Rorschach interpretation* (2nd ed.). Mahwah, NJ: Lawrence Erlbaum Associates.

Winnicott, D. W. (1949). Mind and its relation to the Psyche-Soma. In *Through paediatrics to psycho-analysis* (pp. 243–254). London, UK: Tavistock Publications.

Winnicott, D. W. (1953). Transitional objects and transitional phenomena—A study of the first not-me possession. *International Journal of Psychoanalysis, 34*, 89–97.

Winnicott, D. W. (1956). Primary maternal preoccupation. In *Through paediatrics to psycho-analysis* (pp. 300–305). London, UK: Tavistock Publications.

Winnicott, D. W. (1958). The capacity to be alone. *International Journal of Psychoanalysis, 39*, 416–420.

Winnicott, D. W. (1959). The fate of the transitional object. In C. Winnicott, R. Shepherd, & M. Davis (Eds.), *Psychoanalytic explorations* (pp. 53–58). Cambridge, MA: Harvard University Press.

Winnicott, D. W. (1960a). Ego distortion in terms of true and false self (1960). In *The maturational processes and the facilitating environment: Studies in the theory of emotional development* (pp. 140–152). London, UK: The Hogarth Press.

Winnicott, D. W. (1960b). The theory of the parent-infant relationship. *International Journal of Psychoanalysis, 41*, 585–595.

Winnicott, D. W. (1961). Psycho-neurosis in childhood. In C. Winnicott, R. Shepherd, & M. Davis (Eds.), *Psychoanalytic explorations* (pp. 64–72). Cambridge, MA: Harvard University Press.

Winnicott, D. W. (1962a). A personal view of the Kleinian contribution. In *The maturational processes and the facilitating environment: Studies in the theory of emotional development* (pp. 171–178). London, UK: The Hogarth Press.

Winnicott, D. W. (1962b). Ego integration in child development. In *The maturational processes and the facilitating environment: Studies in the theory of emotional development* (pp. 56–63). London, UK: The Hogarth Press.

Winnicott, D. W. (1963a). Communicating and not communicating leading to a study of certain opposites. In *The maturational processes and the facilitating environment: Studies in the theory of emotional development* (pp. 179–192). London, UK: The Hogarth Press.

Winnicott, D. W. (1963b). The development of the capacity for concern. In *The maturational processes and the facilitating environment: Studies in the theory of emotional development* (pp. 73–82). London, UK: The Hogarth Press.

Winnicott, D. W. (1968). Roots of aggression. In C. Winnicott, R. Shepherd, & M. Davis (Eds.), *Psychoanalytic explorations* (pp. 458–461). Cambridge, MA: Harvard University Press.

Winnicott, D. W. (1969). The use of an object. *International Journal of Psychoanalysis, 50*, 711–716.

Winnicott, D. W. (1971). Mirror-role of mother and family in child development. In *Playing and reality* (pp. 111–118). London, UK: Tavistock Publications.

Index

Note: Page numbers in **bold** refer to tables.

abreaction 5
Abspaltung 83
Acklin, M. W. 128
affect-trauma frame of reference, defense mechanisms in 5–9
aggressor, defense of identification with 29–30
Akhtar, S. 79–81
altruism 24, 30–31
American Psychoanalytic Association 161
American Psychological Association: Code of Conduct 163; Ethical Principles of Psychologists 163
animism 15
anti-cathexis 14, 19
antilibidinal ego 63
anxiety 21, 22; automatic 17; castration 10, 17, 18, 22, 35, 77, 84; depressive 36–38, 42, 43; intolerable 46; moral 13, 18; paranoid 40–43; persecutory 35–40, 42, 74; real 27, 33; of separation 61; signal 17; social 13, 18
Arnow, D. 123
asceticism 22, 29, 31
attacks on linking 80
automatic anxiety 17
autonomy 42, 55, 56, 69, 70
Avoidant Personality Disorder (AvPD) 178
AvPD *see* Avoidant Personality Disorder (AvPD)

Balint, M. 54–57
basic fault 55
Baucom, D. 109
Bayle, G. 90
Beck, S. M. 113
Beratis, S. 83

Bhatia, M. 109, 113
Big Chill, The 118
Bion, W. 94; *Attacks on Linking* 47, 80; *Differentiating the Psychotic from the Non-Psychotic Personality* 46; *Elements of Psycho-Analysis* 51; *Learning from Experience* 49, 50; on projective identification 91; *Theory of Thinking, A* 49; *Transformations* 51; transformative perspective 46–52
Blass, R. B. 84–89
Bond, M. 102
borderline personality disorder (BPD) 108
BPD *see* borderline personality disorder (BPD)
BPI *see* Brief Psychodynamic Investigation (BPI)
BPS *see* British Psychoanalytical Society (BPS)
Breuer, J. 5
Brief Psychodynamic Investigation (BPI) 105, 106
British Independents (aka Middle Group) 53–68; Balint, M. 54–57; Fairbairn, R. 57–64; Winnicott, D. 64–68
British Psychoanalytical Society (BPS) 53, 57
Britton, R. 94
Brook, J. A. 82

Camoirano, A.: "Beyond LDS and RDS: Toward the Development of a Valid and Reliable Measure of Defenses": 1, 129
castration anxiety 10, 17, 18, 22, 35, 77, 84
censorship 11
central ego 63

Chabert, C. 168
childhood: sexual trauma 8
Chilean Psychoanalytic Association 71
Christian, J. 102
cleanliness 18, 136
Collins, R. 122
Comprehensive Rorschach Defense
System (CRDS) 2, 115, 127, 129–155;
concurrent validity 160–168, **165**,
166; convergent validity 168–171,
170; devaluation 147–149; divergent
validity 171–174; high-level denial
135–137; idealization 145–147;
intellectualization 137–138; isolation of
affect 138; LDS *versus* 133; omnipotent
control 149–150; omnipotent denial
151–153; projective identification
139–143; psychic functioning through
175–183; psychotic denial 153–155;
rationalization 138–139; RDS *versus*
133–134; repression 135; splitting
143–145; training 157–160; validation
of 156–174
conceptual mapping 83
condensation 11, 12, 32
conscientiousness 13, 18
Conscious 10, 12–14
constancy, principle of 6
Constantinides, P. 113
container-contained model 51
contempt 43
Cooper, S. H. 123
CRDS *see* Comprehensive Rorschach
Defense System (CRDS)

Dare, C. 5
da Vinci, L. 16
death drive 17, 35, 54, 57, 86
death instinct 36–38, 54, 87, 88
Defense Mechanism Inventory (DMI) 102
Defense Mechanism Manual (DMM)
115, 171
Defense Mechanism Rating Scales
(DMRS) 1, 101–117, 168; future
research directions 114–117;
improvements in defensive
functioning and psychological
well-being, relationship between
111–112; limitations of 112–114;
shifts in defensive functioning
108–110; single-case studies 107–108;
therapist interventions 108–110;
treatment outcomes in clinical
populations 103–107

Defense Mechanism Rating Scales –
Q-sort adaptation (DMRS-Q) 1, 101,
103, 114, 115; convergent validity
168–171, **170**
defense mechanisms 5–20, 78; in affect-
trauma frame of reference 5–9;
defensive measures *versus* 23–29;
motives for 21–22; in structural
frame of reference 16–20; in
topographical frame of reference
9–16; *see also individual entries*
Defense Style Questionnaire (DSQ)
102, 105
Defense Style Questionnaire
(DSQ-40) 172
defensive measures *versus* defense
mechanisms 23–29
defensive passivity 176–177
Defensive Profile Narrative (DPN) 103
deferred action 8
de M'Uzan, M. 168
denial 39, 46, 48, 57, 74, 84; conscious
89; defenses 112, 118; higher-level
123, 127, 130, 132–137; hypomanic
124, 126, 127, 131, 134; low-level
130; massive or bland 124, 126,
127, 131, 134; mature 158, 159;
omnipotent 42, 43, 127, 133, 134,
147, 151–153, 158–160, 164, 182,
183; pollyannish 123, 126, 127, 134;
psychotic 113, 133, 153–155, 164; of
reality 19, 20, 27, 28, 42
denial of aggression 176–177
depressive anxiety 36–38, 42, 43
depressive position 38, 40–45, 60, 119
deprivation 38, 39, 54, 58, 66, 67
de Roten, Y. 112–113
devaluation 59, 73, 74, 102, 106, 118,
119, 121–125, 127, 129–134, 147–149,
156, 164–166, 169, 170, 178, 180, 181
Di Giuseppe, M. 103
disavowal splitting 84–85, 88
displacement 9, 11–15, 23, 25, 32, 102,
112, 171
displeasure 12, 13, 21, 33, 80, 85
dissociative splitting 83–84, 85
distress 24, 47, 73, 81, 91, 100, 106, 166,
167, 171, 179, 182
DMI *see* Defense Mechanism Inventory
(DMI)
DMM *see* Defense Mechanism Manual
(DMM)
DMRS *see* Defense Mechanism Rating
Scales (DMRS)

DMRS-Q *see* Defense Mechanism Rating Scales – Q-sort adaptation (DMRS-Q)
double consciousness 83
DPN *see* Defensive Profile Narrative (DPN)
Drapeau, M. 105, 108, 109, 113
Dreher, A. U. 5
drive: death 17, 35, 54, 57, 86; definition of 10; instinctual 10–12, 16, 33, 66, 78, 81, 84; self-preservative 17; sexual 17
DSQ *see* Defense Style Questionnaire (DSQ)
DSQ-40 *see* Defense Style Questionnaire (DSQ-40)

Eagle, M. 81–83
economic theory of repression 14
ego 6, 16–18, 21–23, 26, 28, 34, 37, 57–58, 60–62, 74, 85, 89, 90; antilibidinal 63; central 63; development 32; ego-instincts 11; immaturity 86, 88; libidinal 63; psychology 69–74; splitting 20, 58, 60, 62, 63; stability 81
empathy 27, 40, 55
emptiness 58
envy 22, 36–37, 40, 48, 50, 73, 91, 92, 147; definition of 36
exchange of opposites 12
Exner, J. E. 128
externalization 26

Fairbairn, R. 57–64
Fechner, G. T. : principle of constancy 6
Feldman, F. 93
Ferenczi, S. 29, 30, 54, 84, 88
Fliess, W. 9
Freud, A. 53, 81, 83, 118; on aggressor 29–30; on altruism 30–31; on asceticism 31; on defense mechanisms 21–34; on defensive measures-defense mechanisms distinction 23–29; *Ego and Defense Mechanisms, The* 21; on intellectualization 31
Freud, S. 2, 35; *Beyond the Pleasure Principle* 17; defense mechanisms 5–20; economic theory of repression 14; *Ego and the Id, The* 16, 85; *Further Remarks on the Neuro-Psychoses of Defense* 7–9; on hysterical phenomena 118; *Inhibitions, Symptoms, and Anxiety* 16; *Instincts and Their Vicissitudes* 12, 85; *Interpretation of Dreams, The* 10, 11; *Loss of Reality in Neurosis and Psychosis, The* 19; *Mourning and Melancholia* 15, 85; *Negation* 85; *Neuro-Psychoses of Defense, The* 7; *Outline of Psychoanalysis* 84; *Outline of Psycho-Analysis, An* 20; *Psychical Mechanism of Forgetfulness, The* 11; *Psychopathology of Everyday Life* 12; on repression 79–81; *Repression* 12; on splitting 83; *Splitting of the Ego in the Process of Defense, The* 84; *Studies on Hysteria* 7; theoy of sexual development 10; *Three Essays* 16; *Totem and Taboo* 15; *Unconscious, The* 13–14
fullness 58

Gacono, C. B.: "Beyond LDS and RDS: Toward the Development of a Valid and Reliable Measure of Defenses" 1, 129
GAF *see* Global Assessment of Functioning (GAF)
Gardner, S. T. 102
Gentlemen's Agreement 53
Gleser, G. C. 102
Global Assessment of Functioning (GAF) 104
grandiose self 73, 75–77
gratification 10, 11, 28, 31, 38–40, 71, 82, 83, 85
Greenson, R. R. 109
Grotstein, J. S. 94–96
guilt 29, 36, 37, 41–44, 62, 81, 119, 123, 178

hallucination 51; auditory 9
hallucinatory psychosis 7, 9
Hampstead Psychoanalytic Index 21
Hartmann, H.: on ego psychology 69–71; *Ego Psychology and the Problem of Adaptation* 69
hatred 15, 16, 24, 36, 37, 41, 42, 44, 48–50, 60, 63, 73
Hébert, C. 109
Henry, M. 109
high-level denial 135–137
Hinshelwood, R. D. 82
Høglend, P. 104
Holder, A. 5
Holt, R. R. 120, 121
horizontal splitting 76, 84
humiliation 178; narcissistic 31

hypnosis 5, 31
hysteria 5–8, 13, 19; sexually traumatic events and 5
hysterical phenomena 118

id 16, 21, 23, 25, 28, 37, 70, 72
idealization 145–147; primitive 73–74; subsequent 74
Ihilevich, D. 102
immature defenses 107, 109, 169–171
infantile sexual curiosity 16
infantile sexual seduction 8
instinctual drive 10–12, 16, 33, 66, 78, 81, 84
intellectualization 22, 29, 31, 59, 64, 102, 106, 119, 120, 123, 124, 127, 133, 134, 137–139, 164
intense desire 42
internal objects 42, 44, 49, 61, 85–90, 93, 134, 181, 182
International Psychoanalytical Association (IPA) 1, 2, 161
intimacy 60, 175
introjection 14, 15, 25, 39–41, 47, 48, 55, 62, 85, 86, 88, 92, 93, 118
IPA *see* International Psychoanalytical Association (IPA)
IRB *see* Italian Psychoanalytical Society (IRB)
isolation 18, 23, 25, 102, 118, 120, 123, 125, 127, 133, 134, 138, 139, 169, 171, 180, 182; of affect 138
Italian Psychoanalytical Society (IRB): Institutional Review Board 163

Jones, E. 53
Joseph, B. 91–93

Kernberg, O. 57, 58, 69, 80, 130, 175; on ego psychology 71–74; object relations theory 71–74; representation theory of splitting 86, 88–89; structural model of personality organization 161
Klein, M. 15, 20, 26, 53, 57, 64, 66, 80, 82, 94, 118; *Contribution to the Psychogenesis of Manic-Depressive States, A* 36; on depressive position 40–45; on envy 36–37; on mature defenses 45–46; *Mourning and Its Relation to Manic-Depressive States* 42; *Notes on Some Schizoid Mechanisms* 36, 39, 87, 91; psychoanalytic theory

35–37; on schizoparanoid position 38–42, 44; *Some Theoretical Conclusions Regarding the Emotional Life of the Infant* 45–46; on splitting 86–88
Kohut, H. 88; and self psychology 75–78; on splitting 84
Kris, E. 69

Laplanche, J. 14, 18
LDS *see* Lerner Defense Scale (LDS)
Lerner, P. M. 1, 118–119, 126–127
Lerner Defense Scale (LDS) 1, 115, 121–122, 127, 156; CRDS *versus* 133; reliability of 129–131; validity of 129–130
Levine, M. 121
libidinal ego 63
libidinal investment 59, 60
Lindfors, O. 105
Lingiardi, V. 112
Loewenstein, R. 69
loss 7, 15, 17, 18, 22, 36, 41–44, 55, 59, 60, 63, 66, 74, 76, 91, 147, 178

Manolopoulos, S. 83
Marty, P. 168
masturbation 84, 85
mature defenses 45–46, 104, 106, 107, 110, 163–165, 169–172, 181, 182
Mayman coding system 130
meticulousness 8, 9
moral anxiety 13, 18
mother–child relationship 70
mother–infant relationship 48
motives for defense 21–22
mourning 15, 20, 44

narcissistic fragility 176–177; Comprehensive Rorschach Defense System for 179–182, 191; DSM-5-TR diagnostic criteria for 178; PDM-2 criteria for 178; Rorschach test—Comprehensive System for 178–179, 184–190
narcissistic humiliation 31
narcissistic personality disorder 73
neglect 55, 79
New York Psychoanalytic Institute 70
North American psychoanalysis 69–78

object relations theory 64, 69, 71–74, 121
obsessive neurosis 8, 9, 13, 14, 16, 18, 19, 23, 26, 37

ocnophilia 55–57
ODF *see* Overall Defensive Functioning (ODF)
Oedipal conflict 10, 36, 77
Oedipus complex 10, 85
Ogden, T. H. 94
omnipotence 37, 42, 43, 45, 49, 56, 64, 65, 67, 73, 74, 102, 124, 125, 127, 134, 169
omnipotent control 44, 73, 74, 133, 134, 149–150, 164, 170
omnipotent denial 42, 43, 127, 133, 134, 147, 151–153, 158–160, 164, 182, 183
O'Shaughnessy, E. 94
Overall Defensive Functioning (ODF) 102–104, 106, 107, 113, 169, 171

paranoia 8, 9, 14, 15, 29
paranoid: anxieties 40–43
pathological narcissism 73
PDC-2 *see* Psychodiagnostic Chart-2 (PDC-2)
PDM *see* Psychodynamic Diagnostic Manual (PDM)
PDM-2 *see* Psychodynamic Diagnostic Manual-2 (PDM-2)
PEP *see* Psychoanalytic Electronic Publishing (PEP)
periodic melancholia 9
Perry, J. C. 104, 107, 109
persecutory anxiety 35–40, 42, 74
phallic phase of sexual development 10
philobatism 55–57
phobia 7, 9, 13–15, 18, 19, 23, 27
Pievsky, M. A. 171, 172
PIRS *see* Psychodynamic Intervention Rating Scales (PIRS)
Pontalis, J. B. 14, 18
Preconscious 10, 11
preeminence 109
primal repression 12, 14, 80
projection 9, 14, 15, 23, 26–30, 35–40, 48, 50, 51, 73, 74, 85, 88, 91–96, 102, 112, 113, 115, 118–120, 124, 125, 127, 128, 131, 134, 139, 142, 152, 171
projective identification: defense 92–94; interpersonal process 92–94
projective transidentification 95, 96
psychic inter-existence 95
Psychoanalytic Electronic Publishing (PEP) 114
Psychodiagnostic Chart-2 (PDC-2) 116, 161–165, **166**
Psychodynamic Diagnostic Manual (PDM) 74, 161

Psychodynamic Diagnostic Manual-2 (PDM-2) 74, 101, 116, 130, 131, 161, 162, 175, 176, 178
Psychodynamic Intervention Rating Scales (PIRS) 108, 109
psychotic denial 133, 153–155, 164
puberty 8, 9, 22

rationalization 138–139
Raven, J. 172–174
Rayner, E. 54
RDS *see* Rorschach Defense Scales (RDS)
reaction formation 13, 14, 18, 19, 23, 25, 70, 102, 112, 118, 123, 127, 133, 134, 137, 169
Reality–Fantasy Scale Version 2 (RFS-2) 167, 168
regression 18, 23, 25, 28, 37, 56, 59, 86, 90, 118, 120
Reich, W.: on character "armor-plating" 23–24
reparation 26, 37, 41, 43–45, 154
representation theory of splitting 86, 88–89
repression 5, 6, 9, 11, 23, 135; Akhtar and Freudian legacy 79–81; with avoidant defenses 82; clinical relevance of 83; conceptual mapping 83; contemporary clarifications of 82–83; economic theory of 14; excessive 16; intentional 7; post-repression 12; primal 12, 14, 80; primary 12–13, 25, 26; proper 12, 25, 26, 80, 82
repressive style 81–82, 121
reverie 96
RFS-2 *see* Reality–Fantasy Scale Version 2 (RFS-2)
RIRS *see* Rorschach Index of Repressive Style (RIRS)
Riviere, J. 64
Rorschach Comprehensive System 115
Rorschach Defense Scales (RDS) 1, 115, 122–127, 156; CRDS *versus* 133–134; reliability of 131–132; validity of 131–132
Rorschach Index of Repressive Style (RIRS) 121
Rorschach test 1, 115, 116, 118–128, 156, 162, 172, 176, 178–179
Rosenfeld, H. 88, 92
Rosso, A. M.: "Beyond LDS and RDS: Toward the Development of a Valid and Reliable Measure of Defenses" 1, 129
Rostand, E. 30
Roy, C. A. 104

sadism 35–38, 40
sadism–masochism 12
Sandler, J. 5, 93; on defense mechanisms 21–34; on defensive measures-defense mechanisms distinction 23–29
Savvopoulos, S. 83
Schafer, R. 119, 183
schizoid personality 59
schizoparanoid position 38–42, 44
Sechaud, E. 89–91
Segal, H. 39–40, 43, 44, 87
self 58; cohesive 75–77; definition of 75; false 66–68; grandiose 73, 75–77; psychology 75–78; true 64, 66–68
self-accusation 8, 9
self-assurance 75, 77
self-confidence 9, 177
self-destruction 35, 67, 88
self-distrust 8
self-objects 69, 75–78
self-preservation 11, 12, 16, 41
self-reproach 13
separation-individuation 119
sexual development, theoy of 10
sexual pleasure 11
sexual seduction 8; in childhood 6; infantile 8
shame 8, 62
Sigal, J. J. 102
signal anxiety 17
Smith, J. M.: "Beyond LDS and RDS: Toward the Development of a Valid and Reliable Measure of Defenses" 1, 129
social anxiety 13, 18
Sodré, I. 92, 134
Spaltung 83
Spillius, E. 93, 94, 134
Spivack, G. 121
splitting 119, 143–145; as disavowal 84–85, 88; as dissociation 83–84, 85; horizontal 76, 84; Kleinian 86–88; meanings of 83; ontological implications of 88–89; pathological 89–91; of representations 85–86; structural 89–91; vertical 76, 84

SPM *see* Standard Progressive Matrices (SPM)
Standard Progressive Matrices (SPM) 172–174
Stelmaszczyk, K. 109
Stenius, J. 172
structural frame of reference, defense mechanisms in 16–20
sublimation 14, 16, 24, 25, 28, 44, 102, 118, 169
substitution 6, 12, 13, 16, 123
superego 16–18, 21, 22, 28–30, 33, 35, 37, 44, 71–73, 75, 76, 81, 88, 89

TAT *see* Thematic Apperception Test (TAT)
Thematic Apperception Test (TAT) 115
topographical frame of reference, defense mechanisms in 9–16
transmuting internalization 75
triumph 42, 43, 92
turning against the self 25, 118
turning into the opposite 25

Unconscious 10–14, 16, 32, 93
unconscious phantasy 35, 41, 42, 87, 88, 91, 111
undoing 18, 23, 25, 26, 45, 91, 102, 118, 119, 169

Vaillant, G. E. 102, 171
vertical splitting 76, 84
Vienna Psychoanalytic Society 69
voyeurism–exhibitionism 12

WAIS *see* Wechsler Adult Intelligence Scale (WAIS)
Wallerstein, R. S. 99, 100
Wechsler Adult Intelligence Scale (WAIS) 172
Winnicott, D. 64–68, 168; *Mind and its Relation to the Psyche-Soma* 68
withdrawal 7, 61, 64, 73, 93, 113

zoophobia 13

For Product Safety Concerns and Information please contact our EU
representative GPSR@taylorandfrancis.com
Taylor & Francis Verlag GmbH, Kaufingerstraße 24, 80331 München, Germany